BUS

8/28/02

ACPL ITE
DISCARD

SIBERIA BOUND

SIBERIA
BOUND

*Chasing the American Dream
on Russia's Wild Frontier*

ALEXANDER BLAKELY

SOURCEBOOKS, INC.®
NAPERVILLE, ILLINOIS

Published by Sourcebooks, Inc.
P.O. Box 4410, Naperville, Illinois 60567-4410
(630) 961-3900
FAX: (630) 961-2168
www.sourcebooks.com

Blakely, Alexander.
  Siberia bound : chasing the American dream on Russia's wild frontier /
  by Alexander Blakely.
    p. cm.
  ISBN 1-57071-944-6 (alk. paper)
1. Capitalism—Russia (Federation)—Siberia. 2. Blakely, Alexander. 3.
Americans—Russia (Federation)—Siberia—Biography. 4.
Businesspeople—Russia (Federation)—Siberia. 5. Siberia (Russia)—
Economic conditions. I. Title.

HC340.12.Z7 S5317 2002
338'. 092—dc21
[B]
                                                                2001055140

Printed and bound in the United States of America
        DO   10 9 8 7 6 5 4 3 2 1

To my parents.

My dad instilled in me the love of travel. He circled the globe several times, but never in a straight line. His credo was simple: "It's all on the way."

My mom instilled in me the love of place. The longer she is in a place, the more beauty she sees there, the more beauty she creates there. Without her, I never would have discovered the subtle charms of Siberia.

Contents

List of Illustrations

Introduction

Five months after the Soviet Union collapsed, I graduated from college with a degree in economics and a surplus of idealism. We had won the Cold War, and with Russia reemerging from seventy years of economic retardation, it was time to win the peace. Freedom and prosperity were surely the greatest weapons we had against a resurgence of Communism, and I could imagine nothing more thrilling and meaningful than helping our former enemies rebuild their country on the solid foundation of democracy and market economics. As with Germany and Japan after World War II, we could secure their stability and allegiance for decades to come.

I assessed my options: 1) travel to exotic, faraway lands; live in a continent-sized economics laboratory; affect events that would affect the world for decades to come, or 2) go work for a bank in St. Paul.

I moved to Novosibirsk, Siberia, on the five-hundredth anniversary of Christopher Columbus's first voyage to the New World. With the hubris of a twenty-two-year-old, I thought this chronological coincidence entirely appropriate. I knew that I wasn't setting out to discover a new world. But neither was Columbus. He was looking for a quicker route to the spices of India. I was looking for the express lane to a spicier life.

In short order, I helped build a tiny Siberian company into the largest importer of cocoa beans and condoms within eight time zones. After just six months, my Siberian partner and I had generated our first million dollars of revenue. Unfortunately, after expenses, payments to the local mafia, and usurious tax rates, only a small portion of this money remained as profit. But it was enough to buy fancy foreign cars: Saabs, Citroëns, and Chryslers. It was enough to take luxurious trips to exotic lands: Germany, England, and even America. It was enough money to build an enormous brick house in the Siberian countryside.

I had left America to get away from the ordinary. Suddenly, I was living the American Dream in Siberia. It felt extraordinary. I couldn't help but think of the real estate cliché about how everything depends on just three things: location, location, and location.

Another cliché says that a rising tide lifts all ships. If true, then a falling tide should lower all ships. But, in our case, it didn't. Even while the rest of the Russian economy was going down the drain, our business kept on growing; our revenues soon surpassed ten million dollars annually. It looked like prosperity, but it was a Potemkin prosperity.

In the pursuit of happiness, we had made a critical and all-too-common accounting error. We hadn't counted costs. If you think that's a minor detail, I'd like to point out that the Soviet Union collapsed because it failed to count costs. Success in the Soviet Union was measured in output, not profit. Five-year plans set output goals, but nobody counted (or reported) the costs of reaching those goals until it was too late. Millions of Soviet citizens died in collectivization, and several million more vanished in Siberia's Gulags. And those are just the human costs.

Soviet factories blackened the Russian skies with millions of tons of heavy metals and toxic pollutants just to produce shoddy products that few wanted. Oil spewed from leaky pipelines onto delicate permafrost ecosystems. The Aral Sea, once the world's fourth largest lake, drained away to a lifeless puddle. Lake Baikal, the world's deepest lake, filled with cellulose from factories turning out obsolete tires. Nuclear power plants melted down.

No matter how the Communists doctored the numbers, the Soviet Union was a horribly unprofitable endeavor. Communist apologists (if any still exist) would argue that you can't make an omelet without breaking some eggs. But if, back in 1917, Russians were shown the future mountain of broken shells alongside the future unsavory Soviet omelet, I suspect that they would have driven Lenin and his Bolsheviks out of town with less civility than they had shown their deposed czar.

Counting costs properly and promptly is the essence of good economics. Proper accounting is also essential in the pursuit of happiness.

In our Siberian business enterprise, we succeeded in generating money and creating wealth in a very harsh environment—and I'm not talking about the weather. Yet despite our success, we needed an ever-increasing level of comfort to isolate ourselves from the increasing destitution around us. And we needed ever-greater amounts of Russian vodka to insulate us, if only temporarily, from our own growing malaise. You can invest only so much of yourself into making a decent living before you realize that you no longer have a decent life. As we narrowly focused on short-term profits, our tunnel vision blinded us to the long-term costs—to our friends, to our families, and to ourselves. It seemed that we, the fortunate few who had prospered during the economic chaos, had paid too high a price for our success.

If, back in 1991, Russians were shown the chaos they would suffer over the next ten years, I think they might have thrown the maverick Boris Yeltsin off that tank during the August coup. They probably would have told him to leave the country and take his corrupt capitalism and his dysfunctional democracy with him. Maybe it was Yeltsin's fault things went so badly. Or maybe it is impossible to make a capitalist, democratic omelet without breaking some eggs.

This book is a look at Siberia through American eyes. It is the story of how the myriad costs of democracy and capitalism affect a Siberian man, his family, his company, his town. It is about events that test an idealistic economist's faith in prosperity.

Siberia Bound is also a look at America through Siberian eyes. It reveals the hidden costs we have paid and continue to pay in order to promote and prolong our prosperity. The Worker's Paradise failed because of unaccounted costs. The American Dream might prove similarly vulnerable if we fail to scrutinize the price tag.

Although I am a dismal scientist, I am not a sadistic author. This book isn't just about costs. It is about hidden reward, unexpected joy, and unconditional love. Read this book for the same reason I wrote it: to better understand the pursuit of happiness and the American Dream.

With every autumn I blossom anew;
This Russian cold is good for my health;
I am in love with life's daily routines;
Sleep and hunger arrive at the proper time;
Blood merrily and lightly flows in my heart,
My desires boil—I am again happy, young,
I am again full of life—that is my nature
(Forgive me this unnecessary prosaic blurb).
                                    —Alexander S. Pushkin

SIBERIA BOUND

1
Pandora's Box of Chocolates

If you can identify what is produced inside a factory by the way it smells outside, chances are the smell isn't a pleasant one. Breweries don't smell like ice-cold beer; they reek of warm, fermenting malt. Paper mills don't smell like crisp sheets of paper; they stink of simmering cellulose. But chocolate factories are exceptions to this rule. They give off the delicious aroma of roasting cocoa beans. They smell good *especially* in Siberia, where city air is usually heavy and dark with a mixture of black coal smoke and bluish-gray car exhaust. The Novosibirsk Chocolate Factory was an oasis for the Siberian nose.

It was less appealing to the eye. With its red brick wall, Russian flag, and metal emblem of Lenin over the front door, the Novosibirsk Chocolate Factory was indistinguishable from the Siberian factories that produced some of the world's worst televisions, refrigerators, and telephones. It was also indistinguishable from the countless Siberian factories that produced the world's best automatic rifles, chemical weapons, and supersonic fighter aircraft. Only the smell set it apart.

Sasha and I stepped out of the comically cramped Russian car and scurried across the slippery sidewalk toward the entrance. We were both hunkered over against the cold. Suddenly, Sasha stopped and bolted upright, his eyes wide open.

"Do you smell that?" he asked me. "That's the smell of profit."

As Sasha and I stepped through the inconspicuous front door of the factory, the pleasant smell of cocoa gave way to the humid stench of bad breath. We stood in a narrow corridor crowded with thick people made even thicker by their bulky coats. We were in chocolate-factory purgatory. Judging by the long faces, some of these people had been waiting here for an eternity. In between the crowd and the door that led into the factory grounds was a turnstile that turned only for a certain few—the chosen people. The factory's version of St. Peter was a large woman sitting behind a plate of glass. Occasionally, she stepped onto a pedal that released the turnstile, allowing in one person at a time. A man screamed at her to let him in, that he had driven all the way from Tomsk, but she yelled back at him with equal venom. She didn't step on the pedal. The turnstile remained locked. The man finally retreated, red in the face. The woman folded her hands and cracked a brief smile.

On the wall was a telephone. Sasha looked at the list of numbers taped to the wall next to the phone. When he found what he was looking for, he took off his black gloves, tucked them into his coat pockets, and dialed (really dialed—it was a rotary phone) the number for the deputy director.

"Do you know him?" I asked.

"Nope," Sasha said with a wink.

"Then why not just dial up the director?" I asked.

Sasha smiled patiently. "Deputies are trying to climb the ladder. They have something to prove. They have to take risks. Directors don't. A smart director would never take a chance on our plan."

Before I got a chance to ask Sasha what our plan was, he stuck his finger in his ear and looked down at the floor.

"Zdrasvuite," Sasha said loudly into the receiver. "I'm here with my American partner."

Dozens of fur hats turned toward me. Wary eyes looked me over, trying to determine if I was indeed an American. I smiled, unintentionally confirming their suspicions.

Sasha continued to yell into the phone, "We'd like to discuss a proposal. Could you arrange for us to get past the front gate?" He nodded twice, then yelled our names into the phone. He had to repeat my name three times. He hung up the phone and punched me in the arm. "Looks like you might owe me a bottle of vodka before the day is done," he said just as the phone rang next to the large woman gatekeeper. She nodded and hung up the phone, then called out our names, mispronouncing mine.

The faces in the crowd glowered at us as we maneuvered toward the turnstile. The woman wrote out paper passes for us. It gave me a sense of déjà vu, as if I were back in high school and had just been handed a hall pass. The feeling was one of simultaneous empowerment and belittlement.

We walked through the door that many of the loiterers would never reach. We found ourselves back outside, but within the factory's walls. As I squinted my eyes against the light and cold, I saw a chaotic and cluttered scene, except for a row of dump trucks so clean they could have just rolled off the assembly line. Why a chocolate factory might need so many dump trucks, I couldn't figure. And if they did need them, why weren't they being used? A large brick smokestack with metal belts circling the shaft every ten feet or so cast a long shadow across the yard. Wooden barrels lay scattered about the grounds. It looked more like a 1920s bootlegging operation than a 1990s chocolate factory. We walked into a four-story brick building on the other side of the courtyard and quickly found ourselves at the door of the Zam Director.

Sasha knocked once, but he didn't wait before opening the door himself. A solid man in his mid-forties sat behind a small desk. A young woman dressed in a chocolate-stained apron sat in a chair opposite him. She had been explaining something when Sasha interrupted her by opening the door. The man instructed the woman to come back later.

She stepped out. We slipped in.

After very brief pleasantries and handshakes, Sasha got down to business.

"Why isn't there any smoke coming from the factory's smokestack?"

I hadn't noticed if there was or wasn't smoke coming from the smokestack.

"We have a raw materials shortage right now," the sturdy man answered. "We are only working every other day."

While I had been busy counting dump trucks, Sasha had been gathering useful clues. I resolved to be more observant.

I surveyed the room and its contents, looking for useful information. The deputy director had four telephones on his desk. Every so often, one of them would ring. He'd hold up a stout finger to pause the conversation, grab the phone, listen for a few seconds, bark out a command, and slam down the phone. He had a receding hairline that he didn't bother to comb over. His tie was loose around his neck and his sleeves were rolled up.

"Vitaly Victorovich, what do you need?" Sasha asked deferentially.

"Cocoa beans," he said.

"Alexander Richardovich," Sasha said, referring to me by my Russian patronymic (my father's name + *ovich*), "represents an American company that can supply your factory with cocoa beans. Isn't that right, Alexander Richardovich?"

"Oh, yeah. Right. Of course we can," I agreed clumsily, then silently scolded myself for being such a dimwit. I was ruining the deal. Wait a second, what deal?

"Well, don't get your hopes up, boys," Vitaly Victorovich said. "We can't pay you money for anything. With all this insane inflation, we can't afford to hold money. As soon as we get any money, we buy something that won't lose its value overnight, like..."

"*Gruzaviki*," I said triumphantly, having finally figured out what all those dump trucks were for.

He nodded once, unimpressed. "So, unless you're willing to accept a dump truck as payment for cocoa beans, I'm afraid we don't have enough money to pay you for any raw materials that you sell us."

Just like I thought. No deal.

Not flustered a bit, Sasha said, "If we supply you with cocoa beans, you could give us chocolate in return."

"There is more than just cocoa beans in chocolate," the deputy director cautioned. "We would have to agree ahead of time on how much chocolate you get for the cocoa beans."

"Details," Sasha brushed off the warning.

"Okay. You write up a contract and come in on Friday. If everything looks okay, we can give it a try," the deputy director said with an unenthusiastic smile. One of the phones rang. He grabbed it and resumed barking. While yelling into the receiver, he nodded and pointed to the door. Our time was over. We nodded back and left.

We had two days to prepare a contract. We wasted forty-five of the forty-eight hours because Sasha had insisted that I pay him the bottle of vodka for the bet I lost. And, of course, one bottle had led to another. So, with only a few hours before we were to be back at the factory, we slapped together a dual-column, Russian-English contract on an enormous and anonymous computer that could barely run the pirated Chinese word-processing software. Needless to say, it was a short contract. We left blank the exchange ratio of beans to chocolate. That we would negotiate on the spot.

Back at the factory, the deputy director looked over the contract quickly, too quickly to read the terse text. After haggling for a few minutes, we came up with a figure that satisfied all parties and filled in the blank spot with a black pen that came from Sasha's briefcase.

Sasha and I got up to leave. Halfway out the door, Sasha turned and said, "It will take several weeks for the beans to get here. Then it will take a few weeks for us to sell the chocolates. How about you start giving us chocolate before the cocoa beans get here. That way we'll have some revenue to buy more cocoa beans sooner."

I wanted to hit Sasha in the arm. It seemed like he was trying to seize failure out of the jaws of success.

"Sounds reasonable," the deputy director said. "I can give you six tons tomorrow. Will that be enough?"

"That should be okay," Sasha confirmed in a matter-of-fact voice.

We shook hands with the deputy director and left.

"Six tons," I said, as we went down the steps. "Sasha, six tons is a lot of chocolate! What are we going to do with it all? And where are we going to get cocoa beans?"

"*Anekdote*," Sasha said, turning to me with a confident smile. "Two guys meet in Red Square. One asks the other if he wants to buy a train full of butter for a million rubles. The second man says

5

he does. The men shake hands and agree to meet again at the same spot in a week. The first goes off to look for a train full of butter and the second goes to look for a million rubles."

We both laughed, Sasha a bit longer than I.

By noon the next day Sasha had sold all six tons of chocolate to his friends and business acquaintances over the phone. Few could pay cash up front, but they all promised to pay us after they had sold the chocolate. Sasha agreed. In the meantime, I made some very-long-distance phone calls. I was trying to find a train car full of cocoa beans. I found a company willing to sell us twenty-five tons of cocoa beans and send them by train from Amsterdam to Novosibirsk. It would take four weeks for the beans to arrive. The supplier expected to be paid in advance, of course.

Sasha and I needed some capital, and we needed it now.

The catch-22 of capitalism was upon us. You can't make money if you don't have any capital, and you can't accumulate capital if you don't have money. The solution, of course, is to borrow your start-up capital. But this was Siberian capitalism. There weren't any banks here that loaned money to budding cocoa bean mongers. No problem. We would simply borrow our start-up capital from a communist.

I glanced alternately at the red-faced man behind the desk and at the portrait of Lenin staring down over his shoulder. Protruding from his desk was a long table. I couldn't tell if it reminded me more of a stage for naked women to strut or a pirate ship's plank. I sat on one side of this plank, Sasha on the other. Sasha and I were quickly becoming business partners, and yet, when I looked across the table, I realized that I didn't know him from Adam. It was Sasha's idea to come here to borrow money. I didn't know if I trusted Sasha, and I certainly didn't trust this crusty man with big red flags on stands in the corners of his office. Our prospective creditor had his back to Lenin. I had to look straight into the Bolshevik's eyes. But Lenin rarely looks you in the eyes. He most often has his severe gaze fixed on the not-too-distant future when communism will rule and the proletariat will be safe from capitalists—capitalists like us.

"We'll need about twenty thousand dollars," Sasha said with a smile that made me want to trust him.

I tried not to look as nervous as I felt. I knew that we needed twenty thousand dollars for the cocoa beans. But now, after Sasha had actually said it out loud, *"dvatzat tyisyach dolorov,"* it seemed a ridiculously large amount of money, especially in a country where the average person's monthly income was about fifty dollars and getting less each day. I was prepared to leave the room before we were thrown out.

All eyes turned to the piece of paper Sasha had pulled from his briefcase.

"We'll return your money in three months, plus fifteen-hundred dollars," Sasha promised. This time I couldn't hide my surprise. We hadn't talked about that! Sasha wasn't looking at me. He had his bright blue eyes and his contagious smile targeted on our potential creditor.

The red-faced man looked pained. Then again, he had looked pained from the moment we walked in. "Agreed," he finally said. "Only, no contract." With his index finger he pushed the paper across the desktop, back to Sasha.

No contract? I bit my tongue.

Sasha, still grinning, ripped the paper lengthwise in two, then ripped the two halves into quarters, then into eighths. He disposed of the ribbons of paper into his case. He then extended his hand to the man. As I watched Sasha's jovial expression transform into a sober, sincere gaze, I realized why a paper contract wasn't necessary. This handshake was the contract. I felt drunk with emotion. In two days, we had sold six tons of chocolate and borrowed twenty thousand dollars without a single lawyer charging two hundred dollars an hour to put words on paper to protect us from any and every eventuality. Even better, there would be no lawyers to siphon thousands of dollars from us when an unforeseen eventuality did occur and a dispute arose, a dispute that only lawyers profited from.

The man extended his hand to me. I grabbed it and tried to look him straight in the eyes but couldn't help stealing a glance over his shoulder at Lenin. He looked different. The great Bolshevik's eyes no longer seemed fixed sternly on the future, but mournfully on the past. We were conducting the most blatant act of capitalism, paying for the use of other people's money, under the nose of the man who tried to eradicate capitalism. It was sacrilege, and it felt good, like sinning should.

Sasha pulled a bottle of vodka from his seemingly bottomless briefcase. His briefcase held all the essentials for Siberian business: a stack of his business cards, leather holders for other people's cards, envelopes with crisp dollars, bundles of worn rubles, several company seals, and a bottle of vodka. Sasha's briefcase was like Batman's utility belt. It wasn't the primary source of his strength, but he could always count on it to get him out of difficult situations.

The red-faced man pulled three shot glasses from his desk drawer. We were soon holding up our full glasses as Sasha toasted to success. We clicked glasses, tossed the vodka back, and chased them with nothing but pained expressions. If the handshake was the contract, then these shots of vodka were the signatures.

Out in the empty hallway lit by only one flickering fluorescent light, Sasha held his right hand up like a traffic cop.

"What?" I asked.

With his left hand he grabbed my right wrist and lifted it up. He grinned and tried to give me a high-five. There was no triumphant slap, only a weak thud as his hand hit my shirtsleeve.

"Come on. One more try," he insisted.

"Okay, but I'm going to show you how to do it right," I said as I grabbed his wrist and guided his hand through a practice run. When we did it for real, our hands met with a loud, crisp *clap!* that echoed down the hallway. That went well, I thought. Now all we had to do was turn this loan into a viable company, not just cheerleading practice.

We walked down the hallway toward a large window. The fluorescent light bulb overhead, flickering and buzzing sporadically, turned the window into a mirror, reflecting the image of a strange pair walking side by side. One man was short and dark-haired, the other over six feet and blond. The sleeves of the short man's suit almost covered his whole hands. The large man's suit barely reached his wrists. I couldn't tell if we looked like bold entrepreneurs or off-duty clowns.

I was twenty-two years old, twenty thousand dollars in debt, and in the middle of Siberia. Despite the prerequisite anxieties of the newly self-employed, I couldn't have felt happier at being right there, right then.

Anything was possible.

2
Sweet Dreams

The idea that became a multimillion-dollar business had originated in Sasha's apartment the night before. Sasha and I were just talking—talking and drinking.

"I think you are the only person, Russian or American, who hasn't asked me why I moved here," I said, then sniffed a slice of dark bread as is Siberian custom after tossing down a shot of vodka.

"I don't have to ask." Sasha's blue eyes looked at me over his rectangle of bread that he pressed to his face like a fake moustache. "I know."

We both sighed as the burn of the vodka faded.

Sasha tipped the frost-covered bottle, filling our shot glasses to the rims for the third time in the past fifteen minutes. Then he grabbed two slices of salami from a saucer and handed one to me. Whimpers and coos came from the next room, where Sasha's wife was tucking in their baby girl. Sasha put a finger over his mouth. "Lyuda is trying to get Alina to sleep in her own room for the first time tonight. She's a little scared."

"Who's scared, Alina or Lyuda?"

"Both," he whispered. Leaning forward as if to confide a secret, he said, "Siberia is the land of future millionaires. America used to be the land of opportunity, but now it's Siberia's turn."

I smiled. "You think that's why I came here? To get rich?"

"Yes," Sasha said without a moment of hesitation, "and I think you were right to come. Today, in order to get rich *from* Siberia, you have to live *in* Siberia. For too long Moscow has taken from Siberia: diamonds, gold, lumber, coal, and oil. And what did Siberia get in return? Criminals and dissidents. But that just made Moscow fat and Siberia strong. Siberia today is a lot like America two hundred years ago, populated by outcasts and ripe with opportunity."

"You're right. Siberia is like America, but not America hundreds of years ago, more like fifty years ago, right after the war," I said, not indicating which war I meant. I didn't have to. In Russia, there is only one war—the war that cost twenty million lives. I took two slices of salami and handed one to him. "Do you know what happened in America after the war?"

"Everybody got drunk, pregnant, then married," Sasha answered with a smirk.

"I mean, what happened to the economy?"

Sasha bobbed his eyebrows up and down in anticipation of my answer.

"It boomed," I said. "Five years of pent-up demand created an unprecedented wave of economic prosperity that shaped an entire generation. Imagine," I paused for dramatic effect, "what will happen here after *fifty* years of pent-up demand."

"What do you mean fifty years? We've been standing in lines forever." Sasha opened his eyes wide and cocked his head back as if both simultaneously offended by my underestimation of Siberia's past poverty and thrilled by the promise of Siberia's future fortunes.

"Now that the cork of communism is off," I said, "this economy could erupt like a bottle of champagne."

Sasha rubbed his hands together. "There are almost two million potential buyers here in Novosibirsk alone. There're another seven million customers in the neighboring cities."

"What neighboring cities?"

Counting in the Russian manner of starting with an open hand and curling one digit into his palm at a time, Sasha recited the "nearby" Siberian cities: "Omsk, Tomsk, Barnaul, Kemerovo, and Krasnoyarsk." He folded his thumb into his palm, making a fist, a physical exclamation point.

"Omsk and Krasnoyarsk?" I questioned. "Aren't those cities in different time zones than Novosibirsk? That's like saying that New

York and Denver are in the same neighborhood as Chicago."

"It's all relative," Sasha laughed. "Siberia's size is as incomprehensible as China's population."

Sasha's real name, like mine, is Alexander. In America, where the variety of names is truly awesome, nicknames are usually shorter and easier to remember than people's real names. In Siberia, however, there is a shortage of original names. Maybe exile in Siberia impressed upon the earlier generations the costs of being original, so they gave their children safe, unoriginal names. When asking a Siberian his name, it's a multiple-choice question, not fill-in-the-blank. Not *what* is your name, but *which?* The choices are very limited.

But after seventy years of chronic shortages, Siberians have learned to make a little go a long way. For every name there are dozens of nicknames. Nicknames are used to help sort out the hordes of Borises, Dmitris, and Mikhails. Each name has a set of generally accepted nicknames. Alexander breaks down into the following set: Sasha, Shura, Sanya, Sashka, Shurik, and Sanka. Each nickname carries a slightly different mood, tone, and character. People's personalities and their relationships with others determine which nickname fits them best. Sasha calls me "Sanya," as if to a little brother or nephew. I call him "Sasha" because it implies friendliness but, at the same time, respect. Sasha is nine years my senior.

Sasha handed me another slice of salami, then poured our glasses full of vodka again. I couldn't tell what he loved more, filling the shot glasses or emptying them.

"*Za zhensheen,*" he said with a wink.

As is customary when toasting to women, Sasha and I stood up like soldiers in the presence of an officer. We clicked glasses, gulped down vodka, and sniffed more bread. The cold liquid sent a cold shiver down my spine. This time my sigh was more of a groan. Either I'd have to eat faster or drink slower.

Lyuda walked into the kitchen. "Why are you guys standing?"

"We just drank in your honor," Sasha reported proudly.

"Thanks," she said, batting her eyelids coquettishly.

Lyuda was tiny. Even in her high-heeled slippers, she barely stood five feet tall. She was wearing a Chinese bathrobe and vivid lipstick. Like many Russian women her age, she was determined not to let the titles "Mother" and "Wife" keep her from feeling like a woman.

"Alina asleep?" Sasha asked as he wrapped his arms around Lyuda's tiny waist and pulled her close to him.

"No, but she stopped crying." She put her head on Sasha's shoulder. The warmth of his wife's cheek on his shoulder made Sasha relax. I, too, relaxed—Lyuda was resting on Sasha's pouring hand.

Despite the eight years that separated them, despite the fact that Sasha was a Tatar and Lyuda was Russian, despite his being a Muslim and her being a Christian, they loved each other. Perhaps their incompatibilities made their love possible. Most good things in Siberia seemed to exist in spite of long odds.

"What are you boys talking about?"

"How we're going to get rich," Sasha said.

"We're gonna be rich?" She smiled slightly. It was as if Sasha had just forecasted next week's weather to be sunny with temperatures in the seventies. She clearly doubted the reliability of her husband's prognosis, but was willing to entertain the possibility, if for the entertainment value alone.

"Really," Sasha said emphatically, then turned to me. "Right, Sanya?"

"It's possible," I hedged.

"You said that the economy would burst like a champagne bottle," Sasha said.

"I said that it could, not that it would."

Sasha looked disappointed, but not defeated.

"Sasha, it might take a while for this economy to make the transition. The American postwar economy was transitioning from military production to civilian production. It was a relatively simple matter to change what to produce. Here the challenge is to change *how* things are produced. The transition here is much deeper, and is going to be a lot more difficult."

"So," Sasha asked, "people aren't going to buy things?"

"Sure they will. People always buy things. We just have to choose the right things to sell."

"Like what?"

I remembered out loud a peculiar economic phenomenon: "During hard times, people indulge in small luxuries. Most Siberians won't be able to buy cars, houses, or exotic vacations for a while, but they will be able to treat themselves to the little things that make them feel a little bit rich."

"Small luxuries, huh?" Sasha looked up at the ceiling and mumbled to himself, "little luxuries, little luxuries."

Lyuda got up and began mechanically maneuvering around the kitchen, opening drawers, pulling out pots from cupboards and bags from the freezer. "*Pelmeni?*" she asked.

"Fine," he answered. "C'mon, Sanya, let's go into the other room so we don't get in Lyuda's way." To my disappointment, Sasha grabbed the vodka bottle and shot glasses. I grabbed a few slices of bread and salami as if they were life preservers and I was on a sinking ship.

"*Davai,*" Sasha said as he got up, "let's get to work."

Lyuda put a finger to her mouth and shushed him loudly, then she forcefully whispered, "*Muzh,* Alina is asleep!" With a wave of her spatula, Lyuda told me and her *muzh* to go to the other room to "work."

As we walked past the door to Alina's room I could hear high-pitched whimpering. Lyuda put down her pots and pans with a clamor and scurried into her daughter's room.

"Maybe we should talk about this tomorrow," I suggested to Sasha.

Without a word, he motioned for me to sit down on the couch. He shut the door behind me.

"So, what are some little luxuries we can sell?" Sasha asked as he took a seat next to me.

Lyuda quietly sang soothing lullabies.

"What about coffee?" Sasha asked.

"Coffee. Sure," I said. "That's big business in America."

Sasha nodded. "That's it," he declared, confident that he had hit the nail on the head on his first swing. "How much does a good cup of coffee cost in America?"

"I don't know. I hate the stuff," I said. "A dollar or two."

"*Two dollars!*" Sasha's jaw dropped. He reached for the vodka bottle. "This will never work. That's over one thousand rubles for a cup of coffee." Sasha shook his head as he poured another round of vodka. "I don't care how good the coffee is; it'll be a long time before Siberians are drinking fancy coffee for one thousand rubles a cup."

"Actually," I said, "if this hyperinflation keeps up, it won't be long before Siberians are drinking *bad* coffee for a thousand rubles a cup."

"Yeah," Sasha sighed, not amused. Then he began looking around the room and mumbling to himself, "little luxuries, little luxuries…" His eye came to rest on the bottle of vodka in his hand. His eyes glimmered. "Alcohol is a little luxury."

Before I could say what I was thinking—namely, that the last thing Russia needs is more alcohol—Sasha shook his head. "No, alcohol is too tightly controlled by the mafia. Besides," he winked, "alcohol isn't a luxury. It's a necessity."

I heard Lyuda leave Alina's room. Apparently she had lulled her daughter back to sleep. Nothing makes a child feel better than mom, except…

"Candy," I said.

Without turning his head, Sasha snapped his eyes to meet mine. He said nothing. I could see that he was considering the potential Siberian candy market. He furrowed his forehead.

His expression made me wonder whether the mafia controlled the candy industry, too.

"How much?" he asked.

"Between twenty-five and forty-five cents for a candy bar," I said. "That's retail, though. We'd be able to buy for a lot less if we buy in bulk."

Sasha did the math in his head. Apparently, he liked the outcome. He broke into an ear-to-ear grin and raised his shot glass. I quickly downed a few slices of bread to soak up the vodka before my liver did.

Before picking up my glass (after which it is considered poor form to put it back down unless empty), I was saved by the bell. The doorbell.

A few moments later, Sasha escorted a man into the room to meet me. "Sanya," he said looking at me, "I want you to meet my good friend Alexander. You can call him Shura."

Shura had been walking by, saw the light on, and decided to drop in. Shura was Sasha's college roommate. He had a thick, black mustache and a wave of black hair on top of his head. He smiled when he saw the bottle of vodka on the table.

"I guess I better warm up another bottle of vodka," Sasha said as he slapped Shura's back.

"Warm up?" I asked. "Isn't vodka supposed to be served ice cold?"

"Yep," Sasha confirmed as he went toward the balcony and opened the Siberian double doors. Siberian double doors aren't placed side by side like French doors; they are placed one right after the other, just like Siberian double-paned windows. Sasha navigated his way across the narrow balcony cluttered with bicycles, skis, and clotheslines, came to a small refrigerator at the end of the balcony, opened it, and removed a bottle of vodka. The refrigerator's power cord was coiled up, unplugged. Retracing his steps, Sasha maneuvered his way back and shut and latched both doors behind him. The tips of his eyelashes were white.

"oooooOOOOAAAAHhh," he let out a yawp. The door had been open for less than fifteen seconds, but the room was now thermally bisected. The temperature near the ceiling was still relatively cozy, but around my stocking feet, it was frosty.

"Watch this." Sasha grabbed the glass of water his wife had been using to spit on clothes before she ran the iron across them. Sasha wiped my forehead with two fingers and smeared my sweat on the table. "Grease. It prevents sticking."

Shura wasn't looking at Sasha; he had seen this trick before and was more interested in my reaction. Sasha poured the remaining water from the glass onto the shiny spot on the coffee table. Placing the vodka bottle on the small puddle of water, Sasha said, "This is why you have to warm vodka up in Siberia before you serve it." He lifted the bottle. The puddle of water, now frozen solid, came with the bottle like a cardboard coaster stuck to the bottom of a beer mug.

"Good vodka served at the right temperature kills you slowly," Sasha said with a smirk. "Bad vodka or vodka that's too cold will kill you quickly."

Just then Lyuda called us into the kitchen for *pelmeni*. I devoured the meat-filled dumplings by the dozen. Unfortunately, Sasha and Shura managed to keep the toasts coming just as quickly, never letting the mitigating effects of the warm food get ahead of the debilitating effects of the frigid vodka. The alcohol, even after warming up at room temperature for several minutes, was so cold that it came out of the bottle slowly, like transparent cream.

"How about some tea?" Lyuda asked, when the bottle was finally empty—the most welcome words of the evening.

Tea in Siberia is not just a drink; it is a ritual repeated several times a day. Lyuda put a pot of water on to boil. Sasha spooned in brown tea from a little red box. She put cups on saucers, and he placed spoons beside them. When the water came to a boil, Lyuda poured the tea into each cup, filling them halfway. Sasha tapped his finger on the table near his cup. Lyuda filled his cup three-quarters full. Then she poured some of the hot water into the cups until the tea faded to a pleasant auburn. Lyuda pulled pieces of a dry lemon from one of the two refrigerators crowding the small kitchen. She dropped the lemon chips into our cups.

"Let's go to one of the factories tomorrow," Sasha said after taking his first sip of tea.

"Factories?" I asked.

"We've got two chocolate factories in town. Why wait to bring American chocolate across the planet when we've got chocolate right here?"

17

"Why would they want to work with us?" I asked.

"Why wouldn't they?" Sasha countered my question with a question.

"I can think of a hundred reasons why they wouldn't."

"And I can think of a hundred reasons why they would." Sasha smiled. "Come on," he said with a wink. "I'll make it interesting. Let's bet a bottle of vodka on it. I bet that we get into the chocolate factory and make a lot of money selling little luxuries. Lots and lots of little chocolate luxuries."

Sasha turned and enthusiastically explained to Shura that the key to success was to sell little luxuries. Shura nodded attentively, taking it all in. Sasha suddenly turned back to me, "Come on. Let's bet."

"I'm not going to bet against us," I said. "That's too pessimistic. That's too…well, it's too Russian."

Both Sasha and Shura laughed heartily. So much so, that Lyuda had to shush them.

"Come on," Sasha said to me, extending his hand. "If you win, you get a bottle of vodka. If you lose, we get rich. It's a win-win situation for you."

"All right." I slapped my hand into his. We shook on it.

Sasha, without letting go of my hand, turned to Shura and said, "Do the honors."

Shura nodded and placed a gentle Karate-chop to our handshake. Only then did Sasha release my hand. "Shura is the witness. He has to enforce that the loser pays up."

I got up from the table. "I'm going."

"*Kuda?*" Sasha looked offended. "Spend the night here." With Alina in one room, there wasn't much real estate left. I wasn't worried that there would be no place for me to sleep; I was more worried that Sasha would give up his foldout couch to me, while he and his wife slept on the kitchen floor.

"Thanks, but no." I slapped him on the back. Then I grabbed his shoulder for stability. "Besides," I said, trying to look him straight in the eyes, "we've got a big day tomorrow. We're going to a chocolate factory, aren't we?"

My Frozen Utopia

What would you be willing to give up in exchange for happiness?

For me, the answer is comfort. Always has been. Ever since I can remember, I have been either happy or comfortable, never both. Happiness isn't some cozy middle ground in between two extremes; happiness *is* an extreme.

While growing up in Minnesota, I thought that summers were fine, but winters were fantastic. My friends and I built elaborate snow forts in preparation for the invasion of an unknown enemy. When no enemy showed, we grew bored and destroyed our fortress like barbarians, screaming and laughing as the walls tumbled into shapeless piles. Winters in Minnesota were never long enough or cold enough for me. If the snow piled up to my waist, I wanted it to rise to my shoulders. When it got cold enough to freeze spit before it hit the ground, I wanted it to get cold enough to freeze pee in midair. On the coldest days of the year, I'd go outside to test whether it was that cold. It never was.

My dad predicted that I would end up living in Canada or Alaska. Latitudinally, he was right on.

By the time I graduated from college in 1992, I had already been to Siberia three times and was eager to go back. Curiosity and an appetite for adventure first lured me there in 1988 to raft down the Ob River, Siberia's north-flowing Mississippi. The next winter I was part of an expedition trekking by horse and reindeer sleigh across a small stretch of Siberia. We went from village to village, spending our nights in places called *Cherepanovo* (Turtleton) and *Zaitsovo* (Hareville). I celebrated New Year's Eve 1990 dancing in the streets of a village about a hundred miles south of Novosibirsk. In 1991, I lived for a few months surrounded by birch forests on the campus of the University of Novosibirsk.

I had finally found a place that could sate my enormous appetite for winter. Winter refines Minnesota. ("It keeps out the riff-raff," my dad liked to say.) But winter defines Siberia. "Ten months of winter and two months of mosquitoes," Sasha would say, adding with a nudge from his elbow, "Don't tell too many people about Siberia or they'll flock here and drive up the price of real estate."

Life in Siberia took effort, but it was well worth it. Life was more difficult, yet more rewarding. Siberia made little sense to most people, including most "European" Russians. But to me, Siberia was about the only thing that made sense. I was a Gen Xer in search of voluntary (or even involuntary) simplicity. Life in Siberia was challenging, frightening, and exciting. Paradise.

Maybe Sasha was right to compare Siberia with an earlier America. My ancestors were surely considered crazy to leave their European homeland for the savage frontier of America. Whether they were running away from nightmares or chasing dreams, they came to America in search of a better life. And that is just what I was doing by leaving behind the comforts of America and moving to the rugged challenges of Siberia. I was simply looking for a better life.

And, for a time, that is exactly what I found. Siberia heightened my senses. I savored every day, starting with the very moment I woke up each morning.

I woke up every morning at the same time—the same time my neighbor's first student began to play the piano. Notes and chords began to seep through the wall promptly at 7:30 A.M. Most days the sounds were as unpleasant as any alarm clock. No matter how tired or hungover, I was up and out of the apartment as quickly as possible just to escape the sounds of the piano students. But Thursdays were different. I went to bed on Wednesday nights eager for the following mornings. Thursday was Olga's morning. (I knew her name because her teacher constantly praised her: "Olga, that was wonderful. Olga, that was marvelous.") Olga's sweet melodies gently swept the sleep out of my eyes and turned my dull routine into a dance. Humming along with the music, I brushed my teeth, folded my bed back into a couch and donned layers of clothing to keep the icy bite of the outside air from gnawing on any exposed skin. Even when I was dressed and ready to go, I couldn't leave the apartment until Olga was done playing. I would sit fully dressed in bulky winter clothing on the creaky chair next to the door and just listen.

When the music stopped, I'd head down the stairwell and out into the street. The frigid air forced me to take short, shallow breaths. Moisture froze to the tiny hair follicles inside my nostrils, creating a tingly sensation with each inhalation.

I set out along the paths of this unique Siberian village. With its crumbling concrete buildings and derelict, half-complete construction projects, this was clearly a Soviet town. But the thickets of birch trees inside the town and the great birch forest just outside city limits made it a druid's dream first and a worker's paradise second. My apartment building was flush up against the forest. Just outside my window, the forest went on, for all intents and purposes, forever. Several trailheads led into the forest. In the evenings, mothers occasionally banged spatulas on kitchen windows to keep their frolicking children from wandering too far into the woods. Once a day, a cascade of bells came from out of the forest, hinting at the location of a secluded church nestled among the protective trees. All winter long, groups of cross-country skiers went into the woods with loud whoops of enthusiasm. They emerged hours later silent, satisfied, spent.

On the other side of my apartment, like the walls of a giant labyrinth, stood dozens of identical four-story apartment buildings laid out at 45- and 90-degree angles to each other. Yes, the buildings were shabby and anonymous, just like all buildings constructed in Russia after the Bolshevik Revolution. Some of the buildings here had been painted loud, primary colors, and yet their intrinsic architectural grayness came through. But the bucolic setting made the village's architectural shortcomings seem tolerable and, with a little help from good fortune and free enterprise, temporary.

Even though I lived at one end of the town and my work was on the other, it took me only twenty minutes to get to or from work if I walked at a steady pace. Instead of traffic jams, morning radio shock jocks, and road rage, during my commute to work I enjoyed a brisk stroll that cleared my head of any hangover. Instead of gridlock, rush hour here meant sidewalks abuzz with people shopping and haggling, gossiping and chitchatting.

The definition of a luxury is something that only a few can afford. By this definition, cars were luxuries in Siberia and walking was a luxury in America. For me, an American, walking to work felt luxurious. I relished the daily regimen of fresh air and exercise. The Siberians thought of walking somewhat differently. In fact, they didn't think about it at all. They just did it. No matter how cold it got, they never complained. Siberians complain about the cold as often as earthlings complain about gravity.

Along my morning commute, the snow crunched and squeaked with each footfall, keeping pace like a rusty metronome. As I walked through courtyards, across buried soccer fields and past little stores, I kept time not by the battery-operated watch buried under layers of clothes, but rather by the world around me. If I was on time, there was a familiar pattern to the events: an old man walking a shaggy German Shepherd; a garbage truck near apartment no. 10; a young man smoking a cigarette as he warmed up the engine of his little red car; people waiting in line outside the corner store. If I was running late, there were different events: a young boy with his Irish Setter; a garbage truck near apartment no. 18; a cigarette butt, but no man or red car. Only the line outside the store looked the same. It was always there.

During my twenty-minute walk to work, I crossed a total of three streets. The widest street was called *Morskoy Prospect* (Sea Prospect), so named because it led to the Ob Sea, a hundred-mile-long reservoir created by damming up the Ob River. Morskoy Prospect was bleak but beautiful, a typical Siberian road—straight, encased in ice, flanked by birch trees, and speckled with over-crowded, rickety buses. There was a bus stop that, even when I was running a little late, I found too much of a spectacle to pass by without a few moments' pause.

By watching the bus stop carefully, I could determine not only the time of day, but the day of the week as well. On Mondays, a middle-aged man stood with his friend. (Friend, brother—that I couldn't tell. Everybody looks related wearing those bulky jackets, dog-hair scarves, and fur hats.) The two men held shopping nets. Inside each net was a frozen pig head. As the men talked, the squinting pig heads, like morbid ventriloquist dolls, seemed to be smiling, waiting to deliver a punch line or sing a duet. Small children standing next to their mothers would stare eye-to-eye with the dead animal heads. Some kids buried their faces into their mothers' coats. Others laughed and pointed.

On Wednesday mornings, an old man who looked like Mother Goose's long-lost Russian cousin waited at the bus stop. His white beard cascaded down the length of his chest. A few minutes before his bus arrived, he would casually step away from the huddled crowd. When he pulled his hand out from his large mitten, it was as if someone had poured a bucket of birds over his head. The old man was immediately standing in a puddle of Siberian Chickadees. As the birds devoured the seeds that fell from his hand, the old man disappeared into the crowd of people. Soon the crowd, too, was gone. Down the street the bus rumbled, a cloud of gray exhaust swirling in the vacuum immediately behind it.

After crossing Morskoy Prospect, I made my way along the snow-packed trails that wove together the village's apartments, shops, playgrounds, and schoolyards. From any one place were half a dozen trails that led to any other place. Traffic levels determined the width of the trail. A surplus of pedestrians inevitably caused footfalls outside the trail, packing down loose snow in the winter and crushing vegetation in the summer, widening the trail where it needed to be widened. Trails with sparse traffic narrowed all year as snow fell deeper and grass grew taller. Trails without any foot traffic disappeared altogether. The transportation infrastructure here was virtually self-regulating, always finding equilibrium, if only temporarily.

To me, this network of trails was a physical metaphor for free market capitalism—high demand increased supply, low demand decreased supply. It wasn't done by one person, but by the collective decisions of many. Paved streets, on the other hand, built by the government, where the government decided they should be, seemed more like a metaphor for communism's clunky command economy. The trails were the sinewy arteries of a vibrant town. They were an organic part of the landscape. The streets, by contrast, were unnaturally straight. They tried to impose a grid on the landscape. Most people stuck to the trails.

There was a point in my walk where a leaning tree formed an arch under which I passed every day. After a few months, I started to suspect that the distance between my head and the top of the arch was shrinking. At first I thought it was my imagination. But, each day, the tree continued to get lower and lower. Then, one day, I actually had to bend down in order to pass underneath. This was definitely not my imagination.

Here we go again, I thought to myself, afraid I was going through another growth spurt. At six-foot-three, two hundred pounds, I was reminded every time I tried to squeeze myself into an airplane seat, twin bed, or telephone booth that the world was designed for somebody else, somebody a little bit smaller. If I grew any more, I would no longer be considered taller than average, I would be considered short for the NBA.

With considerable relief, I realized that I wasn't growing. The village was sinking. As the snow continued to fall, the trails of packed-down snow rose higher and higher. The rising snow created the sensation of living in a frozen version of Venice, in a town sinking inch by inch. Apartment windows that were eight feet above ground in the summertime were waist-high by February, forcing the inhabitants to close their curtains for a few months to protect themselves from the curious eyes of those passing by. The few sidewalks that were regularly shoveled soon became deep trenches that would have been difficult to climb in and out of if it weren't for the steps people carved with hatchets into the snow banks.

About three-quarters of the way to work, I passed the *dyetskii sahd* (kindergarten). Parents and children, gloved hand in mittened hand, came out of the woods from all directions. The parents would walk their kids to the pale green building, bend down to give a few words of encouragement, straighten a hat or clean a cheek with a little spit on the thumb, then head off down the trails on their way to work. This was another way for me to keep time. I knew which kids were dropped off earlier and which ones later. If I saw Vadik in his red boots, I knew I was making good time. But if I saw little Lena with her braids hanging out from her furry hat, I knew that I was late.

I walked on.

After the sounds of children faded, the University of Novosibirsk came into sight. The third most prestigious school of higher learning in Russia, the university was the hub around which the town revolved. Trails radiated out through the woods like spokes, connecting the university with twenty-five scientific institutes. This town, *Akademgorodok* (Academic Village), was designed and constructed for the purpose of conducting practical and theoretical research in everything from nuclear physics to geology. The village was infested with scientists who could split atoms, create or cure diseases, turn oxygen into liquid and mercury into gas. But more than a few of these geniuses had trouble with life's more mundane tasks: I once saw a pair of scientists so engaged in a conversation about thermodynamics that they walked out of the institute without their coats. After only a few steps they were reminded by the sub-zero air that, in their preoccupation with the theoretical, they had forgotten the practical.

The office where Sasha and I worked was located in the university's laboratory building, tucked into the attic—the fifth floor of a four-story building. With its long, straight corridor broken into sections by low-hanging support beams, it looked more like the inside of a submarine than an office. As I walked down the corridor, I had to bend to pass safely under the beams.

During the dark months of winter, when the sun peeked above the horizon for only a few hours a day, I spent ten to twelve hours a day in this submarine. It was dark when I went to work and dark when I walked home. The darkness that hangs over Siberia during the winter can smother your soul with gloom. More than one melancholy novel has been written under the influence of Siberian darkness.

But the darkness was no match for the uplifting power of living in this vibrant village. Twenty minutes of walking along the village's trails infused my soul with vitality. I was rarely comfortable in Siberia, but I was happy. Extremely happy.

4
Beyond the Bicycle Business

Four weeks after they had left Amsterdam, the African cocoa beans finally reached Novosibirsk. A crane snatched the containers from the Trans Siberian Railway flatcars and placed them onto two flatbed trucks. As the red trucks drove through the factory gates, I was awed that the global economy included even Siberia.

But there was no fanfare. Instead, Sasha and the deputy director had been arguing all morning. Vitaly Victorovich claimed that we owed the factory, not the other way around. And he was right. In the past weeks, we had received more chocolate credit from the factory than these cocoa beans were worth. We did owe the factory. Now that the beans were here, we simply owed less.

So we quickly bought more cocoa beans with the revenues from the chocolate sales. We managed to pay the interest on the loan, plus five thousand dollars of the principle, to the red-faced Bolshevik who'd loaned us the money to buy the cocoa beans. But we needed to keep delivering cocoa beans if we were to get out of from under this debt. In the meantime, the factory started working every day. We hired several people to manage the outflow of chocolate and the inflow of beans and rubles. It was a classic bicycle business, one that worked well enough as long as things kept moving. We couldn't stop, however, or it would all come crashing down.

Even though we imported more cocoa beans each month, we didn't see any profit. Just as we were about to pay off all of our debts, the surprisingly shrewd deputy director would offer us more chocolate credit, and we almost always accepted. We were making indecent amounts of money by Russian standards, and decent amounts by American standards. There were big profit margins on both ends of the deal. We profited twice, once when we "sold" the cocoa beans to the factory and again when we sold the chocolate. The chocolate revenues flowed slowly, barely keeping ahead of our cocoa bean expenses. Until we figured out how to speed up the time it took to get paid or delay the time of paying for the beans, all our assets would be frozen, so to speak, in beans and chocolate. It seemed that we would have to be content with the chocolaty smell of profit for a while.

But we weren't content. If anything, we grew more restless. There were too many opportunities out there to sit on just this one. Sasha's friend Shura had recently become the exclusive dealer of Wrigley's products in Novosibirsk. Store windows were quickly filling up with colorful posters showing an absurdly tall woman smiling with her blinding white teeth. She wore shorts (appropriately named) from which extended long, tan legs. Compared to the blocky, furry, Siberian folks, this California girl looked like she was from another planet. She was happy—ridiculously, stupidly happy. The poster implied none too subtly that happiness was only one stick of gum away. Within a month, all the kiosks were selling these chewy happy sticks. The village's trails began to fill up with gum wrappers. Still, nobody smiled or seemed half as happy as the woman in the poster, nobody except Shura. He smiled so much that he hardly looked like a Russian anymore. And why shouldn't he smile? He had a business that was producing more cash than creditors, more dollars than debts.

Whenever Sasha and I had a spare moment from managing the logistical challenges of our chocolate business, we tried to dream up new schemes. If a new product appeared on the Siberian market, we wouldn't rejoice that our choices as consumers had just expanded. Instead, we felt frustrated at the missed opportunity. Standing in front of a kiosk full of colorful lingerie, Sasha and I shook our heads and said, "Of course, why didn't we think of that?"

One day, just when it seemed we'd amassed a sizeable profit, Sasha began removing bricks of rubles from the gray safe under his desk. He tossed them into his briefcase.

"What's that for?" I asked.

Without stopping, he said, *"Dahn."*

"Don? Who's he?"

"Dahn," he said with a smile. "You know, the mafia."

"You mean like Don Corleone?"

"Not *Don*. Dahn." He swung the safe's door shut and turned the large metal key.

"How much does Dahn get?"

"Dahn isn't a person." Sasha laughed as he closed the briefcase with a click. "Dahn is the money we pay to the mafia in order to keep a roof over our heads."

"So, how much does our roof cost?"

"No specific amount. We just pay what we think is fair and hope that it's enough." Sasha slapped me on the back.

"What happens if it isn't enough?"

"I don't know. It's always been enough in the past," Sasha said, trying unsuccessfully to reassure me.

"Are you sure this is enough? Maybe you should put a little more in."

"Don't worry," Sasha said. "I'm practically related to, as you call him, Don. He's a Tatar."

That didn't reassure me either.

But months went by without any negative consequences from Don. So we continued to dream up dozens of ventures, followed through on only a few, and made profits that were quickly drained away to our creditors and protectors. All the while, our chocolate business expanded. The office grew as we hired still more people to sell the increasing amounts of chocolate, to track the containers in transit, to track the money owed to us and by us. Before long, the submarine had two-dozen people scurrying up and down the corridor, popping in and out of the many doors.

Part of me, the economist part, was glad and even a little proud. We were creating jobs. Sure, the jobs didn't pay much, but it was more than most jobs in Siberia paid, if only marginally.

Another part of me, the entrepreneur part, was frustrated. The employees were being paid their wages on time. The red-faced communist-cum-capitalist was getting his principal back plus interest. Don was getting paid for, well, for not doing anything—for not breaking our legs, for not burning our office, for not putting horse heads in our beds. The Russian government was getting paid taxes, lots and lots of taxes. The chocolate factory was getting a steady supply of raw materials, which allowed it to produce chocolate and pay its employees, its taxes, and its Don. The process was working; the wheel was turning. Everybody was getting something, everybody except the entrepreneurs, Sasha and me.

Artists are often willing to work for peanuts if they believe in their work. Their art comes first. But selling cocoa beans wasn't an art. It often required an artist's sense of creativity and passion, but it was not an art. It was a business, and the point of business is not just to stay busy (despite what the word "business" literally implies), but to make a profit—something that had thus far eluded us.

The economist in me was pleased about our success. The entrepreneur in me felt unfulfilled. Only partially satisfied with my job, I considered myself relatively fortunate.

5
After Hours

At the end of every workday, I looked forward to walking home and the search for dinner. I usually started with bread. If I was lucky, there were still a few loaves of Turkish bread left for sale from the back of a truck with the word *khleb* (bread) written on the side. The truck usually sold out and drove away before six o'clock. If it was gone, I had to pick up a loaf of dark rye bread from the state store. The line there was longer; the bread was cheaper, and the cashier was a typical Soviet employee: rude, petty, and slow. Fortunately, there were fewer and fewer of these stores with each passing day. The old Soviet stores with their empty shelves were steadily becoming obsolete. Replacing them were kiosks, street peddlers, and old-lady entrepreneurs. What used to be the black market was now the *babushka* economy.

Outside of every store stood small groups of babushkas selling everything from cucumbers to toilet paper. Often they sold the very same products that were for sale inside the store. And the babushkas charged more for their products. But still they found customers, usually the wives of *biznessmen*. As an economist, I considered this proper. The babushka valued her time differently than the bizness-man's wife. The babushka had time, but little money. The young woman had money, but little time. So, essentially, I considered the young woman was paying the babushka to stand in line. Everybody gained from the trade. It was the free market in its purest form — people trading things they value less for things they value more.

Many evenings I never made it into the stores because I had already filled my bag, pockets, and arms with whatever the babushkas were peddling. The babushka selling sunflower seeds spent most of her time shooing away the ubiquitous Siberian chickadees that frequently dive-bombed her burlap sack, stealing a few precious black seeds off the top. Another babushka sold dirt-encrusted carrots from a rusty bucket. From a large metal canister wrapped in burlap, a heavyset woman sold meat-filled *piroshki* that dripped grease. Except for three old men, the babushkas had a near lock on the street market.

The old men sold three things: fish, tools, and tea.

Next to a tree, a crusty old fisherman stood by himself, smoking a homemade Siberian cigarette made of mystery leaves rolled inside newspaper. Laid out on the snow before his large, furry boots were a dozen fish, mostly perch and an occasional pike. I was warned by my Russian friends not to eat these fish. They came from the Ob Sea, a body of water that the locals said was polluted with the waste from a chemical weapons factory upstream. Of course, the same people that warned of the polluted fish could be found swimming in the Ob Sea during the glorious, albeit brief, summer. There are only so many things you can sacrifice for health's sake in Siberia, and enjoying summer isn't one of them.

Another old man laid out before him a small hardware store: pipes, tubes, hinges, tape, hand drills, washers, bolts, screws, and dozens of other doodads. Whenever something broke in my apartment, which was fairly often, I'd always find just what I needed on the ground in front of the hardware man. His prices were always below what I thought was fair. When buying things on the street, accepting the first offer is insulting. So I usually talked him down a little bit, just enough so that he could say, "Well, okay. I probably shouldn't let this piece go so cheaply. My sick wife will never forgive me." Just as I'm considering giving him an extra hundred rubles for his troubles, he'd say, "But to hell with her. I'm out here every day just to get away from her nagging. Besides, I like you. You're polite, unlike most young people these days."

There was one other old man who peddled his wares just inside the door of the state *produkti* (grocery) store. This old man sold tea.

He stacked a wall of little pink boxes like sandbags in preparation for a flood. Inside the boxes were different kinds of tea, all of which he claimed to have picked and sorted himself. I discovered that one of the best ways to raise my spirits on these long, dark winter days was to buy one of these little pink boxes from him for what amounted to a couple of dimes. He always explained what each tea was good for and when and how to drink it.

"Malissa," he'd say, holding the box in his hand as if it were Aladdin's magic lamp. "Malissa will cure a sore throat. Don't drink it after ten at night. And don't drink vodka for twenty-four hours after drinking malissa."

I bought malissa tea from him fairly often because of my frequently sore throat. My Russian friends said that I had a sore throat so often because I ate too much ice cream. I had no idea if they were right about ice cream causing sore throats, but they were right about my ice cream intake. If ice cream cones were cigarettes, I'd have been a chain-smoker. Almost every day I handed a few hundred-ruble notes plus a plastic bag through the tiny, square window of one of the many ice-cream kiosks. Moments later the bag reappeared filled with a dozen ice cream cones. I could walk around all day with my bag of ice cream. There was no danger of them melting, at least not until May.

Halfway between work and home, I often dropped into my favorite store. It was a tiny shop attached to a flying saucer–shaped restaurant affectionately referred to by locals as the *poganka* (the poisonous mushroom). The little store sold handmade *pelmeni*, Siberian ravioli. *Pelmeni* was the perfect bachelor food. All I had to do was boil them in water for five minutes until they floated to the surface, pour out the water and squeeze a few lines of Bulgarian ketchup onto them. Voila! Dinner. And, on weekends, lunch.

Three large babushkas in greasy white aprons worked at the poganka store. For about a month they thought I was a stupid Russian, because, even though I spoke Russian without an accent, my culinary vocabulary was limited. I had to point at food that I wanted but didn't know what to call. The women behind the counters did what most Russian people do when dealing with dimwitted people: they yelled. "WHAT DO YOU WANT?"

"Red salad," I pointed to the tub full of beet salad.

"HOW MUCH?" the solid woman shouted.

"One kilogram, please."

She held out her chunky hand.

I rummaged around my pockets for a bag.

The woman sighed and shook her head with disappointment.

I produced a plastic bag from one of my pockets and handed it over. She filled the bag with the beet salad, but instead of handing it to me, she gave it to the woman seated behind the mechanical cash register.

"SEMSOTSEMDECYATCHETIRY!" shouted the hefty cashier.

I didn't quite understand how much I was supposed to pay, so I looked at the cash register for some help. Like the keys of a type-writer jammed together from excessive speed, this cash register's display was jammed from excessive digits. The numbers were stuck in between 4,999 and 5,000. A small slip of paper with the words OUT OF ORDER was taped to the machine. Another victim of inflation.

"SEMSOTSEMDECYATCHETIRY!" she repeated.

I played back in my head what she said, "Semsot (seven hundred), semdecyat (seventy)…" I had forgotten the last digit. "How much?" I asked, knowing that this would confirm their suspicions of my stupidity.

Rather than scream at me again, the chunky woman grabbed her abacus, flicked the little wooden rings back and forth with amazing dexterity. She then held up the abacus for me to look at, as if this would make things suddenly clear. "LOOK," she barked. "SEMSOTSEMDECYATCHETIRY!"

I laughed.

"CAN'T YOU EVEN READ AN ABACUS?" she said, completely exasperated by my ignorance.

I shook my head and confessed that I wasn't a foolish Russian. I wasn't a Russian at all. I was an American. There was a pause, then a flutter of apologies. The yelling suddenly stopped and the doting began.

From that day on, I was no longer the village idiot. They adopted me as their collective grandson. They smiled whenever I walked in the door at the end of the day. Sometimes I came a few minutes after they'd closed, but they'd always unlock the door for me. The shelves were empty, but they had tucked away a bag of goodies for me. The bag always had some *pelmeni*, three or four *piroshki*, some cabbage or beet salad and, if they had any, a few chocolates. This care package cost the equivalent of about a dollar, but to me it was priceless. It kept me well fed through the long, cold winters when fat is an asset. I put on about ten pounds each winter thanks to these babushkas (though in their eyes I remained dangerously skinny). I rarely got cold walking home from work. And if I did, there were so many places to drop into along the way that I was rarely outside for more than ten minutes at a time.

I wasn't the only American in this village. In the summertime, American students lived in the dorms, but they came and went so quickly that I didn't have the time or energy to get to know them. They were regarded as tourists, slightly annoying but basically innocuous.

And then, of course, there were the missionaries. They were much more annoying and, as far as I was concerned, far from innocuous.

Like panhandlers, the missionaries hung out in groups on busy street corners and approached strangers. They were polite, happy, and they always smiled. I guess that's why most Russians didn't like or trust them. I didn't like or trust them either. Usually I crossed over to the other side of the street to avoid them. Occasionally, however, I'd take advantage of the fact that I spoke Russian and the missionaries usually didn't. When they smiled at me and quickly exhausted their entire Russian vocabulary in a few words of greeting, I answered like a native, frowning. Then they asked in English whether I had discovered the love of Christ. A young Russian woman, usually a university student who knew a little English, acted as translator for the few bucks a day that the missionaries paid them. I'd listen to these young purveyors of the "Good News," understanding every word they said, but waiting for the translator to finish before I answered, always in Russian.

I said that I had met some Baptist missionaries the other day. "Are you Baptist?" I asked.

No, they weren't. They were Lutheran.

"Well, this was very confusing indeed," I told them through the translator. "Which church did Jesus belong to?"

"Er, uh," they fumbled. The student translator cracked a smile.

I winked at her and walked away.

Some of the missionaries, however, were clearly using God as a pretext to pursue other, less pious interests.

Slava, a physics student at the university whom I taught to play cribbage, had told me once about an older missionary who was "blue." Blue in Russia didn't mean sad or cold. It meant gay. This man, Slava told me, had lived in the village last summer. He preached the virtues of a godly life during the day, but apparently he considered that simply his day job. In the summer evenings, bright and sunny until well after ten o'clock, he often went down to the beach at the Ob Sea to paint various subjects, usually young men. Often the men would be wearing their swimming suits, but not always.

Slava pulled out a bottle of vodka as he told me a story of how his friend had posed nude for this religious painter who was filled with something other than divine inspiration. Slava whispered as he told me how this painter had offered to perform oral sex on his friend.

"How do you know your friend wasn't making all of this up?" I asked.

"Because," he said, "I saw him do it."

"Do what?" I asked, more than just a little nervous about the answer.

"I saw that old man give my friend a *minyet*." Slava gazed into the corner of the room. The expression on his face was something in between revulsion and total absorption, as if he were remembering the sight of a gruesome car accident.

"How did you happen to see this?" I asked, as he poured a round of vodka.

"My friend invited me to watch," Slava said. "I was too curious not to accept."

We both had another shot of vodka without even saying a toast.

Slava shook his head, as if confused. "My friend said that men give better head than women do. But even if they do..."

I grabbed the bottle and filled the shot glasses again.

"I mean," Slava continued, "women are so soft. They smell good. Men are, well, not."

"To women." I raised my glass.

"Amen," Slava said as we stood in honor of women, soft and aromatic.

We drank our vodka and sniffed bread.

"Ask your friend if missionaries give better head than atheists," I said.

We both laughed and then resumed our cribbage game.

At times it seemed as if half the Americans in Novosibirsk were missionaries. I hung out with the other half. Most of us godless Americans, no more than ten at any given time, were sprinkled about the neighborhood known to locals as the Upper Zone. We called it the American Ghetto.

Some expats taught English. Others were here representing one of the many U.S. programs that were supposedly trying to export democracy and promote capitalism. There were a few Americans who were here hiding from the U.S. government, or more specifically, from one of the government's three-lettered agencies. And then there were the oddballs (in whose ranks I placed myself), who weren't exactly sure what they were doing here but were sure that, whatever they did, they wanted to do it here, in this unique town, at this unique moment in history.

On my walk home from work, if I saw the light on in the apartment of one of the Americans, I'd lug my ice cream, bread, cheese, and pelmeni up the steps and pop in for a visit. As often as not, I'd

stay for dinner, which simply meant that we'd boil some of my pelmeni and drink some of their wine or beer, and finish things off by
grabbing a few ice cream cones from the balcony where I had tossed
my bag of frozen treats.

If it was on the way, or even if it wasn't, I would often drop by
Sarah's apartment. Her two-room flat was the most likely place to
find gatherings of Americans and their Russian friends. Sarah was
in her late thirties. Like me, Sarah craved extremes. After years of
living large in both Los Angeles and New York City, she had over-
dosed on America. So she moved to Siberia.

Sarah's relationship with Uncle Sam was like that of a woman
who passionately hates her husband until they get divorced, then
finds that, as an ex-husband, he can be quite charming. America disgusted her whenever she had to go back for short visits (a friend's
wedding, her mother's birthday, etc.). But from a distance—a very
great distance—she found America irresistible and magnificent.
Great works of American literature filled her bookshelves. Stacks of
pulp fiction precariously balanced on top of her coffee table, while
below it were piles of grocery-store gossip rags. Her apartment was a
temple to America.

She supported herself by teaching English. Though the students came to learn a language, they got a remarkably authentic
glimpse into American life. She used texts from the U.S.
Constitution and Declaration of Independence, excerpts from
Playboy, editorials from the *New York Times*, and lyrics from popular music. She said that she wanted "to lead the Russian horses to
the waters of democracy." Getting them to drink, of course, was
another matter altogether. Sarah reveled in teaching a new generation of Siberians about the benefits and responsibilities of civil society. She started each new semester excited about the intelligence
and potential of her students, about the untapped potential of
Russia. But she often ended each semester frustrated. Even in
Russia's youth, apathy, fatalism, and alcoholism ran rampant. It was
overwhelming.

"What's the point?" Sarah complained to me after her star

student got pregnant and dropped out of class. "If they won't take responsibility for their own bodies, how can they be expected to take responsibility for their government?"

As a woman of a mostly liberal to partly radical political persuasion, Sarah had set before herself a difficult task. She was attempting to inculcate the young with the virtues of democracy and freedom while pointing out America's shortcomings. At the same time, she tried to impress upon her students the dangers of communism without slipping over into McCarthyism. She knew that eternal vigilance was the only way to secure freedom. But this generation of Russians didn't thirst for the intangible benefits of freedom as much as they hungered for material tangibles of the West. Most young Russians didn't know or care to know the horrors of communism. Communism had been their parents' problem. As far as the young were concerned, the real tyrants in their lives *were* their parents. What Russia's youth cared about was making money quickly and having fun with their friends. Actually, that's what almost all Russians cared about.

Sarah worked to enlighten, figuring that prosperity would come later. I worked to enrich, assuming that enlightenment would come later. Her means were my ends. My ends were her means. We may have differed on which battles to fight first, but we were loyal allies fighting the same war.

6
Chopsticks

Sasha and I left the submarine one evening after a long day of work. We started walking single-file along the narrow path toward his apartment building. The noise of our boots crunching the snow, the muffling effects of the wool scarves over our mouths, and the fur hats covering our ears made it almost impossible for us to hear each other. We had to yell as we discussed what to do about the latest development at the chocolate factory.

Recently, the Director had been complaining about the high cost of our cocoa beans. Vitaly Victorovich, the deputy director, told us that there was nothing he could do. The Director, a man in his late fifties, had been at the factory since he was twenty. What the Director said was law. Sasha and I both knew that these were classic good cop–bad cop tactics. We also had to admit that it was pretty effective. We needed to sweeten the deal, so to say, or the Director would look for other suppliers.

Rather than finding cheaper beans (my suggestion), Sasha came up with a different solution: a trip to America. More specifically, he wanted to take the Director to America. This, Sasha suggested, would keep the Director happy, smoothing out our working relationship. Over the next few years, this pattern was to repeat itself over and over again. Whenever an economic problem came up (and there were plenty), I usually saw an economic solution. Sasha would see problems in terms of loyalty and friendship—or lack thereof—and solutions were to be found in ever greater acts of loyalty and friendship.

When we reached the door of Sasha's apartment building, we

stood for a few minutes as Sasha's trip to America grew from a mere idea to a vital mission.

"We could claim that the purpose of the trip was to find new equipment for the factory, or something like that," Sasha said. "This would give the Director a convenient excuse to go to America. It would look like a legitimate business trip."

"Maybe we actually could look for some new equipment," I suggested. "Aren't they still using some of the original equipment from the Odessa factory that was evacuated here during the war? After fifty years, don't you think it's time they modernized the factory a bit?"

"Maybe." Sasha shrugged his shoulders indifferently.

An old woman came out of the apartment building's door. Sasha moved to her, took her hand, and helped her down the icy steps. She didn't thank him, but simply mumbled her complaints about how they used to shovel the steps. Sasha agreed deferentially. At the bottom of the steps, she let go of Sasha's arm, turned, and trudged down the snow-covered sidewalk. She was still mumbling to herself as she rounded the corner of the building.

Two dogs rummaged through a pile of garbage nearby, their teeth grinding on whatever frozen scraps they had found.

"Let's go have dinner at my place," Sasha suggested with a nod toward the lit kitchen window seven floors up. "Do you have any plans?"

"I do now," I said. We both headed into the door and up the dark steps.

"Aren't there supposed to be lights in the stairwells?" I asked as I blindly climbed the steps.

"There still are lights," Sasha's voice came from the darkness in front of me, "but the bulbs have been *privatized*."

When we got to the seventh floor, Sasha rang the doorbell. We panted on the dark landing as we waited for Lyuda to answer the door.

The tiny point of light showing through the door's peephole went black for a second. Lyuda's voice came from behind the door, "*Kto* (who)?"

41

"*Svoyee* (your own)," Sasha said.

The lock turned twice. The door opened, spilling bright light into the stairwell. Lyuda didn't seem at all surprised to see me squinting alongside her husband. Sasha was always bringing home friends for dinner and a few drinks. Lyuda walked back into the apartment, freeing up space in the tiny corridor for us to enter. She stood at the entrance of the apartment, folded her arms, and waited for Sasha to give her a kiss. Alina came screaming, "Papa?" Then she erupted into wild giggling when she saw me in my gray rabbit hat. Alina wrapped her arms around her mother's leg. As Sasha was hanging up his coat, he paused and looked around with a smile.

"Everybody's waiting for me?" he said. "I feel so important."

Lyuda hit her husband with her dishtowel. "Hurry up," she said. "The cold air is getting in."

Sasha put on a pair of slippers and finally kissed his wife. Lyuda waved me in. "Your turn."

"Just take off your boots, Sanya," Sasha said. "You don't have to kiss my wife."

Lyuda hit her husband with the dishtowel again, then walked off into the kitchen. Sasha disappeared into the bathroom. Still standing in the doorway, Alina just looked at me and made squeaks and peeps. Suddenly, clearly mimicking her mother, she gave instructions to me in Russian baby talk. She waved her finger up and down at me. Then she darted off into her room.

Lyuda had made a traditional Ukrainian meal, *vareniki*, but Sasha insisted on eating them with chopsticks. Sasha was exceptionally dexterous with his chopsticks, and when he saw that I was also competent, his competitive nature got the best of him. Pretty soon we were trying to one-up each other by picking up heavy or slippery objects with the wooden utensils. Sasha won the competition when I broke one of my sticks trying to lift a champagne bottle.

"Congratulations," I said. "Where did you learn to use chopsticks?"

"Down south," he said as he threw away my broken stick. "China."

Lyuda put a fork on the table in front of me. "No more playing at the table," she insisted.

Sasha laughed and nodded obediently, then asked me. "Where did you learn to use chopsticks?"

"In the West," I said. "America."

Sasha raised a questioning eyebrow.

"There are Chinese restaurants all over America." I explained. "You'll see when we go."

Lyuda shot her husband a look of surprise. "We're going to America?"

"Yes, we," Sasha said pointing at me and then himself. "Not *we*," he said pointing to himself and his wife.

There was a sudden, tense silence. Lyuda got up and started washing dishes. Sasha sighed, then apologized to his wife. Lyuda again sat down next to her husband. She tried to retain her cold exterior, but when Sasha wrapped his hands around her waist, she smiled.

"Speaking of China," Sasha said.

"What about America?" his wife asked, half-heartedly pushing him away.

"Speaking of China," Sasha repeated, squeezing her in his arms.

Lyuda groaned in frustration, but melted into her husband's embrace.

There was a pause as Sasha looked down at the little woman in his arms. Then he went on to tell me of another one of his many business schemes, this one already in progress for a year.

There was only one hotel in our village. Eight stories high, the Golden Valley Hotel stood at the end of the main street like a colossal refrigerator at the end of a giant pantry. It was not much of a hotel as far as comfort was concerned. Then again, not much in the Soviet Union was built with comfort in mind. Since the end of the Soviet Union, however, comfort was now the litmus test of whether something was Western or Russian. The more comfortable, the more Western, and therefore, the better.

43

Sasha's plan was simple. He wanted to turn one floor of the hotel into an oasis of Western-style comfort. It would be like the first-class section of a passenger airplane—not for everybody, just the wealthy elite. Or, as the case may be, the American missionaries. Sasha had negotiated with the owner of the hotel—the same owner of most property in this town: the Siberian Branch of the Russian Academy of Sciences—to let him renovate the top floor of the hotel. No money was exchanged. Promises to share the profits were made over shots of vodka, and that was enough to put things in motion. Sasha determined that importing Western workers and equipment would be too expensive, and Russian labor and equipment too inexpensive. So Sasha decided to use Chinese equipment and labor.

So far, his plan seemed sound enough to my ears. After all, a significant portion of Western comfort is made in China. I asked him how things were going.

Sasha told me about how he had visited China a few years back. While there he had made fast friends with a Chinese entrepreneur, Mahn. Mahn owned several hotels and restaurants in the city of Shenyang. Sasha called Mahn and made his proposal regarding the hotel floor renovation. Several months later, Mahn arrived in Novosibirsk, along with four containers full of rugs, bathroom tiles, mirrors, faucets, and curtains. In addition, eleven Chinese construction "masters" were also on the train.

"That was about eleven months ago," Sasha said.

From the window of Sasha's kitchen, I could see the hotel's top three floors. There were scattered lights in rooms on the sixth and seventh floors. The eighth floor, however, was dark.

Sasha said, "They've been nothing but trouble since the moment they arrived."

I raised a questioning eyebrow.

"When the containers got here, there was more than just building supplies for the hotel," he said as he pried opened a bottle of beer with the side of his knife. "Those sneaky yellow bastards had stuffed in a dozen sacks full of rice, a bunch of their personal

44

belongings, bags of spices, pots and pans. It looked like they were planning on moving here permanently. They've overpopulated their country like rabbits, now they want to come infest ours."

"I'm surprised they didn't confiscate all that stuff at the border. Foodstuffs in a container marked 'construction material.' That's a dream come true for a Russian customs officer."

Pouring the beer into two glasses, Sasha groaned. "We were lucky the customs officer didn't confiscate everything. Never mind the rice. I was able to distract him while those eleven Chinese unloaded their personal stuff from the containers."

"Why did they bring so much rice? There's plenty of rice in the stores up here," I said.

"I don't know," Sasha grumbled. "They are very picky about the rice they eat. For construction workers, they sure do care a lot about food. Must be a Chinese thing."

"So, how's the eighth floor coming along?" I asked after taking a sip of warm beer. It tasted sudsy, like shampoo. In other words, not bad for Russian beer.

"One of these days, I'll take you over to have a look," Sasha promised.

The phone rang. I could hear the angry voice of the chocolate factory director, but not what he was saying. Sasha pointed to the phone then gave me the thumbs up signal as he said, "We were just talking about you. We've got a few ideas that might improve your attitude about doing business with us."

7

Saving Labor

If I woke up to the strange sound of silence, if there was no piano music, then I knew it was Saturday—laundry day.

Of course I had no washing machine in my apartment. There wasn't even a crappy, coin-operated one in the basement. So I had to use a more labor-intensive method of getting clothes clean. Every Saturday, I'd wake up before my hangover arrived and prepare for battle. When the water, which reeked of iron, wasn't dirtier than my clothes, I'd fill the bathtub. The tiny bathroom quickly disappeared into a thick fog. I once tried to keep the steam to a minimum by leaving the bathroom door open, but this filled the entire apartment with steam, causing the wallpaper in the entranceway to peel off the walls and condensation on the cold ceiling to rain down on everything. After that, I kept the bathroom door closed. To endure the heat, I stripped naked except for a bandanna wrapped over my mouth. I dipped the bandanna in cold water so that the steam didn't scald my lungs. It also softened the detergent's nose-piercing fumes.

The bandanna was from America (made in Mexico). The detergent was not. It wasn't even from Russia. When I first saw the blue boxes on the store's shelf I did a double take. There were no boxy Russian letters on it. Instead, flowing Arabic letters decorated its sides. I couldn't read the Arabic, but, at the top, there was one English word: BARF.

I asked the lady behind the counter what was in the box.

"Cleaning powder," she muttered without looking up from her nails, which she was filing with an emery board.

"May I see one," I asked.

With a sigh, she stood up, pulled one of the boxes from the shelf, and tossed it onto the counter with a thud. Bluish-green powder puffed from the corners of the cardboard box. She looked at me as if to say, "Are you happy now?" Another sigh escaped from her blood-red lips. She sat back down and resumed her filing.

I turned the box around in my hand to find more English words on the side panel.

BARF

The Best Quality Detergent

Made in I.R. of Iran

Use BARF with its rich suds for washing silk clothes, cottons, nylons and wollens [sic]. BARF with its cleaning power washes dishes, tiles & bath accessories. To obtain best results soak very dirty clothes in a solution of BARF for a few hours and then proceed normaly [sic].

They cost the equivalent of ten cents per box. I bought forty boxes.

My huge supply didn't even last a year. It wasn't that the Iranian BARF was poor at getting things clean; it was just that the Siberian life was better at getting things dirty. In the summer it was dust and car exhaust. In the winter it was coal soot and body odor trapped by layers of insulation.

Washing my clothes by hand in my tub was backbreaking labor. But that's kind of why I came here in the first place, to do things the hard way. I found the whole sweaty ordeal to be oddly rejuvenating, like visiting a spa and exercise gym all at once. The exercise alone was enough to make me sweat bullets even without the steam. And the steam opened my pores like a faucet. Many American women, and a fair number of American men, would pay big money to have skin as soft and clear as mine was on Saturday afternoons in Siberia. But I didn't expect many Americans would be throwing out their washing machines anytime soon.

Even the other Americans in our little Siberian village didn't do laundry the way I did it. Many, mostly the American women, hired Russian babushkas to do their laundry for them. It was so affordable. Fresh clothes and crisp sheets for only a few dollars a week, who could resist? The American guys didn't usually need to hire babushkas; they had Russian girlfriends. These beautiful women cooked, cleaned, and shopped for their American beaus. Having all the menial domestic chores taken care of by a lovely young woman who laughed at your bad jokes and satisfied all of your sexual needs on demand, who could blame these American guys for willingly traveling back in time to the 1950s?

As an economist, I knew that there was no such thing as a free lunch. There was a cost to this traditional arrangement. I had had a Siberian girlfriend, too, and so I knew the tradeoffs of allowing your mate to be your domestic servant as well.

Throughout my college years, I had maintained a long-distance relationship with a beautiful young Siberian woman. I met her on the rafting trip down the Ob River back in 1988. We had been in the same long-oar boat one lovely day. I didn't speak Russian back then and she didn't speak English. No matter. We were young and she was beautiful. I was content to stare. A month later, I received a letter from her. It was during orientation week of my freshman year in college. Her penmanship was perfect, which didn't matter because I couldn't read it. So I went to the Russian Studies department and asked a professor to translate it. It was a cordial letter. Something along the lines of "My name is Katya, and I remember you." I interpreted it to mean, "My name is Katya, and I love you." I quickly enrolled in Russian 101 and wrote back to her in English.

We wrote back and forth over the years, with professors acting as intermediaries. I continued to study Russian. When I was fluent enough to no longer need a professor's help in translating her letters, I began writing much more intimate letters. Her replies, however, remained reserved. To my disappointment, there was rarely anything in them that I'd have been embarrassed for a professor to read. I decided that she was coy on the page, but would be passionate in person. That's when I took the winter trip to Novosibirsk to go trekking from village to village celebrating New Year's 1990. She was in the Russian contingent of trekkers.

While slowly moving across the whitewashed landscape, I confessed my feelings for her in broken Russian, which made her giggle. While walking down a snowy path in an anonymous village, she slipped and grabbed my arm for support. After steadying herself, she didn't let go; she continued to hold on to my forearm. This, of course, made me weak in the knees.

Back in America, back in college, I kept to what seemed to be the winning formula: I wrote my feelings for her in Russian, bad grammar, fifth-grade vocabulary and all. But her letters were just as reserved as before. The only acknowledgment of my emotional outpouring was a terse statement: "I liked your last letter." Unbelievably, that was enough to convince me to go to Novosibirsk again. Did I mention that she was very, very beautiful?

I spent the summer of 1991 taking intensive language instruction at the University of Novosibirsk. As my language abilities grew, I expected my relationship with Katya to grow as well. We became more physically intimate, which I liked a lot, but we didn't get any closer emotionally, which irked me. Katya wasn't interested in sharing her feelings. "*Ne mogu* (I can't)," she said whenever I asked her to tell me how she felt about me, about us, about anything. She remained a hauntingly lovely, but maddeningly distant enigma.

I knew as early as 1990 that I wanted to move to Russia after I graduated from college. That I moved to Novosibirsk, instead of Moscow, or St. Petersburg, or any other city within the borders of the largest country on the planet, is almost entirely due to love, or rather, the resilient hope for love.

When I moved to Novosibirsk in 1992, Katya and I tried living together. For four years I had studied Russian to be close to this devastatingly beautiful woman. I had made several trips and finally moved to Siberia (to Siberia!), but when we were finally face to face with no language barrier separating us, I felt more distant from her

49

than ever. All she wanted to do was play backgammon. If I nuzzled her neck, or kissed behind her ears, her sighs made me feel like my romantic impulses were a burden for her. On the occasions when we made love, usually after we'd both consumed lots of alcohol, I cradled her head by holding the pillow underneath it. I felt like my hands were too dirty to touch her.

She did my laundry on the weekends. When I suggested that I do the laundry during the week so that we'd have more time to be romantic, she just laughed at the absurdity of my proposal. A man doing the laundry. Ha! That really was ridiculous. She didn't want my help with the chores. She just wanted a man, which, as far as I could tell, meant a provider (financially) and rock (emotionally). I was supposed to bring home the bacon and she would fry it up in a pan. A time-honored business arrangement.

The weekend after I'd watched Sasha and Lyuda harmoniously share the tasks of making tea, I expressed my concern to Katya that our relationship wasn't turning out as I had hoped. She told me that all this soul-searching and relationship talk only got in the way of domestic tranquillity. Although my ancestors were Norwegian—as stoic a bunch as any—I didn't inherit their emotional detachment. I was an Italian trapped in a Norwegian's body. I wasn't so interested in tranquillity as I was interested in passion. When I told Katya that I wanted to love her passionately and to be loved passionately by her, she snickered, "*ne mogu*."

A few hours later, she got on bus no. 8 and headed back to her parents' apartment in the city. Four years of courting, hundreds of letters, immeasurable hopes and dreams—over.

So, in addition to losing the woman I had long fancied as my future wife, I now had to figure out how to do the laundry on my own. That's where the bathtub scheme came in. Sure, it was labor-intensive. But I had no reason to save labor. What was I saving it for? Besides, all the sweating felt cathartic. I was washing the ache out of my heart as I scrubbed the stains out of my shirts.

On most Saturdays, after doing the laundry, I'd usually go for a walk around the village. As I stomped down the four flights of stairs in my heavy boots, the graffiti on the walls came at me with each passing floor.

Fourth floor:

MASHA + IVAN

Third floor:

MASHA LOVES DIMA

Second floor:

SASHA WAS HERE

First floor:

YELTSIN IS A DRUNK. HE'S OUR MAN

On my way to nowhere in particular, I always ran into several familiar faces. We'd stop for some small talk that usually ended with news about what store had Dutch cheese wheels, which one had Hungarian juice boxes, and which had Estonian cookie cylinders. One day I ran into Sarah. She was out looking for a few of the rare yellow cans of Schweppe's tonic water. Had I seen any? I told her I had been doing laundry all morning. I couldn't help her. She laughed sympathetically and asked how I was handling the single life. I shrugged my shoulders. She told me about some German mustard at one of the kiosks down the street. As we parted, she told me to swing by her place that evening. She was having a cocktail party where she wanted to teach the Russians about casual drinking, the kind of drinking where people sipped their drinks during conversation, not the deliberate vodka gulping that usually happened at Russian gatherings. Besides, she said, you might meet a pretty university girl. I thanked her and scurried off to buy two bottles of mustard, one for myself and one for Sasha. He was a big fan of anything spicy. With nothing better to do, I wandered over to Sasha's place to give him his mustard.

I found him tutoring two neighbor boys. The boys weren't old enough to be in high school, but they seemed to be wrestling with some serious material. Judging by the equations and diagrams, it looked like physics, Sasha's specialty. Sasha smiled when he saw me. "We'll be another fifteen minutes. Go to the kitchen and Lyuda will feed you."

As I entered the kitchen, I pulled out one of my bottles of mustard and gave it to Lyuda. She smiled and put the little bottle on the table.

Alina came into the kitchen and started playfully hitting me on the arm as she repeated over and over, "*Dyadya* (Uncle) Xander. Dyadya Xander. Dyadya Xander." With the many Sashas that came in and out of this apartment, calling me Dyadya Sasha had proven too confusing, for her and for just about everybody else.

Lyuda ladled soup into wide, shallow bowls, then placed the bowls on the table. I gladly spooned up the potatoes, carrots, and meat floating in the thick liquid. By the state of the kitchen, I could tell that Lyuda had been preparing this soup for the better part of the morning.

"Good soup," I said.

"See, Alina," her mother said, pointing at me with her long wooden spoon. "See what a good boy Dyadya Xander is." I thought it strange that a woman only one year older than me had just referred to me as "uncle" and "boy" in the same sentence. Alina looked at me with a goofy smile and kicked me playfully under the table.

"Alina, no games!" Lyuda yelled with surprising ferocity, which had surprisingly little effect on her daughter. Alina kept kicking me under the table.

"Alina," I said softly, "take your spoon."

She did.

"That's a girl. Now try your mother's yummy soup," I said. "If you don't, I'll be glad to eat yours."

She started swallowing spoonful after spoonful.

Lyuda laughed, shook her head, and went back to stirring the soup.

Sasha showed the boys out, reminding them of their assignments, then shut the door. He joined us in the kitchen, sat down and began rubbing his hands together.

"oooooooooaaaaAAAAAASUUGGH!!!!" he yawped with anticipation.

Lyuda ladled a bowl full of soup and put it down in front of her husband. He looked at it for a second then handed it back to her. "More meat."

She fished out a few more hunks of meat and dropped them into the bowl. Sasha smiled. When she put the bowl in front of him a second time, there was a moment of tense silence as Sasha inspected his soup. He grabbed a piece of bread in one hand and a spoon in the other. The tension and the soup quickly disappeared.

"Oh, by the way," Sasha said in between spoonfuls, "I'm going over to the hotel this evening. Mahn invited me to have dinner with him. I want to see how the construction is going."

"What?" Lyuda banged the shaft of her wooden spoon against the rim of the kettle. "You're not eating at home tonight?"

Sasha quickly grabbed his wife by the waist. She tried to pry his hands off, but she didn't try very hard.

"Sorry. It's business," he explained.

Lyuda sighed. "You spend so much time working that I hardly see you anymore."

Sasha thought about what his wife said for a long moment. "Lyudechka, as soon as we've made enough money, I'll be able to spend as much time with you as you want. We'll be able to go on long vacations together. But for now, I've got to work hard to earn that money. Okay?"

Now she thought for a long moment. "Okay, but hurry."

"Deal," Sasha said, then turned to me. "So, do you want to come with me to the hotel? I need your opinion on how things are going."

"Sure," I said.

When the soup was gone, we had tea. Then Sasha suggested that we all go for a walk. There were still two hours of sunlight (it was one in the afternoon). It took fifteen minutes to put the layers and layers of warm clothes on Alina. She reveled in all the attention and went limp like a rag doll, dragging out the process. She giggled as Sasha struggled to put on the orange wool tights over her wet-noodle legs. "Alina!" he yelled. At this she giggled even more.

When she was finally bundled up, we adults began taking turns getting dressed in the corridor. Fully dressed, Alina quickly started to wilt for real. She whined and whimpered. The phone rang. Sasha grabbed it. Lyuda rolled her eyes.

We realized by the intensity in Sasha's voice that this was a business call. Probably the Director calling about the trip to America. Rather than having us wait, Sasha waved us on. He silently mouthed that he'd catch up. Lyuda, Alina, and I went down the stairs and out the door.

The street, as always, was buzzing with life. A group of little boys threw snowballs at each other from behind the walls of their snow forts. Some older boys sat on the benches near a stairwell. There was a truck at the end of the lane with a line quickly forming behind it.

"Milk," Lyuda said. She started toward the truck at a fast pace, pulling little Alina along with her. Alina's feet couldn't keep up, so she went limp again, letting her mother drag her. Alina giggled at the great new game she had just invented.

Suddenly, Lyuda stopped and turned to me. "Richardovich, we don't have any bottles. You go back to the apartment and get some. Alina and I will get in line."

"Mama. That's Dyadya Xander." Alina pointed to me.

"Sorry," her mother corrected herself. "Dyadya Xander, go back and get some bottles. Sasha will show you where they are."

When I got back to the apartment, Sasha was still on the phone, but he had already pulled several three-liter glass bottles from the top shelf of an overstuffed closet. He had been watching from the window and knew why I had come back. I grabbed three bottles and headed back down the steps. I met Lyuda and Alina in line. Some of the people behind Lyuda grumbled about me cutting in line. Lyuda barked back that I just brought the bottles. The grumbling subsided, then turned to gossiping and occasional laughter.

This truck came directly from a local collective farm, so the milk was fresher and cheaper than in the stores. The service, however, was a bit crude. The truck had a large tank on the back and a long hose. People put their bottles on a stool while a hefty woman filled them up. Three cats lapped at the puddle of spilled milk before it froze.

When our bottles were full, we returned to the apartment with our liquid treasure. Sasha was still on the phone. Lyuda heaved the heavy bottles into the refrigerator. She nodded and smiled as she looked at the fresh milk snug inside the full refrigerator. Then she turned to me and asked, "What do people in America do on weekends?"

8 Hospitality

Warm, stale air, at once comforting and claustrophobic, filled our lungs as we stepped into the hotel lobby. The guard, a man in a drab blue uniform at the base of the elevators, stopped us without words, just a grim expression. Sasha said that we were going to the eighth floor.

"The eighth floor is closed," he said. He then turned the page of his newspaper, a gesture that said one thing: this conversation is over.

"I know," Sasha said, reopening the dialogue. "I'm the one who closed it."

The guard gave Sasha a questioning look.

"We're here to inspect how the construction is going," Sasha explained. "I'm in charge of what's going on up there."

"You hired those Chinamen?" the guard asked, his expression changing from grim to accusatory.

Sasha nodded, then turned around and began searching the dimly lit lobby. When he spotted a bleached blonde in her forties behind the registration desk, he smiled with a politician's sincerity.

"Alexander Kamilovich, good evening." She almost bowed to him. When she gave the security guard a nod, it was clear that Sasha had her vote.

The guard twitched his head, allowing us to pass.

Sasha pushed the elevator button. We stood there for almost a minute in silence, waiting. The guard eventually said one word: "Broken." Then he turned the page of his newspaper.

"*Kozyol* (goat)," Sasha said with venom when we were on the third floor landing of the stairwell. As we climbed the last few steps before the eighth floor, our hats were in our coat pockets and our coats were folded over our arms. We panted and leaned on the handrails. We reached the eighth floor and opened the door to the construction site. The building's flesh had been ripped away, revealing the skeleton. Both the carpet and the wood planks that the carpet used to cover were gone. When we exited the stairwell, we stepped down half a foot to the concrete floor. Any non-load-bearing walls were gone and, judging by the sagging ceiling, a few load-bearing ones as well. A large stack of lumber surrounded a table saw. A concrete-encrusted wheelbarrow stood in the corner. The wood gave off a pleasant, fresh aroma. Wood in Russia smells the same as in America. The smell of Russian concrete, however, is very different from the smell of American concrete. Russian concrete smells of methane and sulfur, like a match-lit fart.

The dark windows along the opposite wall were completely covered in crystallized moisture. The moonlight outside came through as a frigid blue aura. The hallways in both directions were dark except for a light in the last room on the right. Sasha and I worked our way down the dark hallway, tripping on boxes, stacks of bricks, scraps of wood, and piles of rubble. With each step, the stench of the concrete faded, and a mixture of appetizing aromas intensified. When we got to the end of the hall, we found all eleven workers in one room. They were scurrying around a portable gas stove and a table covered with vegetables, meat, and fish. All eleven of them were wearing shorts, sandals, and loose T-shirts. They were all so busy with their chopping, stirring, and sorting that it took a moment before one of them looked up and noticed us in the doorway. He smiled ear-to-ear and uttered something in Chinese as he waved for us to come in.

The smiling man ushered us through the makeshift kitchen to a door that led to the next room. Before we went through this second door, Sasha said the few Chinese words he knew, causing all the workers to stop and bow in recognition. Sasha bowed in return. So did I. This caused them to begin bowing to me. Now all we needed was some music and we'd be ready to square dance.

"Saasa," I heard from behind us. Turning, I saw a relatively tall man—relative, that is, to the other Chinese men in the room. He had a lime-green suit and a thick mane of black, feathered hair. His suit had long, pointy lapels that made him look like a pimp. His smile affected his whole face, stretching his lips, raising his cheeks and forcing his eyes completely shut. Sasha smiled and shook his hand. Then they bowed to each other.

"Mahn," Sasha said, "this is my partner. He's an American." Sasha declared my nationality as if it were a warning.

Mahn turned his smile on me, then bowed. I returned the bow. We exchanged *ne hows* and *zdrastvuites*. Mahn yelled at one of the workers, who darted out of the kitchen and returned a few minutes later with a tiny Chinese woman with thick glasses. Her teeth were brown. In her small hands she held a Pekingese dog. Small dog, thick glasses, and bad teeth, I couldn't help but think that this woman was even more of a Chinese caricature than Hollywood could ever have dreamed up.

Li Li was the translator.

"I'd like to see how things are coming along," Sasha said, looking at Mahn with a stern gaze.

Mahn, still smiling at us, listened to Li Li's translation of Sasha's sober intentions. The Chinese pimp yelled at his workers. They scurried out of the kitchen. Mahn offered to take us on a tour of the floor with a flashlight. We found the workers conspicuously at their stations, still in their shorts and sandals, mixing concrete, cutting wood, laying tiles, pounding nails. All in the dark.

Mahn took us from one "room" to another. With the walls gone, however, it was difficult to determine where one room began and another ended. Sasha asked fewer and fewer questions as the tour progressed. He squinted his eyes in an attempt to visualize how this chaos would turn into a Western-style comfort zone. He couldn't. Honestly, neither could I.

Mahn recognized our concern and changed his tour route. He pulled us into a room filled to the ceiling with boxes covered in Chinese characters. He ripped open one of the boxes and pulled out a shiny new faucet. By American standards it was tacky. By Soviet standards it was beautiful, with its polished surface and elegantly curved spout. Sasha grabbed the faucet and held it. In the glow of the flashlight, it shimmered. Sasha turned the faucet's handles. They moved effortlessly.

"What do you think?" He handed me this tangible piece of comfort.

When I had it in my hand, I immediately felt that it was light, too light. A lot of this metal faucet wasn't made of metal at all. I looked at Sasha. He wanted good news.

I looked at Mahn. He wanted Sasha to be happy.

"*Khorosho* (good)," I said in Russian. I'd tell Sasha the truth later.

We were ushered back to the room with the kitchen. The six workers had returned from the construction charade and were again chopping, slicing, peeling, boiling, and frying. Mahn invited us to sit down in his room, the only room untouched by the destruction. It had a carpeted floor, a bed, a dresser, and a reading lamp. We sat around a table that had been set up while we were on our tour.

For the next few hours, we were treated to course after course of real Chinese food. No sweet and sour this or that. No chow mein mystery meat. No kung pao or moo goo. It wasn't nearly as attractive as the dishes served in American Chinese restaurants. In fact, some of the food placed on the table was downright frightening. In particular, I remember nearly tipping my chair over backward when a glazed fish head was placed in front of me. Mahn laughed and showed me how to eat it, brains, cheeks, eyeballs, and all. It was all disgusting to look at, but undeniably delicious.

Halfway through the meal, Mahn pulled an elegant bottle from a straw-filled crate. The bottle had grasses and vegetables floating in a clear liquid. Sasha warned me to be prepared when we raised our shot glasses for the first toast, given by Mahn: "*Za Vstrechu*" (to the meeting).

"Be prepared for what?" I asked Sasha. He just winked, took a deep breath, and tossed down his shot. When I downed the Chinese alcohol, I knew. It tasted like hard-boiled eggs soaked in vinegar. It was all I could do not to ruin our party by tossing up all the fish eyes, brains, and cheeks.

Ignoring his usual habit of giving rapid-fire toasts, one right after another, Sasha spent more time talking and eating. Mahn, however, gave frequent and unmercifully short toasts.

The liquor seemed to make Mahn and Sasha understand each other without Li Li's translations. In slurred Chinese, Mahn explained important aspects of the remodeling process. Sasha nodded and agreed, putting his arm around Mahn as he tried to convey in Russian how important it was for them to work faster. The job had to be finished by spring. The hotel owners were pressuring Sasha. Mahn nodded and made gestures of opening and closing the faucet, the faucet he had shown Sasha. Sasha nodded, smiled, and nudged Mahn with his elbow. They both broke into laughter.

Li Li, relieved of her translating responsibilities, turned to me and said out of the blue, "You should marry a Chinese woman." She wasn't offering herself. At least, I hoped she wasn't.

"A Chinese woman." I smiled politely. "Why is that?"

"Because," she slurred, "Chinese women are better than dogs." She covered the ears of her little pooch as she said this.

I raised my eyebrows. "Excuse me?"

"A Chinese wife is loyal and obedient." Her cloudy eyes looked at me through her foggy glasses. "Chinese men are masters of their homes," she declared.

I turned to Sasha and said, "I'm outta here. This is getting too weird."

Sasha nodded and gave me a wink. I gave a quick bow to Mahn. Mahn bowed back. Li Li grabbed her dog's paw and made him wave good-bye. The workmen were huddled around the table, eating rice and vegetables. They all stood, bowed, and barked good-bye. The rich aromas of cooking were too strong. I felt nauseous. I held my breath as I staggered down the dark hallway. When I finally took a breath, it smelled of farty concrete. I had to get out of here fast.

I stumbled my way out of the hotel and found a trail that led in the direction of my apartment. The temptation to lie down in the snow was overwhelming. My apartment, only fifteen minutes away (when sober), might as well have been in a different time zone. The effects of the strange alcohol weren't wearing off. If anything, they seemed to be getting worse with each step. The cold air didn't sober me up either. In fact, I was sweating profusely. I wasn't going to make it home, so I turned into Sarah's apartment, where I found the cocktail party in full swing. There were over a dozen people in the apartment. Sarah was somewhere, but she wasn't the one who opened the door. It was nobody I had met before. I warned him to avoid Chinese vodka at all costs. Then I went into the bathroom and loudly puked seven courses of the best food I'd had in months.

I felt much better, if much embarrassed. I wiped my mouth, dried my forehead, and joined the party. Sarah gave me a look of scorn and disappointment. "Here I am trying to teach these Russians how to drink reasonably, and you come stumbling in and vomit like a hobo sick from drinking turpentine."

"Chinese vodka," I corrected her.

"What does that taste like?" she asked.

"Turpentine."

She shook her head and then laughed at me. "You look awful. Let me make you a screwdriver."

"I don't think I'll be able to drink it."

"Perfect," Sarah said. "I want the Russians to see it's possible to hold a drink without gulping it."

Someone had a guitar. Soon we were singing Russian songs, with the occasional Bob Dylan tune mixed in. The guitar was passed from person to person like a joint. They tried to hand the guitar to me, but all I could do with a guitar was imitate Pete Townshend on a rampage. Not a great party trick, especially if it isn't your guitar.

When I felt my equilibrium had improved enough for me to walk the rest of the way home, I rummaged through the pile of boots by the door, found my footwear, and headed outside.

When I got home, I wanted nothing but sleep. I started taking off my clothes the moment I shut the door behind me. I just collapsed onto the couch without bothering to unfold it into a bed. I was in my underwear and socks. In my hurry to get horizontal, I hadn't even turned on the light. There was just the green glow on the ceiling from the streetlight below my window.

Despite my exhaustion, I didn't fall asleep. Something was different. The wall looked bigger than usual.

I jumped up and turned on the light. The wall wasn't bigger. It looked bigger because the TV in front of the wall was smaller than before. It was a different television set altogether. It was a new, color TV. The old television had been a giant black-and-white set; it took over ten minutes for the vacuum tubes to glow the color of camp-fire embers. The old TV's innards were clearly visible because the back of the set had long ago been removed. Since the V-hold kept slipping and the volume would fluctuate, I had to stick my hand into the TV's innards to adjust knobs and tap the tubes. It was the original interactive TV. But now it was gone.

I stood in my underwear and socks, staring in total confusion at the new color TV. Curiosity turned to horror when I remembered that I had hidden all of my valuables (money, passport, plane ticket to America) inside the giant old television set. As an immovable hunk of worthless junk, it had seemed like the ideal place to conceal the tiny pieces of paper that represented the most treasured things I had: freedom, citizenship, and a way back home. I had stashed the precious papers among the vacuum tubes and wires. At the time, it seemed like an ingenious idea. Now, however, it seemed less clever.

It hadn't been robbed. The door hadn't been forced open; and burglars, even Siberian burglars, don't work on the barter system. The only person who could have done this was my landlady. She had the only other key to the place. I had paid a full year's rent of four hundred and thirty dollars in advance. That would more than cover the cost of a new Korean television set.

I retraced my steps from the couch to the door, putting my clothes back on as I went. I donned my fur hat and darted down the steps. I broke into a run, down the dark paths, through the courtyards, toward my landlady's apartment building. The snow didn't crunch underfoot. Instead, the impacts of my long strides sounded like distant artillery. As I ran, the color of the snow changed, now dark blue in the moonlight, now a cold green from an overhead streetlight, now dark blue again. A dog barked, then lurched at me as I ran by. The owner yanked him back by the leash. The dog gagged and coughed. I kept running, the cold air ripping my throat raw as I panted.

Into the dark doorway and up the steps I bounded three at a time. I reached the fourth floor and banged on my landlady's door with my gloved hand. I banged on the door so hard that I heard coats falling off hooks on the other side of the door. I began coughing violently and gasping for air. The saliva in my mouth tasted like blood.

"Who's there?" my landlady's shaky voice came through the door.

"It's me, Alexander," I said, then erupted in more coughs.

There was silence. I heard her talking to her husband, something about calling for help.

"It's me, Alexander," I repeated, trying to sound calm.

"Alexander who?" she asked, her voice now frantic.

"Alexander," I said. "I live in your apartment."

"Nobody lives in our apartment. It's just me and my husband," she declared.

Her husband's voice suddenly blurted out, "Don't say that! Now he knows it's just a pair of old people in here. Tell him that our son lives here with us."

"We don't have a son," my landlady corrected her husband.

"I know that, but he doesn't," the husband said in a whisper that was crystal clear through the thin door.

I took a deep breath and explained calmly, "Raisa Petrovna, I rent an apartment from you. It's me, Alexander." I paused. "Alexander the American."

"Sasha," she said. The lock turned. She opened the door a crack, casting a beam of light onto my face. I squinted at the brightness. She squinted to see me in the darkness. When she recognized me, the door swung open. I coughed a few more times into my glove.

"*Gospodi* (Lord)!" she exclaimed. "You nearly scared us to death."

I stepped into the apartment and immediately spotted the old television greedily taking up half of the narrow corridor's limited space.

"You nearly scared *me* to death," I said, pointing to the television set. "I thought that I'd been robbed."

"Didn't you see the new television set we put in its place?" she asked.

"Yes, but…." I moved toward the giant old set. Pulling off my glove, I reached my right hand into the black box. My fingers walked over the tubes and wires until they came to rest on the leather case. I sighed with relief as I pulled it out.

My landlady and her husband looked on with interest and curiosity.

"Passport," I said as I waved it in the air.

"*Gospodi*," she said for the second time. She put her palm flat against the center of her chest. "We never suspected. Just think if we had thrown out that TV."

"You, throw out a television set?" Her husband let out a laugh. "Ha!"

She glowered at him. "You see what would have happened if we had thrown it out, like you wanted?"

"Ahhh," he said and waved in the air as if she were a mere mosquito.

"Sorry to bother you both," I said as I pocketed my valuables and put my glove back on.

"Oh, no bother," the old woman said.

"Hhmmph," her husband grunted. "Of course it was no trouble for you. You didn't have to carry that monster."

Ignoring her husband, my landlady smiled at me. "I'm just glad that everything worked out."

"Me, too," I concurred. "Well, I'll be on my way."

"Nonsense. Have some tea," she said. "Your throat needs something warm. Listen to that cough. You probably ran all the way here. If you don't have some tea you'll be sick for a week."

It sounded reasonable. I took off my coat and stayed for a few cups of comforting tea and homemade raspberry jam. My landlady gave me advice on how rubbing mustard on my feet will cure any fever. Her husband insisted that vodka and pepper broke a fever, not mustard. This started another argument between the old couple. When I left, my throat felt considerably better than it had when I arrived. I wasn't tired anymore, or drunk. I decided to go back to Sarah's pad for more singing and flirting with university girls. I was due for a good rebound relationship. Besides, Sarah's place was on the way. Everything in this town was on the way.

9
Promise of America

Since Sasha seemed to have a better grasp of the politics of placation, he was spending more and more time at the factory tied up in tense negotiations over barter ratios and chocolate credit lines. I was relatively free to dream up and explore new opportunities. Learning from Sasha's example of selling what you don't actually have, I was able to sell over one million latex examination gloves to a large pharmaceutical wholesaler.

"Let me see," I said, scratching my head as I examined an improvised spreadsheet I'd typed up on my laptop computer. "It looks as if we pool the inventory from Houston, Los Angeles, and Chicago, we should be able to fill your order."

The company's buyer examined her computer screen and nodded approvingly.

"I'll need a week or so to consolidate the cargo in one location, then another week or so to arrange shipment here."

She seemed willing to give me a few weeks before I produced a bill of lading. She was probably used to waiting months for cargo from the bureaucratic supply monsters of Soviet days. Or maybe she was willing to give me a few weeks because she needed some time to find the money. Regardless, I needed the time to find the gloves.

Back at the chocolate factory, we were losing ground. The chocolate factory had a distinct advantage in our negotiations. The factory was a monopsony (single buyer). Raw cocoa beans are fairly useless to most people. So, if the Director said that our price was too high, we couldn't simply go and sell bags of cocoa beans on the streets. (That's why we didn't worry about our beans being pilfered

66

while en route to Novosibirsk.) On the other hand, if we didn't buy the chocolate from the factory, they could sell their product on the streets. Everybody bought chocolate.

Economic theory said that we were fighting a losing battle. I explained the principle of monopsony to Sasha, and how we were sellers in a buyer's market. If logic said that we were in a vulnerable position, then we wouldn't use logic. We'd use the promise of America.

Sasha wanted to kill two birds with one stone. I could go to America to find the million gloves and prepare for the Director's trip at the same time. Sasha promised that taking the Director to America was the best way to win him over, to turn the bad cop into a good cop.

Rather than improving our business relations with the Director, however, the trip quickly increased tension. Every time we visited the factory, the only thing he wanted to talk about was going to America. What had started out as a means to oil the gears in our frictional working relationship had turned into the biggest wrench, bringing the machine nearly to a halt. Then it got even worse.

Word had gotten around about the trip and soon other important people wanted to tag along. Again, rather than generating good will with our colleagues and customers, the trip created jealousy and petty bickering where it hadn't existed before. Rather than advancing our position with important people, this trip had needlessly jeopardized it.

As with most of Sasha's ideas, this one grew until it was too much for us to handle by ourselves and we had to get outside help. The compulsive entrepreneur thinks that he can do anything. The one who really can do *anything* is the one who knows he can't do *everything*. At least, not by himself. Instead, he hires others to do what he cannot. I realized that I wouldn't be able to prepare for a group of Russians and find one million latex gloves. I needed help. And it came in an unexpected person—a missionary.

Fortunately, this missionary was also a travel agent. He said that he'd take care of everything. All he wanted was a $250 commission per person. Having no alternatives, Sasha and I agreed.

He was in town to change the guard. He had flown in with a dozen fresh, young missionaries. After he'd given pep talks to his young zealots, he would take back the washouts, the ones who had lost their fervor during the dark Siberian winter. I suspected that it wasn't the cold that had tested their faith; it was the darkness—the kind of darkness that makes you feel forsaken. As the gloomy months creep by one after another, doubts grow about whether God cares about you, and finally, suspicion about His very existence takes root in your soul. It's the kind of darkness that makes vodka seem like a true friend, the only true friend.

It was during the dark Siberian winter when the trip to America took over the minds of our colleagues and customers. The group of Siberian businessmen grew in size and scope. Within a week, the group had grown to six people.

Vladimir was the first to join in. Vladimir was a fading, local bureaucrat. He wasn't influential enough anymore to help us, but he was still powerful enough to cause us problems. He had invited himself on the trip by throwing five thousand dollars onto Sasha's desk and saying, "I'd like to invest in your business. I think the interest from this money should cover the cost of going to America. Don't you?"

Sasha bit his lip and agreed, tossing the money into the safe.

The manager of the language program, Zhenya, a man who couldn't even speak English himself, had leveraged himself into the fast-growing entourage. The language program was located behind one of the doors in the submarine, and was partially owned by Sasha. Zhenya insisted that he needed to meet face-to-face with the American organization that sent several dozen students to Novosibirsk every summer. Each student represented $1,300 that went into the coffers of the submarine. The money usually left the submarine to buy cocoa beans, pay for hotel renovations, or other sure-fire cash cows that usually ate up money before regurgitating any profit. The prospect of increasing the number of paying students proved too tempting. Sasha relented. Zhenya would go. Along with Zhenya came Roza, one of the language instructors. She would act as his translator.

Already tired of the whole thing, Sasha just waved his arms and said, "Sure, why not. Anybody else? Maybe your mother-in-law? She'd probably love to go to America."

The places this growing list of people wanted to visit also grew. New York, Washington, and Florida were the highest on everyone's list. We had to make weekly calls to our missionary/travel agent and inform him of our growing size and changing itinerary. He was very understanding and patient. I wasn't sure if his serenity amid our chaos was due to his Christianity or his commission. I didn't really care, either. I was just glad to have his help.

The idea to go to America first came up in early February, and before the shortest month of the year was over I was boarding the first of five flights that would bring me to America. A week later, Sasha and the group would arrive in New York and I would be there to meet them, hopefully having already found and purchased one million latex gloves.

10
Edge of Civilization

My dad picked me up at the Minneapolis airport. He said I had lost weight, but looked healthy, and tired.

I slept for thirty of the next forty-eight hours. The few hours that I was awake were usually between three and six in the morning. I'd find myself riveted to the giant color television set showing infomercials, special offers on decorative plates, and opportunities to start training for an exciting career as a dental assistant. So many choices! It was totally overwhelming, and depressing. I flipped through dozens of channels until my thumb ached from repeatedly pressing the buttons on the remote control. When the sun started to brighten the eastern sky, I fell back asleep. It was easier to have life brought to me on the television rather than go out and live it.

I went outside once or twice. When I did, I was conscious of a severe sense of emptiness. The streets were barren of activity. An occasional car drove by, momentarily interrupting the silence with the engine's whine. Then all was silent again. There were no people walking about. No sounds of laughter. No gossip. Only an occasional dog bark. I went back inside, where the TV promised some intensity, some noise, some color. But the one-way medium that spilled nonstop choices over me, forcing me to say "no" silently over and over again, wound me up as it tired me out. Sleep was my only real refuge from the extremes of boredom and anxiety.

When I woke from my hibernation, I had to ask a question I thought I had asked for the last time during college.

"Dad, can I borrow your car?"

I explained that I needed to drive out to New York and meet

Sasha and the group. No rental car company was willing to rent a car to a twenty-two-year-old without a U.S. address. Dad looked amused that I still needed his help. He gave me the car keys. If he were a true capitalist, he would have charged me money for the use of his car. I was glad he wasn't a true capitalist.

A day later, I was heading east on I-90 toward New York. I went nonstop, except for gas and bathroom breaks. I pulled into the driveway of my aunt's house in eastern Pennsylvania in the middle of the night. I had made it in record time, twenty hours. Rather than wake up my aunt and uncle, I put on my winter clothes and fell asleep in the back of the car.

"You slept in the car?" my aunt asked in the morning. "Oh, heavens. It was below freezing last night."

My aunt put a large, hot breakfast before me, which I devoured. I made a phone call to the missionary/travel agent in upstate New York. Sasha had called him from Moscow to say that the group would be late, by a week! Apparently they needed to get Canadian visas because their flight from Moscow would stop to refuel in the tiny city of Gandor, Newfoundland.

My aunt had an open-door policy. She said I was always welcome to come and stay as long as I needed, and free to leave whenever I wanted. No guilt trips. She didn't charge me rent. Like her brother, she wasn't too much of a capitalist either.

Well, this would give me a chance to track down the medical gloves. For two days, I called around until I had reached the largest producer of latex products in Europe. It was the German branch of an Australian-owned company. They could ship the quantity I needed at a price that left plenty of profit for us.

"Prepayment, of course," the woman said over the phone with a thick German accent.

"Of course," I agreed. Back to capitalism.

That solved, I called the missionary/travel agent. A woman at the church office informed me that he was gone. Gone! Gone where? "To New York City," she said. "The plane with the Russians was going to land today."

Apparently, Sasha had managed to expedite the Canadian visas and the group had caught the next flight. They would arrive in three hours. I slammed the phone down and threw my suitcase in the car. After hurried hugs with my aunt, I was on the road again. Even if I went way above the speed limit, I'd be too late to catch them at JFK. I turned left and headed north to Syracuse, where the church was located. The lady on the phone said that they were driving up today. They'd be there by seven o'clock this evening. I had enough time to get there before they arrived, but just barely.

I made it to Syracuse and found the church fifteen minutes before a minivan pulled up filled with Russians. It was a strange sensation to see Sasha jump out of the minivan. Up until that moment, a part of me suspected that Sasha was just a figment of my imagination — that the whole seven months I'd spent in Siberia had been just a dream. A great dream, but a dream nonetheless. Now, here Sasha was, in a church parking lot in upstate New York. My two worlds had collided.

Out filed six Russians, tired from a long flight and an almost equally long car ride. The Director, however, looked relatively perky. He took a deep breath of air and nodded approvingly, then started doing calisthenics by swinging his arms about.

The Russians, all of them, greeted me with hugs and slaps on the back.

Within a few minutes, several cars arrived at the parking lot. We were divided into groups. The arrangements were for everybody to spend the night in the homes of the church's congregation. It was a great way for us to save on hotel expenses, explained the missionary/travel agent. It was a great way for these zealots to have captive audiences for their Christian babble, I thought to myself. I remembered with significant relief that nobody understood English except Roza. Everybody else would be immune to any attempts at conversion tonight. And Roza, well, she was in her sixties, headstrong, and dead set in her ways. I sort of hoped that whoever took her in tonight would try to convert her. They'd be sorry.

The Director and Vladimir went to the house of one of the choir members. Roza went with a middle-aged woman in a station wagon. Sasha and our missionary/travel agent went to the director of the church's outreach program. I was paired up with Zhenya. Our host, John, was the missionary/travel agent's assistant, like Dr. Frankenstein's Igor. I learned with horror that he was going to be with us the entire time; not just tonight, but the entire two weeks. From New York to Miami, he would be our chaperone. On the one hand, I didn't want him around, inserting Jesus into every conversation. I wanted to show off my America, not the America of these Bible thumpers. On the other hand, it was thanks to the missionaries that we had such good hotel rates in New York, Philadelphia, Orlando, and Miami, plus cheap plane tickets from Philly to Orlando. I decided that it would be best to not rock the boat and go with their itinerary, but I was determined to prevent things from becoming a two-week Christian sing-along.

I left my dad's car in the parking lot and got into the minivan. Zhenya was quickly asleep in the back seat, so I talked with John. John was in his late fifties, as best I could tell. He giggled a lot. He was friendly enough, but then again, all missionaries are friendly.

After nearly an hour, we ended up at a small house in a distant suburb. The house was a one-level ranch immaculately well kept. There were little shelves all over the walls; on the shelves sat cute little porcelain figurines and knickknacks, the kind I'd seen advertised as special collector's items on late-night television. John pulled out the hideaway couch and said we were welcome to wash up. There was a shower down the hallway.

Halfway through my shower, John walked into the bathroom.

"Here's a towel," he said with a giggle.

Rather than just putting the towel down and leaving, however, he stayed and tried to strike up a conversation. He talked to me through the foggy glass door.

"How long have you been living in Siberia?" he asked.

"Half a year so far," I said as I turned my back to him, hoping he would take the hint and leave. Then I realized that he might not consider this the hint I'd intended. I turned again to face him, but that felt even more awkward. I turned the temperature up to produce more steam, to conceal myself in the fog.

"Don't you miss America?" he asked.

"I'm sorry, what about Miss America?"

He squealed. "Not *Miss America!* I asked if you miss America?"

"Sometimes less than others," I said.

He finally said good night and left. As I toweled off, I found myself smiling in the mirror. Maybe he wasn't gay. Maybe I was just tired. Yeah, that was it. I went back to the fold-out bed and told Zhenya that the shower was free.

I immediately fell asleep only to be woken by the sound of a woman's scream. There was nervous laughter and a flurry of apologies in English and Russian. Zhenya came walking into the room. His cheeks were flushed. He got into bed and turned out the light.

"What happened?" I asked.

"That John is a strange fellow."

"Did he bring you a towel?"

"Yeah."

"But he didn't leave," I said.

"Nope," Zhenya said, still a little flustered. "I didn't want to get out of the shower, but there was no hot water left. I didn't know you Americans had shortages of hot water. I thought only in Siberia people had to take cold showers."

"Is that what all the screaming was about?"

"No. John finally left the bathroom when I gestured that I needed to use the toilet. When I finally came out of the bathroom, everything was dark. I wandered around, feeling the walls until I found the bed. I started to get under the covers, but something was wrong."

"What?"

"Wrong bed," Zhenya said. "The light came on and I was in some old lady's bedroom. I don't understand English well enough, but I think John said that the woman was his mother."

We both erupted in laughter that we smothered with our pillows.

"Sanya, this isn't what I expected. All I've seen so far are blue men and the inside of cars," Zhenya said.

"Welcome to America."

11
Border Crossing

Zhenya and I were introduced to John's wife and still-flustered mother-in-law during an awkward breakfast of cold cereal and milk. We then climbed back into the minivan and drove to the church parking lot, where we met up with the others.

The plan for the day was to go to Niagara Falls, a mere four-hour drive from Syracuse. There was a collective groan from the Russians when I translated the agenda.

"I know that you've spent all of your waking hours so far in cars," I told them. "But, trust me, Niagara Falls is worth the trip. Really."

Grudgingly, they agreed.

If we were going to be Americans by spending the day in the car, I figured we might as well be ugly Americans and take two cars. I drove Sasha, the Director, and Vladimir. John drove Zhenya and Roza in the minivan.

We got on the interstate and I hit cruise control, which aroused my passengers' curiosity. They all leaned over to look at my foot, which, to their disbelief, wasn't on the gas. When we climbed a hill, the car's engine roared in order to maintain a constant speed. My passengers all shook their heads with amazement.

"Why are you holding the steering wheel?" Vladimir asked.

"I still have to do that part," I confessed.

"So, what's the point of cruise control?"

"To keep my leg from getting tired."

"Tired? Walking makes your legs tired. That's why people drive," he said, shaking his head. Cruise control had gone from miraculous to ridiculous in a matter of seconds.

"I haven't seen a single Lada," Sasha remarked as he watched the flow of oncoming cars.

"And you won't see a single one in America," I told him. "There are no Russian cars on American roads."

"No way. I don't believe it."

"Let's bet on it," I said, holding out my hand. "I guarantee you will not see a single Russian car during the entire time we are in America."

Sasha grabbed my hand. "A bottle of vodka to the winner."

We shook. The Director karate-chopped our hands apart, sealing the deal.

We stopped after an hour at a "travel oasis" for gas and bathroom breaks. Everybody started taking pictures of each other, not of the scenery, of which there wasn't much; we were on an interstate highway, after all. Sasha watched as I filled the car up with gas. He looked confused.

"What's the matter?" I asked.

"What about money?"

"What about money?" I topped off the tank. Ninety eight. Ninety nine. Click. Twenty dollars even.

"Don't you have to pay?"

"Of course," I said as I twisted the gas cap back on and returned the nozzle to its holster. "Now we pay."

Sasha stood still, stunned. "What's to prevent people from pumping gas then driving off without paying?" he said as he hurried to catch up to me.

I looked around for a moment, found what I was searching for, and pointed to the video cameras mounted on the wall of the building.

"What's a camera going to do?"

"Take your picture," I said.

"And so? They've got my picture and I've got their gas."

"It's not just a picture of you. It's a picture of your car and license plate. Several miles down the road, you'll be pulled over by a police car. And you're going to have a hard time pleading your innocence when the cop is holding a computer printout with a picture of you committing the crime."

"Sounds worse than the KGB," Sasha said.

When we walked into the building to pay, I pointed out the height measurements on the doors that allowed a video camera to determine the height of any would-be robber.

"Definitely worse than the KGB," he said.

I told the heavy-set clerk my pump number. The clerk, without looking up at me, mumbled, "Twenty dollars." I handed over the money and the transaction was complete. Well, not quite. "Have a good day," the clerk mumbled, still without looking up at me.

Sasha, the Director, Vladimir, and I went into the bathroom together like girls on prom night. There was a wall of identical white urinals. The Russians were a bit hesitant to urinate into something so clean, but when I stepped up, they followed my example. When I stepped back, my urinal clicked, then flushed automatically. Vladimir contorted himself in order to look into the urinal I had used as he continued to use his.

"They're automatic," I explained. "Kind of like toilets with cruise control."

Vladimir raised his bushy eyebrows. "Don't tell me that Americans get tired from flushing the toilet?"

"No," I said. "It keeps your hands from getting dirty."

"Then why are you washing your hands?" he asked. "Did you pee on them?"

Vladimir stepped away from his urinal, which flushed on cue. He laughed. There were two more flushes when Sasha and the Director finished. They went to the sinks to wash their hands, but Vladimir continued to look at the urinals. He had a mischievous expression on his face. He walked up and down the wall of urinals as if he were a general inspecting his troops. They didn't flush as he walked by them, which disappointed him.

Suddenly, he pulled his penis out again and walked up to the first urinal on the wall. Then he sidestepped to the urinal next to him. The porcelain apparatus flushed dutifully as if he had actually used it. Vladimir laughed with satisfaction. He had conned the machine. With his penis still out, he sidestepped like a country line dancer across the whole wall, setting off every single toilet.

John was eager to get back in the car; our Russian guests were not. They were far more interested in exploring the curiosities of this travel oasis. The Director stood in the candy aisle. Surrounded by a cornucopia of chocolate bars in flashy-colored wrappers, he wore a tired expression on his face. It was the first time I'd seen him look tired, ever. Zhenya watched the sweaty hot dogs going around on the rotisserie. Roza leafed through a clothes rack of Harley-Davidson T-shirts. Vladimir was nowhere to be found. I assumed he was still in the bathroom playing mind games with the toilets. John nervously waved for everyone to get back into the car. We ignored him.

Sasha grabbed my arm. "Let's go for a walk."

The monotonous whir of traffic surrounded us as we walked on the grassy island with a sign that read PET EXERCISE AREA.

"Two thousand dollars." Sasha handed me a wad of bills. "Hold this for me for a while. I've got too much cash on me."

"You're sure you don't work for the mafia?" I asked.

Sasha smiled. It was a proud smile, as if I had just paid him a huge compliment.

"Looks like business is going well." I said.

"Well, as always, we've got our fair share of problems." His face suddenly snapped, as if he just remembered something. "By the way, did you find the gloves?"

"Yes. We need to transfer twenty thousand dollars to a company in Munich and they'll ship them out to us."

Rather than relieved, Sasha looked more troubled at hearing this.

"What's the matter?" I asked.

"We're kind of short on cash right now," Sasha cautioned.

"So what's all this?" I said, patting the two-thousand-dollar wad in my pocket.

"*Myeloch* (chump change)," he said.

"What about the hotel?"

Sasha didn't say anything.

"I've been meaning to bring this up with you for a while but I haven't had a chance. Do you remember when Mahn took us on a tour of the eighth floor?" I asked.

A nod from Sasha.

"Do you remember when he showed us that faucet? The shiny one?"

Another nod.

"It felt like plastic to me. I'm afraid Mahn isn't using the highest quality materials."

Sasha laughed. "I know. He wasn't just cutting corners with materials either. I had to send them all back to China. The hotel reconstruction is temporarily on hold until we find a new team of workers."

"Back to China! Why?"

"Remember that delicious meal they made for us?" Sasha asked.

Now it was my turn to nod. "Best Chinese food I've ever had."

"Well, there's a reason for that." Sasha let out a few puffs of disgusted laughter. "Those Chinese construction workers weren't construction workers at all. They were cooks. It turns out that Mahn is a restaurant owner, not a hotel owner. I must have missed that in Li Li's translation."

From the pet exercise area of an American interstate highway, our Siberian business endeavors seemed less like cutting edge free enterprise and more like comical caricatures of capitalism.

"Well, how about the chocolate factory? Has our friend," I nodded in the Director's direction, "finally softened his tone? Can we at least expect to make a profit on the chocolate any time soon?"

"Yep," Sasha nodded. "That wad in your pocket is a small sample, just the tip of the iceberg. Let's be sure that he enjoys this trip," Sasha said with particular resolve.

We reached the end of the pet exercise area, a grass island in a sea of asphalt. For a few moments, we lingered on the beach, the curb. Then we turned and started walking back.

"Come on, campers. Let's get a move on," John shouted. He was honking the van's horn and laughing nervously. He had lured his passengers back into the minivan by holding up two six-packs of soft drinks.

"I've got Coke and I've got root beer," he said. "Come and get it!"

The Russians, of course, only heard the word *beer*.

"It's not real beer," I tried to tell Vladimir as he made a beeline to John.

"Ivan," Vladimir said as he pointed to the cans. "*Pivo* (beer)."

John shrieked with delight. "Here you go, you rascal." He handed over the six-pack.

Before we were out of the parking lot, Vladimir had taken a sip, spit it out, and launched the can from the car window. To keep him from throwing out the other five cans I had to tell him that we could get a five-hundred-dollar fine for littering.

"How would they know who did it?" Vladimir asked.

"KGB," Sasha said. "I think that after the Soviet Union fell, all of our KGB agents moved here to became policemen."

I turned onto the entrance ramp of the interstate and came to a stop just behind John's minivan. I stared at the minivan's brake lights while we waited at the short traffic light that rationed the number of cars entering the highway.

"Why are we stopped?" Vladimir asked.

"Red light," I said, pointing.

"But there is no cross street. How can there be a red light if there is no cross traffic?"

The brake lights went off and the minivan accelerated away from us.

"Go," Vladimir said excitedly.

"I can't. It's red again. See." I pointed.

"So what? There is no reason to stop." He was genuinely frustrated. "Don't tell me there are more KGB cameras watching us."

"These lights regulate the number of cars that can enter the highway at a time. Without these lights, there wouldn't be any room to build up speed. It's safer and more efficient this way."

"*Strana svobodi* (country of freedom). Hmmph," Vladimir grumbled. He saw the point of the light. He just didn't agree with it. It might be safer and more efficient, but it was still an infringement on freedom, his freedom.

A couple of hours later I followed the white minivan into an empty parking lot. The mist from the falls pushed upward at the edge of the parking lot. As we exited the car, I realized something was wrong. We were on the U.S. side. From the Canadian side, you could see the falls. But from this side, all you could see was a river end abruptly in mid air.

John had obviously forgotten this detail. He tried to make the best of it by pointing out the wonders of the mist cloud.

After four hours in the car, our butts were sore, our legs were stiff, and our minds were hungry for stimulation. But John wanted to do it all over again. He looked at his watch, then whispered to me, "We have to get going pretty soon if we want to get back on time."

"What if we don't want to get back on time?" I put my hands in my pocket to prevent myself from strangling him. He was making it very difficult for me to show the Director a good time.

"We have to get back by seven. The church has planned a dinner and party for us." John was on the verge of becoming hysterical.

"A church party. I'm sure the Russians will be eager to get back for that," I said.

My sarcastic remark was lost on John. He smiled, as if I'd just reassured him that the Russians weren't going to mutiny.

"John," I said calmly, "these people have been in planes or cars for the past three days. If this wasn't such a disappointing view of the falls, I'd insist that we stay here for at least an hour."

"But we have to go. I promised I'd have them back by seven."

I looked over and saw Sasha and Vladimir tiptoeing like mischievous teenagers over to the minivan. They were carrying the remaining root-beer cans. A moment later, they tiptoed away with four cans of Coke. Suddenly, I felt my anger fade entirely. "Okay, John. Let's go. There isn't anything to see here anyway."

John bounced back to the minivan, herding his confused Russian passengers as he went. I did the same with mine. As we drove toward the highway everybody in the car was silent. I could see in my rearview mirror that Sasha was mad. How could I have let this happen? A long road trip for nothing. I smiled to myself. John's blinker lights went on as he approached the onramp. A police car drove by.

"You guys have your passports?" I asked.

Everybody said yes as they patted the pocket of their jacket or pants.

The minivan turned and started accelerating down the on-ramp. I turned toward the on-ramp and then kept on turning, making a complete U-turn.

"You guys want to make use of those Canadian visas?" I accelerated toward the Canadian border.

"You've got a light hand," the Director said, his broad smile framed in my rearview mirror.

Sasha gave me an approving punch on the arm.

"Enjoy your visit," the border guard said after he examined the passports of my Russian friends.

Minutes later we were standing in Canada, looking back at Niagara Falls. Now this was a glorious view!

"America sure looks nice from here," Sasha said. "We were beginning to think that the U.S. was made out of nothing but roads." A bottle of vodka rose from an inside pocket of Sasha's jacket. He asked me if I could get some glasses; we needed to celebrate our successful jaunt into Canada.

I bought a can of Coke from a concession stand nearby and asked for three extra cups.

"Have a good day, eh?"

We stood in a circle on Canadian soil, holding Russian vodka in plastic cups made in China and toasted our good fortune. Sasha, the Director, and Vladimir drank one more round in my honor.

We stayed for about an hour, marveling at the glory of the falls. Sasha kept looking away from the falls. When I asked why, he said that Alexander Mogilny, his favorite Russian hockey player lived here. Sasha was trying to determine which of the penthouses on the ridge belonged to his hero.

I was glad to see the three Russians gradually empty the bottle of vodka. It meant that I wouldn't have to worry about having an open bottle in the car, and it also meant that my passengers would sleep like babies all the way back. The idea of subjecting them to another four hours of interstate on their second day of America seemed cruel.

Before we left, I took one last look at the impressive falls. Sasha was right; America was beautiful, especially when you're standing in a foreign country.

12

Swiss Chocolate and Cheese Steaks

The next day our missionary/travel agent arranged for us to visit a nearby factory owned by Nestlé, the Swiss chocolate giant. The visit to the factory lasted for just over an hour, but it seemed longer. I found myself checking my watch every five minutes. Our host's business card read "Manager of Operations." Specifically what operations he managed it didn't say. He was barely past forty and yet he seemed much older. He had a belly that pushed outward, giving his tie an almost horizontal surface to rest on. The skin on his face hung loosely, as if gravity were stronger wherever he stood.

In comparison to the American factory manager, our enthusiastic Siberian Director, in his early sixties, was the picture of vitality. His stomach was flat. In the factory's sauna (that's right, the factory had its own sauna), I'd seen him roll his stomach muscles like a belly dancer. The Director's face and high forehead were covered with smooth, taut skin. His skin had a healthy tan, even in March. The Director released a nonstop torrent of questions. Roza, acting as translator, couldn't keep up with him. She would be halfway through a question when the Director would ask a follow-up question. Roza flailed her arms, which caused him to laugh and put his hands on her shoulders. He apologized. She accepted his apology and quickly went back to translating.

The Nestlé factory was a model of efficiency. The candy bars whizzed by on mechanical causeways that descended from the ceiling, circled around through a series of machines, and then disappeared through the floor. The candy bars moved so fast that the red, white, and blue wrappers blurred into an endless streak of purple.

Quite a contrast from the Siberian chocolate factory. That factory's old equipment roared and whirred, but produced very little motion. Sturdy women dressed in chocolate-stained uniforms operated the machines. One woman, the one who made the cornstarch forms for the chocolate to be poured into, was covered in the cornstarch dust. Every time she blinked, yellow dust puffed from her eyelashes. Another woman held a long blade with handles on both ends. She cut the whipped egg-yolk and sugar filling that, once covered in chocolate, became the highly-prized Russian treat called *ptichi moloko* (bird's milk). Dozens of women sat beside conveyor belts, occasionally reaching out to remove a misshapen chocolate. These women took fierce pride in the chocolates that rolled by them at a leisurely pace. Whenever the Director led me past one of these workstations, the women would pull a few of the brown morsels from the belt and hand them to me.

"*Nash luchee, da* (ours is best, right)?"

I always nodded. It was only later that I realized that when these women asked whether their chocolate was the best, they weren't comparing it to American or Swiss chocolate. They were comparing it to the chocolate coming off the conveyor belt just on the other side of the factory floor, where other women would soon force some of their chocolates on me, insisting that they made the best in the factory.

At the Nestlé factory, however, the production floor wasn't teeming with burly women who forced chocolate on you. In fact, the production floor was nearly deserted. There was one woman with a hard hat, safety goggles, and a clipboard. She walked around the floor inspecting the machinery. The factory was fully automated and remarkably efficient.

At the end of our tour, the manager of operations grumbled a few words, then gave each one of us a complimentary candy bar, the same kind you can get at 7-Eleven. Our Siberian Director made a long speech about how grateful he was for the tour, what an excellent manager our host must be to keep a factory like this in operation, and, in short, that he wished our host to be healthy, happy, and successful. The Director then reached into a bag he had been carrying and pulled out a large box of chocolates that made all the Russians gasp. This box of chocolates was as rare and treasured to Siberians as a Babe Ruth baseball card is to an American. The manager of operations accepted the box with a polite smile and then tossed it onto a nearby table. Some almond shavings came out of the box's corners. "You should really consider plastic shrink wrap," he said.

The Siberian Director accepted the obvious advice with a polite smile.

I was glad when we got back into our cars and drove away. We kept on driving until we were in Newark, where our missionary/travel agent had made reservations for us at the airport Days Inn. For the next few days, this was our launching pad into New York City.

Manhattan—America's pedestrian utopia. Here the drivers were at a disadvantage. Here the sidewalks never ended. Here the streetscape was a flow of human activity, not just automobile congestion. We walked and walked, stopping every so often to sample pizza slices, hot dogs, and pretzels. The Russians kept getting sucked into electronics stores, where, to my surprise, the salespeople could speak a little Russian. "*Dyoshovo* (cheap). *Kupite* (you buy). *Dlya vas* (for you)."

In every store, Vladimir walked up to me, clutching something in his hands. He gave me a peek of the item. Whispering, he asked me how much it cost.

"Let me see the price tag," I'd say. This was obviously hard for Vladimir. In order for me to appraise the item, he had to let go. He'd have to relinquish his booty. Reluctantly, he handed it over.

"It's a portable camera. Ten dollars," I told him at one store. The price tag read $9.99.

"It's so small," Vladimir said. "It must be a spy camera." He quickly grabbed the camera back.

Even though all the prices were clearly marked, Vladimir continued to bring things to me for appraisal.

"Sixteen dollars, Vladimir," I said. "See, it's written right here, fifteen–ninety-nine." I wanted to teach this man to fish, but he just wanted me to keep giving him fish.

Later, we ducked into a dollar store.

Vladimir walked up to me, cradling a pair of sunglasses in his little paws.

"Sanya, how much do these cost?"

"One dollar," I said. "Everything in here costs one dollar."

He walked off, only to return a few minutes later with a set of color pens. "Sanya, how much do these cost?"

"One dollar," I said. "It's a dollar store. Everything in here costs one dollar." I grabbed a polyester sailor's cap. "See this?" I shook it. "One dollar!" I grabbed a three-pack of Cracker Jack boxes. "Guess how much these cost?"

He looked at them, trying to determine what they were.

"ONE DOLLAR!" I screamed.

"One dollar?" he said, oblivious to my anger. He grabbed them from me. "I think I'll buy these." He walked off toward the cash register.

The next day we drove to Philadelphia, my college stomping grounds. I showed off the City of Brotherly Love: Independence Hall and Old Town, Market Street and the waterfront.

Vladimir was entranced by African-Americans, especially African-American women. "I want to get my picture taken with her," he said, pointing to a young woman sitting alone on a bench near a tinkling fountain. He handed me his newly purchased "spy" camera and walked toward the fountain. Slowly, he took baby steps toward the unsuspecting woman. I pointed the camera. Just as he and she were in the frame together, she noticed him.

"Oh, I'm sorry," she apologized. "Let me get out of your way." She got up and moved away. I snapped a picture of a broken-hearted Vladimir, alone.

That night we ate at a restaurant where I ordered Philadelphia cheese steaks for everyone. During dinner Vladimir asked, "Why are your doors made out of glass?"

"What are you talking about?"

"All the doors in America are made out of glass," he said in his baritone voice. He pointed to the glass door of the restaurant and then to a small house across the street. The house's door wasn't made entirely out of glass, but it did have a large window at face level. "It's almost as if you're asking people to break in and rob you," Vladimir said.

"I guess Americans don't want to feel like they live in a vault," I said, alluding to my own aversion to the latest Siberian trend: steel doors. The doors were welded together in place and bolted directly into the concrete doorframe. Scarred by welding burns, the doors had no redeeming aesthetic value. They made the sound of a prison cell slamming closed. Locked down.

Roza said that she didn't have a steel door and wasn't going to get one.

"Weren't you robbed recently?" Sasha asked.

All heads turned to Roza, who smiled politely. "No, Alexander Kamilovich."

Sasha looked puzzled.

"A prowler did break into my apartment," Roza said, restoring Sasha's faith in his own memory. "But I wasn't robbed."

Roza looked around the table to see that everybody was waiting for her to elaborate. She acquiesced. "A man broke into my apartment earlier this winter. When I heard the noise I thought it was my son. So I got out of bed and went to make him some tea." She paused, still wearing her dignified smile. "I turned on the light and there was a strange man in my apartment. He had a knife in his hand."

Everybody had stopped eating by now and listened with terrific interest.

"He didn't say anything. I realized that he was disturbed. So I took on a motherly tone. 'You look hungry,' I said. He still didn't say anything. So I walked by him and his knife and went into the kitchen. I started making tea. He got a little nervous when I pulled a knife out of the drawer."

Vladimir shouted, "*Oookh ti.* That was sly. Did you stab him?"

"No, I cut some bread and buttered it. After a while I got him to sit down at the kitchen table. He was angry—angry at everything and everybody. But he was more hungry than angry. So I fed him slowly and tried to calm him down. He told me about how his wife had died and how he had lost his job. I just listened and fed him. After a few hours, he said that he belonged in a hospital. So, with his permission, I called the police to have them take him to the hospital."

Everybody nodded in silent awe and admiration.

The next day we drove on to Washington, D.C., where we visited the Smithsonian museums according to our interests. I took the men to see airplanes and rockets at the Air and Space Museum. In the lobby of the museum were two large intercontinental ballistic missiles: one American and one Russian. The text on the plaque before the rockets explained that these weapons were dismantled as a part of the Strategic Arms Limitation Treaty.

"Look," Sasha said, pointing to the Russian rocket, "they cut ours up to get it in here." He pointed out the weld marks on the hull of the larger rocket. He inspected the American rocket. No weld marks. "I bet your rocket still works. You guys aren't complying with the treaty," he said in an accusatory voice, then nudged me in the side with his elbow and gave me a wink.

Next stop: Orlando.

As we stepped from the plane and into the tunnel, the dry, cool air aboard the plane was interrupted only for a moment with a whiff of thick, humid air. Moments later we were in the conditioned air of the airport terminal. Even to my American eyes, the Orlando airport looked less like an airport and more like a shopping mall. We packed ourselves into another rental minivan equipped with cup holders and ashtrays. On the way to the hotel, John made a pit stop at McDonald's.

As everybody sat on plastic chairs and picked at the McFood on plastic trays, Sasha grabbed my arm. "Let's go for a walk."

But again there was no sidewalk to walk on. Parking lot after parking lot stretched down both sides of the wide street. After our brief respite in New York City, we were again in America, where a person's foot spends less time pounding the pavement than it does pressing on the gas pedal. And if even that proves too strenuous, there is always cruise control. With nowhere to walk, Sasha and I ended up straddling the Hamburglar and Mayor McCheese, two of the many McCharacters with giant springs coming out of their stomachs that corkscrewed into the sand of the restaurant's fenced-in Playland.

"So, how do you like America?" Sasha said in Russian but with an exaggerated American accent. He grabbed the metal handle-bars protruding from the Hamburglar's head and leaned back. His weight bent the spring so that his back nearly touched the sand. "That's the first thing Americans ask when they hear that I'm from Russia. Nobody ever asks, 'Do you like America?' or 'What don't you like about America?' They just assume that I'm going to like America. I do like America—parts of it, anyway—but I don't like the assumption that I have to like," he paused, looking around, "all of it."

A minivan full of squabbling children pulled away from the drive-through window. "Who ordered the McChicken? Who ordered the strawberry shake?" The kids screamed, "I did! I did! You didn't order that. That's mine. Mom, Timmy took some of my fries." The dad yelled for everybody to quiet down or they were going to go right back to the hotel and nobody would see Mickey Mouse. The bickering didn't stop. As the dad tried to turn left across the fast moving traffic, he yelled, "I want food going in your mouths and nothing coming out! Food in! No words coming out! Got it?" The minivan lurched across the oncoming lanes and then merged into traffic with a screech and a honk from the car behind it.

I leaned Mayor McCheese forward until his lettuce lips kissed the sand. "All Siberians ask me the same question: 'Why did you come to Siberia?' I've never had anyone ask me, 'So, how do you like Siberia?'"

We both rocked our metal steeds back and forth for a bit.

After a long pause, Sasha said, "I just figured out where this sense of déjà vu is coming from. Ever since we landed in America, I have had this feeling of familiarity, as if I have been here already."

"This isn't your first trip to America?"

"No, it is. I've never been here before. But I've been told about this place so often that I feel like I know it intimately. It was all the communist propaganda. They talked about this place all the time."

"Communist propaganda talked about urban sprawl?"

"No," he said. "I'm talking about the communist propaganda touting the future wonders of the worker's paradise. This," he said with a wave of his hand, "is what they had been promising us for seventy years. America has achieved communism." Sasha looked around and nodded. "Yep. You've made it. Congratulations."

I laughed.

Sasha, to prove his point, began reciting the signs that America had evolved into the perfect communist state. "How about all of those houses we saw on the way from the airport. Row after row of virtually identical houses. Nobody but a communist could have conceived such ugly uniformity."

I couldn't argue with him on that point.

"And they promised no shortages under communism," he continued. "I haven't seen any empty shelves since I got here. Under communism the government is supposed to fade away as the people govern themselves. From what I've seen, you all follow the rules and obey the laws, even when there is no chance of being caught. Under communism money becomes irrelevant. You Americans all have your plastic cards to pay for everything. How much money do you have in your wallet right now?"

"Seven dollars," I said, "not counting the two thousand you asked me to hold on to."

"I've got over a thousand dollars," Sasha said. "Who is the communist and who is the capitalist here? Admit it, Sanya, America is a communist utopia."

"Maybe you're right," I grumbled. "But if this is utopia, then utopia is way overrated."

We spent the entire day at the closest thing America has to utopia: Disney World. I stood in more lines in one day at the Magic Kingdom than I did all year in Siberia. The good part was that we were on foot, not crammed into the minivan. The bad part was that every line ended with us piling into a vehicle in which we sat, while the boat, train, or submarine took us on a tour of a magical place with dancing pirates, menacing monsters, and singing dolls.

We stood in lines that wrapped back around themselves, forcing us to see the same people every time we doubled back. In one of these lines I noticed Roza mumbling to herself. I moved in closer to hear what she was complaining about.

"*Kak grubo* (how rude)," she said.

"What's rude?" I asked.

"Forgive me for saying this, but you Americans have really disgusting eating habits. Americans always have to have something in their mouths. It's either green ice cream, a twisty plastic straw, or a—what do you call that?" She pointed to a young boy stuffing his mouth with a cylinder of meat nestled in fried dough atop a rolled-paper stick, all smothered in sugary, red tomato paste.

"A corn dog," I said as my eyes panned across the rest of the waiting crowd. Roza was right; nearly everybody's mouth was busy either licking, chewing, sipping, or swallowing. There weren't any idle mouths. I spotted a pair of teenage boys with still mouths. I was about to point out these two sophisticated gents, but I noticed that they both had small lumps in their cheeks. They frequently spit brown liquid into Coke cans.

"Most people are probably just trying to save time," I said, trying to find a rational defense for such behavior. "They're eating lunch and standing in line at the same time. Killing two birds with one stone. They're just being efficient."

"If that," Roza said, pointing to the a girl holding a quaff of bright pink cotton candy larger than her own head, "is lunch, then you Americans are even more disgusting than I thought. That's why all Americans are fat, except the people in New York City. I didn't see as many big butts there as I do here."

"Forgive me for saying this," I said a bit defensively, "but Russians aren't exactly slender."

"*Bolshie* (big)," Roza said, "*ne tolstie* (not fat). There's a difference."

She was right. A large Russian woman gets her figure not from high quantities of food, but from moderate amounts of food with a singular quality: starch. A scale might not differentiate a Russian grandma from an American grandma, but a squeeze could. When you hug a Russian babushka, it's like hugging a tree. There is no give. Her sturdy frame stands its ground. Siberian *babushki* are toned up from all the physical exercise it takes to get through the average day: walking, climbing steps, walking, hauling groceries, walking, doing laundry, walking, walking, and more walking.

I was embarrassed when I looked up at the crowd of Americans passing by. They were fat—car-sitting, junk food–eating, TV-watching fat. Obese. Blubbery. Even the seven-foot-tall Donald Duck had a potbelly. The only one who wasn't fat was Goofy.

13
Good-bye, America

We returned to the hotel in the evening and collapsed from exhaustion. Having fun is hard work. Expensive, too. Sasha had made a significant dent in his wad of cash when we left Disney World.

After one night's rest, we packed up the minivan again and headed for Miami. Because the Russians had been buying souvenirs, trinkets, and doodads all along the way, each time we got into the minivan, there was more and more stuff and less and less room for us. Elbows were everywhere. It was hard to determine which of the tangled legs belonged to whom.

It is a five-hour drive from Orlando to Miami along the Florida Turnpike. Fortunately, Siberians are masters of self-entertainment. Jokes, songs, and stories made the time fly by a lot faster than did the monotonous scenery of swamps and suburbs. Every time we passed another ugly housing development, Sasha would look at me with a triumphant grin.

"*Ti prav* (you're right)," is all I could say.

As we approached Miami's city limits, Sasha told a joke:

"A Frenchman, an American, and a Russian are in a bar. They get to talking about which country had the most beautiful women. The Frenchman says, 'If a Frenchman puts his hands around a Frenchwoman's waist, his fingers will touch. And it's not because Frenchmen have such big hands. It's because Frenchwomen have such slender waists.' 'That's nothing,' the American says. 'If an American woman gets on a horse, her legs will touch the ground. And it's not because American horses are so short. It's because

American women have such long, sexy legs. 'Ha,' the Russian laughs. 'If a Russian man slaps his wife's ass on his way to work, when he comes home after work, her butt will still be jiggling. And it's not because Russian women have such big butts. It's because the Russian workday is so short.'"

As we pulled up to our hotel, everybody was laughing, even Roza.

Being bilingual has its perks, especially in Miami, unless, of course, your second language isn't Spanish. I tried to remember my three years of high school Spanish, but the Russian words came first, then the English, and finally a few sprinkles of Spanish *palabras*. Interestingly enough, the Russians were disappointed, even a bit angry, that so many people in Miami spoke Spanish, not English. After all, if the Siberians wanted to hear people speaking Spanish, they could have gone to Cuba!

It was March. There was still plenty of snow on the ground in Siberia. But here, it was eighty-five degrees at night. Even though it was already past nine P.M., everybody wanted to go to the beach. John, as always, was nervous. He wanted to wait until tomorrow. So we let him wait until tomorrow. We, however, were going swimming now.

The minivan, emptied of all cargo except a few beach towels, seemed ridiculously roomy. All the personal space each passenger now had felt somehow lonely. The smell of saltwater filled the van as we got closer to the ocean. The Russians started to sing. They all moved forward onto the first bench and snuggled up together. We drove toward the beach like kids on the way to the circus. The songs were lovely. I felt blessed to be in a car full of people that could create beauty so easily. And, yet, the music seemed out of place. Halfway into the third song, Sasha stopped everybody by waving his arms.

"Why are all of our songs so sad?"

"Hey," the Director said, "he's right."

"They're not all sad," Roza protested.

"Then sing a happy Russian song," Sasha challenged her.

"The sun shines clearly," Roza began alone. *"Hello, beautiful country,"* everybody joined in.

Suddenly Sasha waved them off again.

"A happy song that isn't about the great October Revolution."

There was silence. A man wearing a bushy mustache and a Kaiser helmet with a spike on top drove by us on a Harley Davidson motorcycle. The thunderous roar engulfed us as he accelerated by.

"Kharley, Kharley," Vladimir yelled as he strained to watch the hog pull away, its red taillight shrinking into the distance.

Unwilling to sing melancholy Russian songs, the beach-goers settled for upbeat songs that extolled the virtues of the benevolent Communist party. Each song ended in a round of laughter.

The road ended in a "T." I stopped the car at the intersection. We could hear the waves but couldn't see them. In between the beach and us stood a wall of high-rise condominiums. I looked left; the wall went on to the horizon. I looked right—same thing.

"Right or left?" I asked.

"Right," Sasha said, in between Bolshevik verses. "We've erred enough to the left."

"Right it is," I said and pointed our festive van south. The solid wall of condos was perfect, impenetrable. The beach had been divided up and turned into private property. All of it.

Frustrated, I finally gave up searching, parked the van and walked my six Russians into an upscale building. If somebody in this carpeted lobby asked us what we were doing in sandals and T-shirts, I probably would have babbled at them in Russian about what a crime it is keep people from the beach so that rich people can have a good view. Fortunately, nobody stopped us. I found a door that led outside. Actually, it didn't lead outside, but poolside. The glow from the underwater lights made the side of the building ripple.

"Why is there a pool here?" Vladimir asked. "Who needs a pool when the ocean is within spitting distance?"

Through another door we went, our sandals snapping against our heels, spelling out in Morse code: "W-E D-O-N-T B-E-L-O-N-G

H-E-R-E." The blue aura of the pool vanished as the blackness of the ocean opened up before us. Everybody broke into a run. We had the beach entirely to ourselves. We laughed and frolicked like kids playing hooky from school, only we were playing hooky from winter. Eventually, hunger reminded us that we had skipped dinner. Smelling of salt and sand, we drove back to the hotel and ordered three pizzas.

"If they don't deliver it within thirty minutes, it's free," I said after I hung up the phone. I could see from the expression on Sasha's face that the pizzas were already of secondary importance.

"Let's all go wait in another room. The delivery guy won't be able to find us. And after the thirty minutes are up, we can claim our free pizza." He beamed with mischievous pride.

"Sasha, are you hungry?" I asked.

"Oh, come on," Sasha said. "Only one thing tastes better than pizza."

"What's that?"

"*Free* pizza!"

"Sasha, you're about to get hot pizzas delivered to you in the comfort of your hotel room. You don't have to risk frostbite or stand in lines. You don't even have to get into a car. In fact, you don't have to lift a finger. You want all of this, *and* you want it for free?"

Sasha laughed. "Yeah. If they are dumb enough to offer such a deal, I'm going to take advantage of it."

"It's not a game. It's a business," I said.

Sasha didn't seem to acknowledge the difference.

We went to the next room. The pizza guy found us anyway, with seven minutes to spare. After eating his third slice, Sasha complained that the pizza tasted too salty.

The next day we found public access to Miami Beach. Sasha and I left the group on the white sand surrounded by pastel buildings. He and I took the minivan to do some errands. We went to a pharmacy to pick up some medications that Sasha couldn't get in Siberia. The names of the medications, of course, were Russian.

They meant nothing to the pharmacist; he didn't speak Russian — or English. After a lot of pantomiming sore throats, stomachaches, and an irritation below the belt-line, the Spanish-speaking pharmacist nodded that he understood. We left with a bag full of pills, powders, and elixirs. When we returned to the beach, our group was huddling under a beach umbrella. Except for the bronze-skinned Director, everybody looked like strawberry short-cake, a random patchwork of red and white skin, either savagely burned or still Siberian pale. Everybody was eager to leave, to get away from this cursed sun.

"Okay, okay," Sasha promised. "But I want to get wet first. Five minutes." We pulled off our shirts and walked across the sand. My pale legs protruded from my swimming trunks. Sasha, like all Russian men, wore briefs. As we floated around, I noticed that there were very few women at this beach. In fact, there were exactly zero women. Just guys.

"I think this is a gay beach," I whispered to Sasha in Russian.

Sasha jerked and spun in the water, as if a shark had brushed up against his leg. "You're kidding?" he said after he recovered from the shock.

"Nope," I said. "Take a look around."

There were guys wearing very skimpy briefs, rubbing oil on each other, playing volleyball, swimming in pairs just like...well, just like us.

"Definitely gay," I said. "And I bet they think we're gay too."

Sasha laughed. "No doubt John picked out this spot."

That night everybody ached with red, tender skin. But the next morning, they insisted on going back to the beach. It was our last full day in America, our last day of summer before the Siberian version arrived in three months. Within seventy-two hours, we'd be back in Siberia, trudging through the snow with wool scarves scratching against our sunburned noses. But today, everyone wanted to cheat winter one last time.

That night I reminded Sasha of our bet. We hadn't seen a single Russian car during our entire time in America. Sasha had lost.

Graciously, he presented me with a large jug of Russian vodka that he had been lugging around in his luggage the whole time.

"Unless you plan on hauling that thing back to Russia, I suggest we drink it tonight," he said.

We gathered ingredients from a deli and had a Russian picnic right in our hotel room. Roza let down her prim and proper façade and revealed her Russian roots by tossing back a few shots with us.

John even joined in on the pagan feast. He came over to me and started yammering in my ear. He told me that he was going to miss us, that he was envious because we were going back to Novosibirsk, and he was returning to upstate New York.

You should be envious, I thought to myself. Instead I told him, "There is still snow on the ground back in Siberia. In a couple of weeks the swarms of mosquitoes will be out in force."

John laughed. "I know, but…" He paused. "It's such a great place to paint."

The next day, we boarded an Aeroflot jet bound for Moscow.

As the plane left the ground, I turned and asked Sasha, "So, how did you like America?"

He groaned and said, "Sanya, have you heard the song 'Goodbye, America?'"

"Yeah. They play it all the time back in Novosibirsk on that new radio station *Yevropa Plus*."

"Do you know what it's about?"

"No," I confessed. "I haven't really listened to the lyrics."

"You should. It's about a guy, a Soviet guy, who dreamed of America all his life. For him it was a magical place—freedom, streets of gold, all that crap. Well, the Soviet Union collapses and the Iron Curtain lifts. The guy pools his money, buys a ticket, and goes to America. But it isn't like he dreamed. It's suburbs, fat people, and endless highways. So, in the song, when he sings 'Goodbye, America,' he is saying good-bye to America the adjective, America the dream."

As the plane gained altitude, the wall of condos faded into the distance, and the blue ocean moved like a curtain closing after a grand spectacle.

14
Spring in Siberia

A sense of serenity came over me as I looked out the window of our descending plane. The view of the landscape below looked like a fly's view of a Holstein cow. Dark, irregular patches of trees interrupted the expansive snow-covered Siberian landscape. The plane descended slowly, gradually, and in a straight line. It was very different from the dramatic way American planes swerve, dive, and slalom in a futile attempt to avoid making noise over the sprawling residential areas along the plane's landing pattern. In Siberia, nobody lives underneath the landing pattern. There was more than enough open land here. No need to build houses near the airport, or airports near the houses.

Once on the ground, as everybody split up to go their separate ways, the Director turned to Sasha and told him that it had been a good trip. The price of chocolate would remain low. Our profits would stay high. Sasha's irrational plan had worked.

For the next month, whenever we visited the factory, all the Director wanted to do was reminisce about sneaking across the Canadian border to see Niagara Falls, or sneaking through a ritzy condominium to take a night swim in the ocean. We had made friends with the Director, and now we were making money. Lots of it.

We had enough free capital to forward the prepayment for the million gloves, which earned us enough profit to order a second load of twice as many. Our unexpected glove business caused the German supplier to sit up and take notice. Soon she was sending us other products, including sterile surgical and extra thick autopsy gloves. The sterile surgical gloves were desperately needed in the local hospitals, but the hospitals simply didn't have the money to buy them. The autopsy gloves, however, were a huge hit. No sooner did we get a shipment in and they were sold out. Could there be that many autopsies going on? Maybe there were, but that's not what the gloves were being used for. It turned out that people were using them as gardening gloves at their dachas, their summer cottages. Who were we to argue with paying customers?

Sasha and I had spent so much time and energy over the past year trying to earn a profit that when we finally did have, in Sasha's words, a positive "delta," we weren't sure what to do with it. At least, I didn't. I wasn't earning money toward some end. Earning money was the end. For Sasha, however, it was only the beginning. He was able to spend everything he earned, and more.

Despite his jokes about how suburbs in America were like a communist utopia, he didn't waste time before making a down payment on his own suburban dream. His excuse: he was once a communist himself.

He and his friend Shura decided to buy a duplex in a housing development fifteen minutes south of our village. The house wasn't finished; it had no roof. In fact, none of the houses in this future Siberian suburb were even close to complete. But the house cost the equivalent of ten thousand dollars for each half. Sasha found out that the seller was trying to buy a Russian jeep but couldn't find one. Sasha offered to buy a jeep for him if he'd knock five thousand off the price of the house. Agreed. Sasha called a friend who knew a friend who sold Russian jeeps for the equivalent of four thousand dollars. Sasha talked him down to thirty five hundred plus twenty-five boxes of chocolate.

To make the down payment, Sasha asked my permission to borrow some money from our business. I agreed. Like I said, I had nothing on my shopping list. Besides, I figured that this would be a good test of my partner. If he didn't return the money, I would know that he wasn't trustworthy, and I could leave the business before I lost anything more than time and a few thousand dollars. If he paid it back, I'd know that Sasha was trustworthy and I could invest myself into this business with confidence.

Sasha took me with him to buy the jeep. With his briefcase full of cash, Sasha knocked on the steel door of a rusty military trailer. The door opened with a waft of warm, smoky air. We ducked into the small room made even smaller by five burly young men with crewcuts. The eldest, probably in his early thirties, sat on an upside-down crate behind a rickety desk. The rest of the men stood around him. Bodyguards. Sasha was offered a crate to sit on. I wasn't. They probably assumed that I was Sasha's bodyguard. So I played the part, folding my arms and trying to look as tough as I could. Sasha pulled bundle after bundle of rubles out of his case. He pulled off the paper seal of each bundle and counted the bills one by one, pushing the tallied bills across the desk. The man offered Sasha a cigarette. Sasha refused and kept on counting.

The pile of money in Sasha's briefcase shrank steadily as the pile of money grew on the opposite side of the table. When Sasha got down to the last bundle, the heads of the bodyguards bounced in unison to Sasha's counting. Sasha's voice got louder as he counted out the final few bills. He held up the very last banknote above his head.

He slapped it down on the desk. *Whap!*

A key slid across the desk. *Zing.*

There was a flurry of hand shaking and head nodding, but no smiles.

One of the bodyguards opened the door to the trailer. We found a tan UAZ at the base of the trailer's steps. The key didn't open the jeep's door, but the door did open. There were no locks on the doors. That's the way these vehicles came off the assembly line. The key connected the battery to the electric motor that cranked the engine a couple of revolutions until sparks ignited the mixture of air and gasoline in the pistons, setting in perpetual motion the repetitive cycle of intake, compression, explosion, and exhaust.

"Now this is a jeep!" I climbed in, slamming the slab of metal generously referred to as a door. It latched shut only with the proper balance of respect and violence.

"Not like those four-wheel-drive limousines I saw everybody driving on the smooth streets of America," Sasha said.

There were no leather seats in this little UAZ, no stereo system with CD player, no air conditioning, and certainly no cup holders.

The dashboard had a total of three dials: a speedometer, a gas gauge and a temperature gauge. There weren't any microchips in this car's brain. This metal mule didn't have a brain. It was a machine. You were supposed to drive it, not live in it.

"What does this do?" I asked, reaching up for the switch on the little metal box above the windshield.

"Go ahead." With raised eyebrows, Sasha encouraged me to flip the switch.

I tried, but it didn't budge.

"Harder. Don't be shy." Sasha laughed. "The UAZ doesn't respond to politeness."

I pushed with my thumb until the metal switch began to dig into my skin. Suddenly, there was a "click" as the little box began to buzz like a bumblebee stuck in a soda pop can. The windshield wipers jerked back and forth sporadically. We both laughed at the pure functionality of this vehicle.

"Uaziks are so simple you can fix any problem with a hammer." Sasha hit the dashboard with his fist so hard that I gave him a look of concern. "Don't worry," Sasha said. "It's a tough machine."

"I wasn't worried about the machine. I was worried about your hand."

"Look," Sasha said as he wedged his briefcase onto the gas pedal and pulled his foot aside, "Russian cruise control."

We both laughed our way right through a red light, nearly hitting a motorcyclist wearing red-baron goggles.

Sasha removed the briefcase as I looked around for traffic cops.

We got back to Sasha's apartment and parked the UAZ just below his kitchen window, seven stories up. I instinctively went to lock the door, but remembered that there were no locks. I noticed another UAZ parked down the street, also without locks. The owner of that UAZ, however, had removed all the door handles. The doors simply had holes where the handles once were. I assumed that the guy had a door handle attached to his key chain. We left our tan UAZ and went up to have lunch and a glass of tea with Lyuda and Alina.

For the first time in months, it was warm enough to open the windows and let in some fresh air. It was still cool out, but not dangerously cold. The sun beamed into the kitchen. Wearing sweaters, we sat around the table sipping spoonfuls of steaming soup and periodically looking down at the UAZ to make sure it was still there.

There are two sounds that announce spring in Siberia. The first is the *thwump* of people beating a winter's worth of dust out of their carpets. The second is the thunderous crash of giant icicles shattering on the cement below. Above every entranceway to these bleak rectangle apartment buildings is a thick concrete slab. They were not to keep the snow off the steps but to prevent falling icicles from skewering residents. You knew it was spring if you slammed the door behind you and, as you tucked in your scarf, a six-foot icicle exploded on the concrete above your head, scattering frozen, glistening shrapnel in every direction.

After lunch we drove the UAZ a few miles out of town to the real estate salesman. Again Sasha counted out bundles of money. When Sasha showed him the UAZ, the balding man complained that he had wanted a green one. They only came in two colors: green and tan. Sasha said that a tan UAZ was more distinctive. But the man didn't seem to think that distinctiveness was inherently desirable. Sasha changed his approach. He said that Americans drive around in tan jeeps.

"If you don't believe me, you can just ask him. He's an American," Sasha said, twitching his head in my direction.

I backed up Sasha's story. "Ever since Operation Desert Storm, Americans prefer tan jeeps."

The man nodded. That was good enough for him. He accepted the jeep and the cash. Half of the brick shell now belonged to Sasha.

Shura didn't have any trouble coming up with the money to pay for his half. He was in business by himself and, therefore, could take as much money out of his business as he wanted. And it looked like he did just that, and often. Shura drove a black BMW around town, all bought with the revenues from his growing gum empire. He paid for his half of the brick structure and became a homeowner or, at least, the owner of half a roofless home. The up-and-coming Siberian gum emperor and the budding Siberian chocolate emperor had the beginnings of a joint castle.

Sasha and Shura took me out to their new estate on the first day that the snow had receded enough to allow Shura's BMW to get within walking distance. The snow had melted back to reveal sticky, heavy mud. The weight of the mud plus the airtight suction made it nearly impossible to lift my leg without leaving a shoe behind.

We eventually slogged our way up to the house. Not only roofless, the structure had no steps, doors, or windows. We used a wood plank to climb up from floor to floor, taking the plank with us as we went. On the top floor, Sasha pulled a bottle of vodka from his coat pocket. The sun burned its way through the thin clouds. I could smell everything thawing. We each took swigs from the bottle, then spit it out on the bricks of the house. It was tradition in Russia to *obmyit* (cleanse) any major purchase with a spray of vodka from the mouth of the new owner and his friends.

When we got back to the village, I spotted a young woman mounted atop a horse in front of the university's main entrance. Long, wavy, strawberry blonde hair flowed down her back. There was a crowd around her. They were all singing and laughing.

"What's going on?" I asked Sasha.

He let out a laugh. "April first. Today is Math Day. Those are the math majors. It's their day to celebrate. Don't you guys celebrate Math Day?"

"Nope. Today is April Fool's Day in America."

"I know that Americans don't like mathematics, but isn't that a bit extreme?"

When we got back to Sasha's place, Lyuda told her husband that, rather than just letting all the fancy Chinese faucets and carpets intended for the failed hotel project sit around collecting dust, she should use them to furnish her beauty salon.

"What beauty salon?" Sasha asked with genuine curiosity.

"The one I want to open," she answered. "You've got your chocolate business. I want a beauty business."

"Why not?" Sasha said. "A trip to the beauty salon could be considered a small luxury, right?" He looked at me for confirmation.

I shrugged my shoulders and nodded. "Yeah, I guess so."

Lyuda let out a squeal of excitement and gave her husband a kiss. But the moment was short-lived. Domestic matters trumped business matters. "You and Richardovich, take out the carpets and beat them till they're clean."

Alina repeated her mother's instructions, waving her finger at us.

"Party's over," Sasha said, getting up from his chair.

We had to hold our breaths as we worked because of the dust cloud that enveloped us. Finished and filthy, we returned to the apartment along one of the slowly melting trails.

The paths of packed-down snow that crisscrossed our village melted much more slowly than did the rest of the fluffy snow. Consequently, what used to be trenches in the deep snow quickly became elevated walkways of dirty snow. People continued to walk on them to avoid stepping on the seven months of frozen dog shit now reappearing and thawing on both sides of the paths. The trails continued to melt until they crumbled from the weight of the footfalls. Soon, everything was mud. For a few days, everybody walked on the village's few paved streets, taking twice as long to get from any one place to another. The trails dried up about the same time that the swarms of mosquitoes came.

Having grown up in Minnesota, I was no stranger to mosquitoes. But Siberian bloodsuckers make Minnesota mosquitoes seem cute and courteous. The Siberian mosquito is easily twice as large as the pests of my childhood. When a Siberian mosquito pierces your skin with his nose, it isn't merely annoying; it is painful. As if their size wasn't impressive enough, they swarm like bees, descending on you in such quantities that two slapping hands can't possibly keep up with the plethora of needle pricks. It used to be a common form of torture in the Siberian gulags to send a shackled, naked prisoner outside in the springtime. Within ten minutes, the most hardened criminal went insane from the frenzied assault.

Rather than let the pests destroy my mental health, I let them improve my physical health. I took to running through the woods in the mornings. I'd wear just a short-sleeve shirt and shorts. If I kept up a decent pace, I could outrun the swarm of bloodthirsty bugs. But if I slowed down, my elbows would swing back into the swarm that was closing in on me. If I tired, I would be devoured. Adrenaline prevented me from ever getting tired. So, with a little help from these hungry insects, I burned off my winter fat in a matter of weeks.

I was ready for summer. I wasn't ready for what summer would bring with it.

15

The Capitalists

I was in the submarine when I got a call from Sasha.

"Are there any cars there?" he asked.

"Yes. You've got the *Lada*, but the *Zhiguli* is still here," I reported. We didn't drive ourselves. With all the drinking that was an integral part of Siberian business, it was necessary to have not only company cars but company drivers as well. We had two company cars, both Russian. We had two company drivers, both Russian, both named Sergei. Unlike the cars, these two Russian men were big, powerful, and reliable. Whatever happened to those little metal pieces of crap, these large guys could fix.

"Good. Get to the factory right now. I'll wait for you here. It's an emergency."

It took an hour for Sergei to slash and dart through the chaotic traffic until we reached the factory door. Sasha was waiting outside. He was smoking a cigarette and pacing. He instructed Sergei to drive back to the office. The other Sergei, tinkering with something under the hood, would drive us both home later. Then Sasha grabbed my arm. "Let's go for a walk."

We walked around the factory as he explained the situation. Our competition had arrived.

"Two guys showed up while I was talking to the Director," Sasha said as we walked past a short line for ice cream. "The guys offered to deliver cocoa beans, lots of them." Sasha held out a cigarette for me.

"Let's get some ice cream," I said after declining the cigarette. "It's summer. All kinds of people are going to show up and make promises. But who is willing to stay here all winter long and follow through on their promises?"

Sasha nodded. He wanted to believe me. I bought two ice cream cones that were pulled out of a cardboard box with a pair of tongs by a solid woman in her forties. I handed one cone to Sasha.

"Winter keeps out the riff-raff," I repeated my dad's favorite Minnesota catch phrase. "Pretty soon, it will be winter again. There's nothing to worry about."

"Maybe you're right," Sasha agreed as he flicked his cigarette and turned his attention on the ice cream.

Of course I was right. Western companies weren't a threat, at least not yet. This market was still too wild, too risky for them. Russian companies weren't a threat either. They didn't have the capital necessary to keep this bicycle business moving. But in the Director's office, I met the competition, and they were definitely a threat.

On one of the walls of the Director's office was a huge mural of a tropical beach, complete with white sand, palm trees, and clear blue water. The opposite wall was a large bank of windows, revealing gray concrete buildings and red smokestacks billowing out thick, brown smoke. The Director's desk, like all desks of important people in Russia, had several telephones and no computer. Jutting out from the desk was a long conference table with chairs on either side. This was where the Director received his regular guests. Special guests were invited through a hidden door into a smaller room, a secret room of privilege and comfort. It took several months and a trip to America before Sasha and I were shown this special room. But as we walked into the office, we saw that the Director had opened the hidden door for these unexpected guests on their first visit.

"Come, join us," the Director said with a smile and a welcoming wave. As I passed by the Director's desk, I saw a picture lying flat. It wasn't of his wife or kids. It was a picture of the Director, Sasha, and me standing in front of Niagara Falls with plastic cups of vodka in our hands.

We entered the secret room and were introduced to the visitors. They were Russian capitalists, straight from the financial centers of

Russia and the U.S. One lived in Moscow; the other lived in New York. They were a powerful team. Unlike most Russians, they had access to capital. And unlike most Americans, they were willing to risk their capital in Russia. They understood that great profit requires great risk.

The Moscow man, Dmitri, was huge—as tall as I was and twice as wide. When he learned that I had been a swimmer in college, he bragged that he had been a champion swimmer at Moscow State University. Whether the desired effect was to put me in my place as the second fastest swimmer in the room or simply to put me at ease being with a fellow swimmer, the result was neither. I suddenly felt my physical immunity to obesity vanish. Dmitri had been a swimmer, but now, only in his mid thirties, he was fat. He was fat like an American. He was all belly. Up until that moment, I thought that I would always be reasonably fit and trim because I used to swim over four miles a day for six years. I quickly made a silent vow to myself never to let my body swell up like that.

The New York man, Yuri, was small, well dressed, bald, intense, and confident. This guy worried me the most. He was definitely the brains of their operation. If this were a James Bond movie, he'd be the one with the white cat on his lap.

There is an unspoken rule among bilingual people for determining which language is spoken. As in dancing, you work around the weakest partner. After only a few sentences, or sometimes only a few words, it usually becomes clear who was less fluent, and you spoke in that person's native tongue. In this case, it was clear that we should have been speaking in Russian. But Yuri refused to speak to me in Russian. I couldn't tell if he was trying to downplay my ability to speak Russian, or if he was showing off his ability to speak in English in front of the Director—a pretty easy thing to do since the Director didn't speak English at all.

Refusing to concede that his English was better than my Russian, I continued to speak in Russian. For a few minutes it was quite an odd scene, a Russian businessman who lived in New York speaking in English to an American businessman who lived in Siberia speaking in Russian.

Like a beautiful woman watching two men verbally spar for the privilege of her affection, the Director sat with a contented grin on his face. All the while, Yuri and I, like rutting caribou, sorted out who had bigger antlers.

I changed tactics by switching from Russian to colloquial English.

"So, what pipe dream brings you out to this neck of the woods?"

In the time it took to empty a bottle of vodka and a box of chocolates, Yuri and Dmitri revealed their intentions. They were on a tour of Siberia and the rest of Russia. They wanted to woo as many chocolate factories as possible. Their pitch was concise and convincing. They purchased lots and lots of cocoa beans and, therefore, got a good price. They could not only pass on these savings to the factories, they could ship the beans in advance and take payment later, months later if the factory needed it. Of course every factory in Russia desperately needed in-kind loans. Sasha had just spent the morning pestering the Director to prepay for the next shipment of beans. (Our capital was tied up in latex gloves and an unfinished house in the suburbs.) The Director didn't want to cough up the money. And now he didn't have to. He could eat his cake and have it, too.

A thought suddenly occurred to me. Maybe Yuri and Dmitri were simply friends of the Director, planted to give us a scare so that we'd relax our payment conditions on the factory.

Dmitri and Yuri left for the factory in Barnaul. They didn't seem the slightest bit afraid to walk away, to leave us alone with the Director. They knew that we'd try and talk him out of buying from them, but they were confident that their offer spoke for itself. Beans now, money later; the Director would be a fool not to take them up on the offer. Even a trip to America couldn't compete with that. Suddenly, managing our fortunes seemed less urgent. We had to figure out how to stay in business.

We got back to our village in the evening.

"Come on," Sasha said. "Let's eat dinner at my place. I'm probably in big trouble for being late. If I bring a guest to dinner, Lyuda won't yell at me." He paused. "Not until it's time to go to bed. Then I'll really get it."

"Or you won't get anything at all," I said with a smirk.

"Exactly." He laughed and shook his head.

Lyuda opened the door and glowered at her husband, then smiled as she saw that he wasn't alone. Sasha nudged me in the side and gave me a wink. Then Lyuda let him kiss her on the cheek. Sasha was truly a master of getting out of tough situations, at least temporarily.

We ate dinner, which led to drinking vodka.

"Do you think the Director will stop buying cocoa beans from us?" Sasha said as he poured the first round of icy vodka pulled from the freezer. Lyuda, at the first sight of the bottle, left the kitchen with an exaggerated sigh.

"Yes," I said. "I sort of hope that he does."

"Why?"

"Because if he doesn't, then he is a fool. And I'd hate to think that we've been doing so well thus far because we've been working with a fool."

There was a pause while we both stared at the vodka in our shot glasses.

"After all we did for him, too. We treated him like a friend," Sasha bemoaned. "Well," he picked up his glass, "to friendship."

"To friendship."

Click.

I looked out the window. The sun was close to the horizon, but it would be another hour or so before its slanted course took it over the edge, and even then only for a few hours.

"Let's go for a walk," I said. "It's too nice to sit in here."

Sasha got up from the table. "Mind if I bring my wife and kid? It might get me off the hook for being late."

"Sounds good. But if it doesn't, tell Lyuda that you'll be coming home early from now on, seeing as our chocolate empire has been conquered by somebody else."

"We'll figure something out," Sasha said confidently.

The four of us went for a walk through the birch forest. We came to the movie theater. It was always something of a guessing game to try and figure out what movie was playing. The theater didn't have a brightly lit marquee above the door. Instead, across the wide but lightly traveled (at least by cars) street stood a long wooden sign. Actually, it wasn't one sign, but seven signs put together. Each sign advertised a movie that would be playing for two or three days. Every few days, the sign on the left was removed and a new one placed on the right; all the ones in between slid over one place.

Each sign was made out of a square, three-foot-by-three-foot plank of wood. The name, year, and country of the films were painted by hand in vibrant colors. If you looked at the wood squares from the side, you could see layer upon layer of paint, evidence of dozens of movies gone by. Occasionally, the sign artist would brush in the names of the movie stars.

It was amusing to see the names of American movie stars hand painted in Russian. It usually took a few seconds before I could recognize the names. Willis became "Villis," Hanks became "Khanks" and Jack became "Djek" or "Yak." But the distortion of Hollywood's most popular stars was nothing compared to the way this little theater took poetic license with the actual movie titles. Marilyn Monroe's hit *Some Like It Hot* was advertised as "In Jazz, Only Women." Bill Murray's comedy *Groundhog Day* was translated as "In Bed with a Groundhog." Lots of American boys saw the movie *Die Hard*. Lots of Russian boys saw the movie "Tough Nut."

"*Izvenetye* (excuse me)," I heard somebody say with an American accent.

We all turned around to see a young man standing with perfect posture and a Bible in his hand. The familiar university student translator stood at his side. She wore a slightly embarrassed smile on her face. I didn't recognize the missionary. He must have been new.

Alina hid behind her mother. The young man smiled at Alina as she poked her head out from around her mother's hips.

"Read any good books lately?" I asked him in Russian.

After listening to the translation, his eyes lit up. He clutched the Bible in both hands.

"*Nyet*," I said. "I know that you've read that book. Shakespeare. Have you read any Shakespeare?"

"A little," he said after waiting for the translation. "But I'm more interested in…"

"What about Dostoyevsky?" I interrupted. "You're in Russia. Have you read any of the great Russian writers? Tolstoy? Gogol? Chekhov?"

"I'm sure they are fine writers, but I'm more interested in reading about the soul."

"The soul? What the hell do you think good literature is about? It's all about the soul! Especially Russian literature!"

He said in a pathetic attempt to be respectful, "I don't read Russian novels because I'm afraid that too much gets lost in the translation."

I looked at the English-language Bible in his hand. I didn't know what to say. Wasn't it obvious to him?

He laughed, "Maybe someday I'll learn Russian well enough to read Dostoyevsky in the original."

"Maybe someday you'll learn Greek well enough to read the Bible in the original," I said in English.

His smile vanished.

"Let's go," I said in Russian to Sasha, Lyuda, and Alina. And off we went, taking our damned souls with us.

"I've got it," Sasha declared suddenly as if he'd been struck with a divine revelation. "We'll join them."

16

If You Can't Beat 'Em...

I felt triumphant in defeat. Market competition had won. Sasha's faith in friendship over economics had lost. Part of me, the economist part, wanted to say, "I told you so." But I didn't, partly because I hadn't insisted on competing on purely economic merits, and partly because Dmitri and Yuri didn't compete strictly on economic merits either. In addition to giving raw material credits, they also promised to take the chocolate factory directors on trips to America. They had outdone us in every way. But we weren't dead yet. We still had one card to play.

"When problems come up," Sasha said to Yuri over the phone—"and, trust me, there *will* be problems—you are going to need local people to make sure things get resolved. Listen, you guys can out-finance us, which means you can out-supply us. We're not even going to try to compete with you in that game. Why work against someone when you can work with him? Am I right?"

Sasha nodded his head as he listened to Yuri's reply. Sasha winked at me. Sasha and Yuri were both yelling. They weren't angry; that's just the way most Russians talk on the phone. It was impossible not to overhear the conversation from across the room.

"Let us be in charge of Siberia," Sasha said. "That will allow you to concentrate on European Russia."

Yuri and Sasha negotiated like Hitler and Stalin, dividing up their empires before they had actually conquered them. They formed a pact. Yuri would ship the cocoa beans to Dmitri in Moscow. Dmitri would ship them on to us in Novosibirsk. We would distribute them to the Siberian factories. We would also be in charge of collecting the money from the factories and sending it to Dmitri. "After all," Yuri confessed, "this is where we plan to make most of our money. Late fees. None of those factories know how to pay on time." He laughed. Then he got very serious. "But they will pay. Your job is to make sure of that. We'll have to agree on what percentage of the profits you will get."

Our chocolate empire had grown sevenfold almost overnight. We would be supplying seven Siberian factories with a variety of raw materials, and not just cocoa beans. Our assortment had grown to include sugar, peanuts, and coconut oil. The next month we spent on the road, getting to know all the Siberian factories and, more important, establishing a rapport with the directors. It was our turn to use good cop–bad cop tactics. Sasha was the good cop; I was the bad cop. Sasha could give (raw materials, favors, trips to America, etc.), and I could take it all away. At least, that's what we wanted them to believe.

Every director had a large, fairly austere office where he conducted routine business. Some had pictures of Lenin still hanging on the wall. But every office also had the obligatory hidden door that led to a plush room with comfortable furniture. Lenin's portrait was never found in here; the communist charade had collapsed decades ago in these rooms. Capitalism, however, didn't quite reign here either. Paranoia did. Business was rarely discussed in these rooms. Oddly, most of the serious negotiations were carried out in the backseats of cars. All we were doing was supplying factories with raw materials, and, yet, I felt less like a chocolate baron and more like a loan shark.

Whenever I needed a break from talks about interest rates and late fees, I visited Sarah's apartment. I told her of the former communist pleasure domes I'd been to in the past week. She just shook her head as she listened. The blatant hedonism that the Bolsheviks practiced while they preached the virtues of austerity in the name of building a worker's paradise was enough to make even a bohemian embrace global capitalism.

"The worst part is that they're the same people," Sarah laughed. It was a bitter laugh. "I bet half of those directors you work with were once communist big wigs."

"Probably more than half," I said. "Even Sasha belonged to the Communist Party."

"No!"

"Yep, he showed me his old membership card the other day."

"So your partner was once a card-carrying Communist." Her smile snapped into a confused expression. "But Sasha is Mr. Entrepreneur. How could he have ever been a Communist?"

"He said that it was the only way to get ahead. If you had any ambition, you had to be in the Party."

"So, are you two ambitious guys getting ahead?" she asked.

"I can't tell. We're definitely moving. I just can't tell if we're moving forward."

All the factories shut down for the summer. It was too hot to make chocolate. The chocolate would have melted before it reached the end of the conveyor belt. So, like school kids, we had a summer vacation.

With all the down time, Sasha and I assessed our situation. We weren't enjoying our jobs much anymore. Since we teamed up with Yuri and Dmitri, we weren't really entrepreneurs anymore. We were their point men. On the plus side, we were making steady money. We decided that we wouldn't bite the hand that fed us, but we also wouldn't stop looking for ways to regain more control of the situation.

With some of the money we'd earned, Sasha paid me back for the house loan I'd given him. He also chipped in half of the money to pay for having a roof put atop the shell of bricks out in the nascent suburbs. Shura paid for his half. Shura was also doing well. His business had expanded from just gum to another little luxury: lady's nylons from Italy.

I spent much of my free time at the beach—usually the nude beach. The nude beach was where all the Americans hung out. Actually, the nude beach was by far the more family-oriented beach.

The "clothed" beach was full of young Siberian bucks trying to impress bikini-clad damsels. If you looked too long at any of the tanning beauties, you might find yourself toe to toe with a muscular young man with too much vodka and testosterone in his bloodstream. Or, even worse, a group of missionaries might gather around you, block the sun, and preach to you about how they wanted you to feel the radiance of God's grace.

The nude beach, on the other hand, was sprinkled with people of all ages. Kids ran around naked, splashing and frolicking. Adults did pretty much the same thing. People were there to see and be seen, to play, to sing, to tell stories, and most of all, to soak up as much sun as possible. It was the perfect place to spend the entire Siberian summer, all seventy-five days of it.

Shocked by Dmitri's fit past and flabby present, I often dove into the water and swam straight out toward "Taiwan," the island about one mile offshore. There were no white lines roping off a swimming area, and no lifeguards who blew their whistles at anybody having any sort of fun, the kind of fun that led to accidents and lawsuits. I was free to swim wherever I wanted. So I swam straight out. I never made it to Taiwan, but I was free to try and that was more important than actually doing it.

The risk of living in Siberia made everyday life precious. Hangover or not, I was always glad to wake up in Siberia. Here, in this place with a horrific history and an unknown future, life was urgent without being frantic.

17
Security Matters

With the sudden surge in raw materials coming to Novisibirsk, we needed to find a warehouse. Fast. Even though it had a large enough warehouse, the chocolate factory wasn't an option. Storing cocoa beans there would be like hiding sheep in a wolf's den. The Director himself had pointed this out. "In a pinch," he said, "I'm afraid we would probably take a pinch."

We had to find a more secure place.

Fortunately, Vitaly Victorovich, the deputy director, had an idea. We drove to another anonymous factory on the other side of town. Just before we entered the factory, Vitaly Victorovich turned to me.

"You're Russian," he said, grabbing my arm. "You can't let anyone know that you're an American."

"Why?"

"This is a military factory," he said as we approached the gray concrete walls tipped with barbed wire. "Top secret stuff."

He walked on, leaving me stunned in the middle of the street.

"Come on," Sasha waved for me to catch up.

There was a guard standing by the door. He couldn't have been more than twenty. He wore camouflage and held a *Kalashnikov* (AK-47) machine gun in his arms.

The woman at the front gate wanted to see some identification. I had my U.S. passport. That wouldn't go over very well. Fortunately, I had a fake student ID from the university that Sasha had arranged for me; it allowed me to fly on Aeroflot for student fares. (I once flew to Moscow and back for thirty-five dollars.) I never expected this fake ID to get me into a military factory. Vitaly Victorovich called the military director on the lobby phone. He handed the phone to the sturdy gatekeeper. After receiving a one-word command from the phone, the stone-faced woman waved us through.

Vitaly Victorovich presented a box of chocolates to the military director. They shook hands like long-time friends. Sasha introduced himself; then he introduced me as Alexander Ivanovich Popov.

"So, you want to store some cocoa beans in our warehouses?" the white-haired military director asked. He didn't give anybody a chance to answer. "I never thought that the day would come when there would be candy in our warehouses." He shook his head and put both hands on his desk. He was still standing. We had all taken our seats around his desk. We looked at each other nervously. Our hands were on the backs of our chairs, poised to push us up again in case we had prematurely made ourselves comfortable.

"There's no money to pay my employees. I'm not allowed to fire them, but I have nothing to pay them with. I can't just pay them with what we produce. This isn't a chocolate factory!" he shouted.

There was a tense pause.

"I'm sorry," he whispered as he sat down. "These are my problems, not yours."

Everybody nodded with a little sympathy and a lot of relief.

"You want to know what the worst part is?" he asked.

Nobody answered.

"It isn't the market that's killing us. They say that our products aren't competitive, but they are. Our products are the best in the world. Our missiles are better than American missiles." He looked right at me. "Our missiles have to be better; the American spy planes are better than ours. But our missiles can get them."

"Even their stealth planes?" Sasha asked. I felt like kicking Sasha under the table. I wanted to keep the conversation on innocuous subjects, like chocolate, sports, weather, anything but military matters. I didn't want to hear, learn, or know anything about this place. I was like Schultz from *Hogan's Heroes*. I wanted to know nothing.

"Stealth, shmealth," the military director said with a wave of his hand. "Trivial."

This was way more than I wanted to know. I felt like sticking my fingers in my ears and singing a few bars of "Stars and Stripes Forever."

Standing up again, the director lost himself in a tirade: "We're dying because we're not allowed to sell our products to anybody but those pinheads in Moscow. And they don't pay us. They talk about the pressures of the free market." He let out a bitter laugh. "Ha! How free is the market if we aren't allowed to sell what we produce? The Soviet Union never produced anything worth a damn except weapons. Now we're not allowed to sell the one thing that we make well. Free market. *Ptu*," he spit on the floor behind his desk. "Does that seem like the free market to you, Alexander Ivanovich?"

Pause.

"Sanya?" Sasha said, reminding me that I was Alexander Ivanovich; the director was talking to me.

"It's bullshit," I said, then laughed nervously.

"It's not funny, Alexander Ivanovich."

"Of course not," I said. "Sorry."

The director finally sat down again. Without breaking eye contact with me, he bent slightly and pulled a bottle of cognac from his desk drawer. His other hand put a four-leafed clover of shot glasses on the table. Moments later, they were full of amber liquid. We all drank to the bad health of, as he put it, "those bastards in Moscow."

We chased the cognac with some chocolates.

The glasses were immediately filled again. Sasha proposed the next toast: "To those bastard Americans and their fucking free market." He winked at me.

We all clicked glasses and mumbled, "Bastard Americans. Fucking free market." Everybody except the military director. Three glasses hit the table empty; the fourth glass remained full. With three fingers still wrapped around the full shot glass, his index finger pointed to Sasha. "You shouldn't badmouth the Americans.

If it weren't for the Americans, our weapons industry would be as backward as all our other industries. Look at all of our great social-ist industries. They're crap! Even the chocolate industry."

Vitaly Victorovich shot his head backward as if his nose had just been flicked.

"Oh, come now, Vitya," the military director said. "How old is the equipment you have at your factory? Do you think that your chocolate could compete on the international market? How many tons of chocolate did you sell this month in Germany? Argentina? Australia?"

"None!" Vitaly Victorovich looked like a pupil caught red-handed cheating on an exam.

"So," the military director said, turning again to Sasha, "don't badmouth the Americans. They provided the only competition that those bastards in Moscow couldn't isolate us from. The Americans pushed us forward, forced us to be better, all the while those morons in Moscow kept the rest of the country from moving at all. *Pteew.*" He spit on the ground again. "I'll drink again to the bad health of those bastards in Moscow." He tossed down his shot of cognac.

The military director pulled out some pictures of the weapons produced in the factory. He passed them around the table as if they were pictures of his grandkids. I did my best to look interested while simultaneously trying not to look at them at all.

Sasha said, "Alexander Ivanovich, show the director your watch."

My face burned red. I prayed that the director would assume it was the cognac coloring my face and not my bubbling panic.

"Watch?" the director asked.

My watch had an analog display, but it flipped open to reveal a tiny calculator underneath. With all the hyperinflation, I used the calculator frequently. Whenever I did, however, people looked at me like I was a spy.

"Go ahead, show him," Sasha said with a little laugh. Had the cognac already gone to his head? No. Sasha, despite his small size, could drink me under the table any day.

I turned my wrist. The director looked at the slim black watch.

He seemed duly impressed. "I bought it in Moscow," I lied, hoping to end the matter then and there.

"Open it," Sasha said, laughing mischievously.

The director looked at me, then at my watch.

I shot a venomous look at Sasha as I clicked open the watch.

"Opa!" The director shouted with sudden enthusiasm as he stood up again and moved around the desk to get a better look. He examined it, pressed the buttons, and, for almost a full minute, forgot about the rest of us in the room.

The military director turned my wrist around, obviously looking for something.

"It's Japanese."

"Japanese, uh?" He nodded, as if he had known the answer all along. "This is what I'm talking about. I'd like to see one of our Soviet factories build something like this. They can't! They haven't had to compete for fifty years, so they produce crap like this," he pulled the large metal watch off of his wrist and let it drop onto the desk with a loud thud. "That's what you get without competition. Competition," he declared loudly. "That's the key."

I, the only trained free market economist in the room, couldn't have said it better myself.

Sasha looked at me, then at the watch on the desk, then at the director. He nodded.

I pulled the watch from my wrist and gave it to the director. "Here. I'll get another one next time I go to Moscow."

The director didn't hesitate. He grabbed my watch and went back to his seat. A few moments later, as if snapping out of a dream, he grabbed his discarded metal timepiece. "*Na*," he said as he gave it to me. "Barter. Now that's the free market."

Without even looking at the watch, I put it on my wrist. It was heavy. It felt like a clock, not a watch.

After a few more shots of cognac, the director agreed to let us store cocoa beans in one of his many empty warehouses. The price he wanted for the space was reasonable; it was competitive. We three took turns shaking his hand and then left. When we exited the factory, I breathed a sigh of relief. The lump in my stomach faded as I saw the soldier with the automatic rifle fade in the rearview mirror.

"Sasha," I said.

"What?" He turned to listen to me.

I slugged him in the arm. "That's from Alexander Ivanovich."

Both Sasha and Vitaly Victorovich burst out laughing.

I looked at my new watch. It had two crossed Arabian sabers, an American flag, and six words: OPERATION DESERT SHIELD across the front and MADE IN USSR below the number six.

"I'm going to give this to my brother," I said. "He's a pilot in the Marine Corps. I'm sure he'll be the only one in his squadron with a Russian made 'Desert Shield' watch."

"You better tell him not to fly over Russian air space. 'Our missiles are the best in the world,'" Vitaly Victorovich said, mocking the gruff voice of the military director. "Tell your brother that he isn't safe in his 'shmealth' plane."

We all laughed.

On the day before we planned to move the cocoa beans to the warehouse, we learned that the military factory had stored chemical weapons in the warehouse. "It's been cleaned. It's perfectly safe," the military director insisted. Regardless, we decided not to store the beans there. The idea of kids getting sick from eating anthrax-contaminated chocolate didn't seem worth the risk. Besides, the competition (Nestlé, Mars, and Hershey) would take advantage of any health risks—perceived or real—associated with Siberian chocolate. The kiosks were already filled with Snickers, Bounty, and Mars bars. There were also huge television ad campaigns associating their chocolate with everything flashy, glitzy, cool—in short, everything Western.

We couldn't risk contaminating the already colorless reputation of Russian chocolate. We couldn't let the competition gain an even greater edge. After all, competition was the key.

18
The Currency of Desperation

"There once was a prince who lived in a tiny kingdom," Galya, a dark-haired woman who worked in the submarine, said during a tea break. "There was a tradition in this kingdom," she continued, not indicating whether this was a fairy tale or one of her anecdotes, both of which she told at any given opportunity. "Tradition dictated that the prince had to marry the woman who could boil water fastest. When the prince reached marrying age, there were only two unmarried women in this tiny kingdom: a beautiful young maiden and a haggard woman past her prime." Galya, at thirty-four years of age, heavy-set, and the mother of a fourteen-year-old son, was, by Siberian standards, past her prime; and yet, her large blue eyes and low, sultry voice still commanded attention from the stronger sex in a way that made the young, trim beauties envious. At office parties, Galya would frequently break into song as if she were on Broadway. Her flamboyant gestures were all at once arousing and ironic. She, unlike many women her age, had a healthy sense of humor about physical beauty, especially its inevitable departure.

"Who do you think married the prince?" Galya asked me, barely holding back her own laughter.

I shrugged my shoulders.

"The beautiful lass." She smiled brightly.

I didn't get it. Was I missing something?

"Do you want to know why?" She asked.

I nodded, hoping for a punch line.

"Because the haggard lady kept taking the lid off the pot to see if the water was boiling yet." Galya frantically picked up the lid from the electric teapot, letting out puffs of warm steam. Then she burst into a rolling, full-body laughter.

The rest of the women in the room—the majority of them beautiful lasses—laughed politely, uneasily, then quickly changed the subject. Galya's ironic jokes tested the sanctity of beauty. In a world where everything man-made was functionally adequate but aesthetically barren, women shouldered a heightened responsibility to create beauty, to embody it. Galya's ability to joke about the fickleness of beauty caused other women to both admire and despise her. It was heresy. But the underlying truth was hard to ignore.

Galya once showed me a photograph of an attractive girl in her late teens sitting on a large rock next to a large body of water. The girl was wearing shorts and a bikini top. Her hands cupped her knees. Her gaze was both alluring and innocent. I recognized the body of water as the Ob Sea.

I was afraid that Galya was trying to set me up with one of her neighbor's daughters. It wouldn't have been the first time I'd been introduced to a young woman by a middle-aged woman. But my heartbreak with Katya had left me weary of Siberian women.

"Who is she?" I asked.

"That's me," Galya said with a snicker. Suddenly, her eyes brightened, as if possessed. She awkwardly worked herself onto a chair, then gingerly—as gingerly as a woman her size can manage—stepped onto the nearest desk. As if the desk were a rock on the shores of the Ob Sea, Galya sat down and struck the same pose, looking into the sunset with the same Mona Lisa smile. "Don't you recognize me?" Then she burst out laughing, cackling.

Nikolai, a chocolate salesmen whose desk Galya had commandeered for her brazen display, ignored the woman sitting on top of his papers. He simply put one finger in his ear, pivoted in his seat to the side and continued talking loudly on the phone. Not even a hint of an amused smile or annoyed grimace cracked Nikolai's stoic face. It was as if Galya didn't exist, which made Galya laugh even more.

"I once was quite the looker," she said, pointing to the photo in my hand. I looked again. She really was a "looker" back then.

"I bet you never thought fifteen years could do so much damage," she said, then reclined back on Nikolai's desk as if she were a lounge singer sprawled out on a polished black piano in a smoke-filled room. Nikolai pivoted another ninety degrees away, turning his back on the supine woman sprawled on his desk. The other women in the room were giggling nervously at Galya's latest show.

"Don't laugh too much, girls," Galya said in her booming, theatrical voice. "Someday men will turn their backs on you too."

The women stopped giggling. They wiggled about in their chairs, suddenly uncomfortable.

Galya rolled over on her side, sending a flock of white paper fluttering to the floor. "Don't hang on to your beauty. It will leave you anyway. It *will*—along with whatever man who chose you for your beauty." She looked at the women with as serious an expression as Galya ever gave. "There is nothing sadder than a woman who spends her life trying to save her beauty, instead of spending her beauty to save her life." She shook her head as if her last comment had taken her by surprise. Then she laughed again. "I'm quite the philosopher, no?"

Just then, Nikolai hung up the phone, stood up, put his hands on his hips and looked down at his desk. Galya batted her eyelashes at him. She lifted one leg and placed her foot firmly on a pile of papers. Her dress tumbled down from her elevated knee, revealing part of her thigh. Nikolai looked confused for a moment. Then his face lit up suddenly. He bent over, opened the drawer of his desk and pulled out a pack of cigarettes (Marlboro) and a lighter (Zippo). Saying nothing, he walked out of the room.

Galya chuckled out loud, then jumped up suddenly. "Kolya," she cried out, "spare a cigarette for a lovely damsel?"

"*Da.*" His voice came from the corridor "Do you know any?"

"*Sveenya* (pig)," Galya said as she scurried after Nikolai.

I was left alone in the room with four beautiful Russian women, women whose expression made me fear they were suddenly determined to spend their beauty.

Although we called our office the submarine, the crew bore little resemblance to a group of young men with crisp uniforms and shaved heads. We few men were the ugly minority. For the most part, women manned our submarine. From the recently graduated university students who worked as assistants and gophers to the middle-aged women who worked in accounting, every woman in the submarine, even Galya, made an extra effort to be attractive, to be feminine. They wore clothes that accentuated curves and revealed plenty of smooth skin. They wore lipstick as alarming as blood and perfume as subtle as a migraine. There were times when the long corridor of the submarine looked like a runway full of fashion models. The clickity-click of so many high-heeled shoes sounded like a hundred Shakespeare-wanna-be monkeys typing away at a hundred typewriters.

In addition to Galya's stories and antics, tea time was also when the women in the office loved to crowd together and thumbed through a magazine that I had brought back from America. It was *Playboy*. These women made no pretenses about reading the articles. They just wanted to see page after page of semi-naked women. Each turn of the page produced a wave of enchanted *ooooooohs* and *aaaaaaaahs*. I had bought the magazine at the request of Sergei, one of the drivers, but he never saw a single page. The women had confiscated it for themselves. Whenever one of the men in the office asked to have a look at it, the women greedily clung to the magazine, defending it with the ferocity of a dog guarding a bone.

The cornucopia of cleavage in the office excited and concerned me. These Siberian women had trapped themselves in the same conundrum that most farmers faced—the plight of the one-crop producer. These women relied exclusively on beauty.

With demand relatively stable (this is before the advent of Viagra), these women, by working harder and harder to increase the supply of beauty, were simply driving down the price of their output. It was a vicious, self-defeating cycle. And yet, just like American farmers, these women kept at it with desperate stubbornness, further worsening their situation. By making physical beauty all-important, they were making it ever more impotent.

Knowing nothing else, the Siberian man became insensitive to the brilliance of the Siberian woman's plumage. For the unprepared foreigner, however, such an onslaught of raw beauty could be dangerous.

A young Dutch man from our cocoa-bean supply company flew out to visit us. His assignment was to inspect the new warehouse facilities where we kept the beans. We told him that we paid the salaries of the armed guards posted at the doors. That seemed both to scare and relieve him. We told him that this warehouse was more expensive than the first one that we had found, which had once housed anthrax and mustard gas. That we had even considered a former chemical weapons warehouse to store beans seemed to scare the poor Dutchman even more. But he quickly found something else to examine other than warehouses. When he left three days later, he was suffering from a very sore neck from all the gawking at long, slender legs; ample, exposed cleavage; and luscious, lurid lips.

As distracting as the women were at work, the women I encountered after work were downright disturbing.

Living as an American bachelor in Siberia has a way of warping a man's ego. Beautiful women—too beautiful to give me the time of day in America—treated me here as if I were charming, gallant, and irresistible. It made me feel like Pam Anderson on an Army base. Foreign men, especially Americans, could do no wrong here. There were no negative consequences. No checks, no balances.

I could have been fat, ugly, and even cruel, and these women would still be attracted to me. Even though the rules had changed in my favor, I felt cheated somehow. I wasn't fat. I had broad shoulders, well-defined arms, and a flat stomach (at least in the summertime). Russian women didn't seem to care about these assets. Good looks and clean living seemed insignificant next to my U.S. citizenship.

I cringed whenever I saw a stunning Russian woman standing too close to a plain American, Irish, or German guy. In the real world, this Russian woman was obviously out of his league. Could he possibly believe that she was attracted to him as a man? But it was clear that either he believed the sincerity of those seductive Russian eyes, or he simply didn't care whether they were sincere or not. They were looking at him. Why she was looking didn't matter.

I tried to speak only in Russian whenever I was in the company of an unmarried Siberian woman. If she figured out that I was a foreigner, it wasn't long before she'd press both of her hands flatly on the lower part of her back, her elbows almost touching behind her. The effect was to stretch her blouse smoothly over her forward-thrusting breasts. It was about as blunt an invitation as any young bachelor could hope for. But her eyes were not full of lust. They were both desperate and calculating, like the eyes of a chess player who was down to a few pieces, mostly pawns. She was running out of good moves.

Whenever one of these beauties stood flirtatiously close to me, or caressed my arm gently with the flats of her fingernails, I'd say something that turned her off in an instant. I'd tell her that I loved Siberia—that I planned to live here forever. Often she wouldn't even excuse herself. She'd just turn and walk away toward some of the other foreign guys in the room.

For the most part I avoided these women because I knew that their affection, although seemingly free for the taking, actually came at a high price. I'd fallen once for the seductive beauty of a Russian woman, and wasn't about to do it again. Sometimes strength is when you can do something you thought you couldn't. Sometimes strength is when you know you can do something but don't.

19
The Entrepreneurial Spirit

The obsolete infrastructure of the communist economy was both a burden and a blessing.

The burden: almost nothing worked. It wasn't like America where everything seemed to happen automatically, effortlessly, for a fee. In Siberia, we didn't have legions of service providers to take care of our every need—no Kinko's to make copies of important documents and no Federal Express to rush those documents to the next town. Most of life's challenges and obstacles we had to solve ourselves.

The blessing: to live in Siberia is to know the satisfaction of self-reliance.

When the arid winter air had me waking up with a parched throat, I invented a humidifier out of water jugs, towels, and a fan. It was ugly, but it worked. I also invented a water filter: three glass containers connected by a rubber tube bought from the old man who sold hardware doodads on the street. I put boiled water in the first jug. The water had a brownish tint. Gravity slowly siphoned the dirty water from one jug to the next through the tubes. By the time the water had reached the outflow spigot I put into the last jug, it was relatively clear. Once a week, when I cleaned the sediment off the bottom of the jugs, I felt a combination of pride and relief that my contraption had kept all that gunk out of my gut. My apartment wasn't very cozy; it had the ambiance of a mad scientist's laboratory.

In Siberia, function trumped form and severe scarcity bred intense ingenuity.

But things were changing. Now Siberians didn't have to make do with so little. The market had arrived, and it was time for Siberians to embrace the possibilities, the opportunities, and the freedom to do and buy anything. The only thing that was scarce now was money. Not surprisingly, most Siberians channeled their creative energy into money-making pursuits. The entrepreneurial spirit was suddenly rampant in Siberia.

A large shipment of autopsy gloves arrived just in time for potato-picking season. In the very back of the container, our German supplier had stuffed in some complimentary condoms. Five thousand latex compliments. I divvied up several dozen among the company employees. We decided to see if the rest would sell in the local kiosks. They did. More often than not, women bought them. It always amused me to stand in line at a kiosk and hear a middle-aged woman in front of me ask for a pack of *prezervativi*. (*Prezervativ* means "condom," and *profilaktika* means "maintenance." Mixing the two is a good way to get a laugh, or a slap on the cheek.)

Sasha had a love-hate relationship with these condoms. They brought us needed revenue, but they literally got between him and his wish to have a son. Sasha was pressuring his wife to have another kid, preferably a boy. Lyuda was pressuring her husband to finance her beauty salon. She wanted to be an entrepreneur, too.

Shura, a pathological entrepreneur, had built his gum empire by taking out a few high-interest loans. He was unable to make the payments and sold the business to pay his debts. The Italian panty-hose business, however, was taking off. Shura was an entrepreneur, not a manager—an explorer, not a settler.

Another entrepreneur walked into our life that summer. His name was Sergei. His greasy blonde hair was short, too short to bother putting a comb through. But it wasn't Sergei's hair that most people considered his defining characteristic. A diplomat would say that Sergei was sturdy. Clothes labeled him "XL." Russians described him, oddly enough, with the word *healthy*. Ignoring their own dimensions, most Americans would simply call him fat. I pre-ferred the word *big*. He had large, blue eyes that oozed sadness. He looked exhausted, always. And yet, he was one of the most tireless men I ever met.

He came to the office and made us an offer: if we bought a Kamaz (a Russian cargo truck), he'd drive any cargo we had. And when we didn't have any cargo of our own, he promised to find cargo to haul and we'd split the profits. A new Kamaz cost about fifteen thousand dollars—coincidentally, about the same amount of money Lyuda said she needed to open her beauty salon.

Sasha bought the truck.

In the following month, Sergei spent a week and a half customizing the truck, a week looking for cargo, and two weeks hauling books to and from Moscow. He turned in the equivalent of eleven hundred dollars in profit. If things kept up at this pace, we'd have our initial investment back in a year. Even better, we now had a ten-ton truck at our disposal to haul beans, gloves, chocolate, and condoms.

Soon after Sergei and the Kamaz became a regular part of the office, Ivan Ivanovich walked in. Ivan Ivanovich was a short, sturdy bald man with a voice like Darth Vader's. When he talked, you felt it in your chest. He wore thick, square-rimmed glasses that made him look like a professor. The missing fingers on his right hand betrayed the fact that he was not a man of books, but a man of power tools.

Ivan Ivanovich approached us much as Sergei did. He wanted us to pay for a machine that he would operate. When private property was reintroduced in Russia, Ivan Ivanovich gathered all the money he had and purchased an old boat. The economic chaos that followed privatization caught him off guard. Consequently, he didn't have enough money to make the necessary repairs to his vessel. That's why he had come to us. In exchange for the money to fix up the boat, Ivan Ivanovich promised to work for us as the company boat captain. He said the boat would be a great way to entertain visiting foreign guests and business partners.

Again, the money necessary was about fifteen thousand dollars. Lyuda lobbied for it. Ivan got it—even though it would be a year before the boat was ready to go. But soon there would be no place to go. Summer was coming to a close.

When Lyuda heard that we'd given money to some strange boat captain instead of her, she was furious. Sasha hemmed and hawed, and eventually calmed her down by promising that the beauty salon would be next. The next time we had a spare fifteen thousand dollars, we'd open a beauty salon. One morning as we were walking to work, Sasha turned to me and said, "Remind me never to have an extra fifteen thousand dollars lying around."

"You don't want Lyuda to open a beauty salon?"

"Not right now. I want her to get pregnant. I want a son. If she opens a beauty salon, she'll be too busy to have kids. What's the point of earning a lot of money if you don't have a big family to spend it on?"

The entrepreneurial spirit had even gotten into Sashka, a five-year-old boy who lived in an apartment on the first floor of my stairwell. He rented his older brother's Dendy (a Chinese version of Nintendo) cartridges to kids in the neighborhood. Sashka used the same strategy as Yuri and Dmitri, our cocoa bean loan sharks. He rented the cartridges out for a day at a reasonable price, but he charged high late fees. For those who refused to pay up, he threatened to tell his brother who had "stolen" his cartridges. In addition to video game rentals, he collected bottles for their deposit. Rather than picking up bottles that were discarded on the street, little Sashka went door to door. He was too cute to refuse. He made a deal with me: I was to leave my bottles outside my door on Thursday mornings on my way to work. When I came home, they were gone. In short order, he had made enough money to buy a dog, a purebred Irish Setter. He named it Philip.

But for every person who saw opportunity in the market, there were many more who saw their freedom shrink, their opportunities dwindle. Scientists, once the elite of this town, were quickly becoming the underclass. Funding had dried up for the dozens of institutes scattered about the birch forest. A small minority of institutes adapted and attracted foreign sources of money.

For the most part, however, the scientists hoped for money from whence it had always come: Moscow. But it came slowly if at all. The only freedom the market brought them was the chance to rent out space in their institutes to *biznesmeni*. Scientists whose last names once commanded respect and awe were forced to double and triple up in cramped basement offices.

All the while, uneducated, undisciplined men colonized the spacious rooms on the first floor of these concrete castles of science. These young men—young enough to be the scientists' children— sat alone behind gigantic desks and drank vodka with every client that walked through their doors. Talking on cordless phones, the new elite paced up and down their large offices making deals. They didn't discover anything. They didn't produce anything. They bought low and sold high. At the end of the day, the scientists had no money in their pockets while these *biznesmeni* had enough money to afford Italian suits, sweet-smelling prostitutes, and December vacations in Cyprus.

For a few, the market was the means to obscene, limitless wealth. For many, the market was simply a cruel word that brought destitution. For some, the market was a way of life. For others, it was just a four-letter word.

20 The Road to Nowhere

One of the things I learned fairly quickly in Siberia was not to worry about the destination whenever an opportunity to go on a trip presented itself. It's trite to say that the journey is more important than the destination. It's trite, but it's true.

So when Sasha invited me to take a trip down to the southwestern edge of Kazakhstan, I didn't even ask him why. He told me anyway. He was moving his parents out of the utter destitution of his dying hometown. They were Tatars, not Okies—and moving north to Siberia doesn't have the same ring of hope as moving west to California does—but the similarities were there.

Shouldering a duffel bag that looked as heavy as five bowling ball bags, Sasha walked into the kitchen on the morning of our departure. "The kiosk around the corner didn't have much," he said, panting. "I had to go to the one by the post office." As he carefully set the bag down on the kitchen floor, glass clinked against glass. He unzipped the bag to reveal more than a dozen bottles of vodka.

"It's a long drive to Kentau. We're gonna need these for bribes along the way." Sasha smiled as he pulled out one of the bottles. He handed it over for me to inspect.

My first impression was disbelief. On the label was the familiar picture of Arnold Schwarzenegger with half his face ripped off, revealing a red-eyed robot within. In Arnold's robotic voice, Sasha said, "Tarmeenator Vohdka. Da Last Vohdka You'll Eveh Drink."

I told Sasha that I was a little concerned about not having a visa for Kazakhstan.

Sasha looked at me and smiled. "Don't worry about pieces of paper, Sanya." He smirked as he patted his duffel bag full of Terminator Vodka. "We've got all the authorization we need right here."

Sergei picked us up in the red Kamaz. The Kamaz, with its ten wheels, three axles, and diesel engine, was the king of the Russian road. Sergei was a real truck driver; he drove fast, cussed often, and smoked constantly. Sergei got us onto the main road and pointed the truck south.

The differences between traveling in America and Siberia became apparent right away.

On America's highways, it's impossible to pass by a building without large, brightly colored signs insisting that strangers know who produces what inside. Before your curiosity even raises the question, the answer is loudly volunteered: Anderson Windows, Goodyear Tires, Redwing Shoes. Along the Siberian roads, however, buildings remained nameless and made no effort to reveal what goes on inside their crooked, cracked, concrete walls.

As with buildings, so with entire towns.

American towns brag of their distinctiveness with signs that entice drivers to stop, to have a look around, or even better still, to buy something. Siberian villages, on the other hand, didn't feel the need to boast to passing motorists. They didn't call attention to themselves, preferring to remain nameless and without distinction. The population and elevation of each town were never volunteered on reflective metal road signs. It's the nail that sticks up that gets hit by the hammer, or so goes the Russian saying.

But Siberian villages were not completely anonymous. Groups of old women with colorful scarves on their heads revealed what made each village special. In one town, the old ladies sold three-liter jugs of cream. In the next village, the old women sold fresh loaves of bread; near another, assorted sausages were offered to hungry motorists. Whenever we stopped, the old women erupted with high-pitched calls and songs about the quality of their products. Sergei ignored the loud, skinny women and went straight for the quiet, heavy-set women who, according to him, sold better food.

"You don't buy clothes from a naked person, do you?" he asked as he got back into the truck with an armful of bread, cheese, and scallions.

Where the road crossed a river, young boys hung freshly caught fish on strings from low tree branches. This was the Siberian lemonade stand—the first experience many Siberian kids had with running a business. Three boys caught fish; one ran the fish to the road; a fifth boy did the selling. Some enterprising boys even cooked the fish on a stick over an open flame. By late afternoon, we had traveled several hundred kilometers and eaten several hundred calories each of homegrown vegetables and fresh fish.

In the late afternoon, we pulled off the main road and drove into a tiny village.

Dark gray in its own shadow, a birch forest guarded the horizon like a distant army. The nearby fields were spotted with people stacking piles of hay higher than the rooftops of the village's little white cottages. A light breeze carried into the air dry grass, brown leaves, and tiny insects stirred up by the hundreds of stabbing pitch forks and slashing scythes. Reigning over the blue-green fields at a sharp angle, the sun lit up the airborne particles, making them appear like millions of meandering fireflies. The moist aroma of freshly cut hay was so thick that I could taste it on my tongue.

In the dust cloud behind our Kamaz, a dog dutifully barked at our wheels, giving up pursuit once we'd passed his territory, at which point another dog darted out from behind a pile of wood and gave chase. Joining in the chase were groups of laughing, screaming children. When Sergei stopped to ask directions from a square-shaped woman carrying milk in two metal buckets, all the commotion quickly evaporated. With tails waving proudly, the dogs retreated with occasional backward glances, just in case we decided to launch a counter attack. The children, too, were suddenly silent and shy; they hid behind large stacks of firewood, crooked telephone poles, and even a grazing cow.

"*Dyen dobri* (good day)." Sergei regarded the woman. "We're here to pick up some potatoes."

The woman put her milk buckets down, but not because they were heavy for her—with those arms she probably could have carried the cow that produced the milk. She didn't approach the truck, and it didn't seem that she wanted us to get out and approach her. She bent down. With her sausage-shaped fingers, she separated a long blade from a tall clump of grass and plucked it from the ground.

The three of us all looked at each other in confusion.

She slowly straightened up as much as her stout frame allowed, bit off the bottom of the blade of grass, spit it out and began picking her teeth with her improvised toothpick.

Sergei turned the engine off.

"Potatoes?" she finally said. Her voice didn't match her frame. The pitch was piercingly high. "You're lucky you ran into me. I'm the only one here. Everybody else is in the fields."

She paused as she worked the stem of grass over her molars. Once done, she spit out little pulverized pieces of grass, then resumed her monologue: "We have to get the hay stacked before the snow comes or, of course, our animals will starve. You never know when winter is going to show up. I remember one year when it snowed in September. We thought we weren't going to survive." She shook her head. "Two days later summer came back. It was as hot as Tashkent. We walked through the melting snow barefoot." She folded her hefty arms over her mighty bosom and let out a puff of laughter. As if to explain the unexplainable, she said one word: "*Sibir.*"

Our Kamaz clicked and crackled as the engine cooled in the evening air. Looking out the window, I tried to imagine what this village looked like covered in snow. Sasha looked down at his hands thoughtfully. Sergei lit up a cigarette and scanned the horizon. Occasionally brushing flies away from the milk buckets with her meaty paw, the woman looked over at the lone cow.

"Maria, get out of here! Get back with the herd!" Heeding the woman's first command but ignoring the second, the cow meandered a few feet in the direction of a broken-down tractor engulfed by tall grass.

"Over there," the woman pointed. "See the trailer in that field? Those are your potatoes."

"Thanks," all three of us said in unison.

"*Nezashto* (it was nothing)," she said without picking up her buckets.

Less than a minute later, Sergei stopped the Kamaz near the trailer stacked high with potatoes. I jumped out to stretch my legs, all the while looking around to see if any dogs intended to make good on their threats.

Silence.

I glanced back to see that our talkative guide was still watching us.

"She isn't in much of a hurry, is she?" I commented to Sasha as he jumped out of the truck.

"Life goes at a different pace here," Sasha said without even looking to see what she was doing, or rather, what she wasn't doing. He just explained how the Russian word *seichas* (now) is the combination of two words: *sei* (this) and *chas* (hour). "When a Russian tells you he'll do it *seichas*," Sasha said, "he literally means 'within the hour.'"

"Maria," I said to nobody in particular. "Not a very Russian name for a Siberian cow."

"It's Spanish," Sasha said. "It's from the—"

"Catch," Sergei said as he tossed two buckets to us and kept one for himself. "Let's get to work."

Sasha and I stood in the trailer and scooped bucket after bucket of potatoes. We handed the full buckets to Sergei, who stood in the back of the Kamaz and dumped the spuds into the cargo section, then gave back the empty buckets. As we worked, the red sunset bled into the golden sky, then drained away, leaving only darkness. I caught out of the corner of my eye a cow meandering by our trailer. When I stood up, a pulse of pain shocked my lower back. I massaged the sore muscles with grubby fingers as I watched a herd of cows come out of the darkness. They gradually worked their way up to our trailer, then surrounded us, some going by on one side, others on the other. For a minute or two it was a surreal dream of us aboard a potato barge drifting slowly along on a river of cows.

A pair of younger cows came right up to the trailer. They started to eat some of the potatoes that had fallen to the ground. It sounded like they were munching on crisp apples. A loud bellow came from out of the darkness. "Eden! Gina!" The young cows scampered off. I looked out into the darkness to identify the mysterious herder. A tiny old woman moved by us with purposeful speed, saying nothing as she passed. Then she and her herd of cows were gone.

"Gina? Eden?" I asked, looking at Sasha. "What is it with these cow names anyway?"

"They're names from those *teleserials* that all women are addicted to nowadays," Sasha explained.

"From the Mexican soap operas?" I laughed.

"They're not all Mexican," Sasha said. "*Santa Barbara* isn't Mexican. Is it?"

"No," I confessed, "I'm afraid that one is from Hollywood."

"Look!" Sergei said, pointing to something behind us.

I turned around to see what looked like a giant spotlight. Was it one of the Siberian gulags? The light grew steadily. It took a moment because of its enormous size, but I eventually recognized the harvest moon coming up over the horizon. It was so bright I had to squint. Eventually the entire white disk rose above the birch trees. The sky was now dark gray and the ground light blue. I turned to look at the surrounding fields now visible under the intense moonlight. I recognized the herd of cows floating across the countryside like an amorphous patch of white fog.

I looked down at the trailer. It was almost empty. Sasha and I scooped the last dozen-or-so buckets of spuds. We sat, tired and dirty, on the edge of the trailer and watched the moon in silence. Sergei lit up a cigarette, smoked it to the butt, then lit up another with the red tip of the first.

"Sasha, what are these potatoes for anyway?" I asked.

Sasha, ever the entrepreneur, explained that, since we were driving all the way to Kazakhstan, we might as well make some money while we were at it. "Potatoes grow better in Siberia than in Kazakhstan," he said, "which means they tend to cost more down there. Buy low, sell high. That's the way it's supposed to work, right?"

"Yeah, but…" I paused. "Who are you going to sell the potatoes to?"

"Selling them won't be a problem. Selling is never the problem. It's the money that's going to be the problem," Sasha said as he bummed a cigarette from Sergei.

"So don't sell on credit, or will it be hard to find someone willing to buy the whole batch for cash?" I asked.

"Cash *is* the problem. Kazakhstan isn't part of Russia anymore. They don't use Russian rubles. They still use Soviet rubles. Even if we find someone to buy these potatoes for cash, Soviet money will be worthless up here. We're going to have to buy something down there with our potato revenues and bring that back here to sell for Russian rubles."

"Like what, gold?"

"Yeah, maybe."

"You're making this up as you go along, aren't you?"

"Of course," Sasha said as he let out a cloud of smoke through his toothy smile. "That's what business is all about, right?"

I laughed, shaking my head.

"What are you laughing at?" Sasha asked, also laughing.

Scratching my dusty head with my dirty hands, I said, "I remember how we discussed in my college economics courses how Russia would never develop a market economy without an entrepreneurial class. We thought that the entrepreneurial spirit had been snuffed out by seventy years of communism. That's part of the reason I came here, to help a few Siberians develop into entrepreneurs."

"Sanya, don't take this wrong—I don't want you to pack up your bags and go back to America—but communism didn't snuff out the entrepreneurial spirit. It promoted it. The best way to promote alcoholism is to ban alcohol. And the best way to promote capitalism is to ban free enterprise. No, Sanya, communism was the ultimate school for entrepreneurs. Do you know that a few years ago it was a serious insult to wish someone to live on just his salary? Everybody had to be an entrepreneur. I bet Russian businessmen are more creative and willing to take risks than American businessmen."

"From what I've seen, that's true," I said. "Unfortunately, too much energy and creativity is wasted trying to cheat the system."

"Sanya, you don't know what you're talking about. There's a Russian saying: 'Naïveté is worse than thievery.' If the system is crooked, you *have* to cheat the system. You forget, it was only yesterday when it was illegal to sell something for a profit."

"Actually, Sasha, I do know what I'm talking about. I studied economics for four years."

"There is a difference between what you learned in textbooks and what's going on here," Sasha said.

"I'll give you that. But the principles are the same. Do you remember when you found out that American supermarkets give discounts on damaged goods? You asked why people don't just rip labels and hammer dents into cans in order to get a discount. That isn't being an entrepreneur, that's being a crook."

"In a crooked game, you have to play by crooked rules."

Frustrated, I shot back, "What's the point of having a free market economy if everybody is still playing by communist rules?"

Looking up at the moon for a moment, Sasha said, "It's a temporary problem. My generation was rewarded for cheating the system. Perhaps it's too late for us to change our ways. But who knows? A lot has changed already. Now it's against the law to sell something for a loss."

"Against the law?"

"That's right," he said with a nod. "Now we're legally bound to turn a profit. That's to ensure that every business transaction is taxable." He paused. "But if the new system rewards people for doing things within the law, I think the next generation, at the latest, will have a chance to build a normal society."

Sasha's optimism always surprised me.

We were completely grimy and savagely hungry. Clean streaks, where the sweat had trickled down our brows, went down our filthy foreheads like icicles. Our stomachs growled like angry dogs.

Fortunately, Sasha knew somebody in the village. She was the mother-in-law of a friend. She was the one who had organized the potato sale from the village's collective farm. We cleaned up in a homemade *banya* and were treated to peasant's wages: food, and lots of it.

Sasha added one of the bottles of Terminator Vodka to the table setting. Even though Sasha insisted, Sergei didn't drink. We (Sasha, myself, and our host) had to make up for his abstinence. A few hours later, the bottle was empty and our stomachs were full. Sergei went out to sleep in the truck. Sasha collapsed on an old couch. I was offered a place to sleep in a windowless room. In a bed a few inches shorter than I was, in a room a few inches longer than I was, in complete darkness and total silence, I fell asleep.

21
Trouble Ahead

I woke up and stepped outside just before sun up. The village was already stirring with sounds. The neighbor's rooster warmed up his voice. In a distant field the little old lady yelled at Maria, Gina, Eden, and the rest of the herd. A gentle breeze floated over the tree-tops, sprinkling yellow leaves down onto the brown ones already scattered about the ground. For someone addicted to the excitement of city life, this bucolic village would be unbearable.

I washed my hands and face with mineral-rich well water. Sasha poked his sleep-wrinkled face out of the cottage's door. His eyes squinted at the sun just appearing over the horizon.

"*Peet menshe* (drink less)," he said, rubbing his eyes, "*no chashe* (but more often)."

I snickered as I spit out the ice-cold water.

"Morning, Sanya."

"Morning."

We shook hands.

"*Na*," he grunted, holding out a bottle of beer for me. "Always save a little beer for the morning after. It's the best hangover medicine."

I took his advice, the bottle, and several sips of the warm, sudsy liquid. (It sure tasted like medicine.)

Sergei had been up for hours already. While we slept, he had tended to the Kamaz like a beaver tending a dam. Because his hands were greasy with Kamaz fluids, Sergei offered his wrist, which Sasha and I shook dutifully.

"We should buy an American truck," Sergei dreamed out loud as he washed his hands under the trickle of well water that I poured from a bucket. "You know, like a Mack truck, a big rig that can haul forty tons. We've only got eight tons of potatoes and we're more than full. Think about the kind of money we could make with a *bigamerican* truck."

As we drove south again, Sergei explained why a Mack truck would be more profitable, while Sasha, who would have to front the money, argued that bigger isn't always better.

In a nameless town, a pair of young women walked on the side of the narrow, dusty road. They wore the standard Siberian fashion ensemble: dark leather jackets that barely covered their behinds but completely hid their mini skirts. They strutted in leather boots that rose above their knees and flared just below their bare thighs.

They're not objects, my politically correct conscience whispered in one ear.

Look at those legs! my hormones screamed into the other ear.

Sergei tooted the horn and made the sound that Russians use to call cats: "Kssss, kssss, ksssss."

To my surprise, instead of the insulted frowns I expected to see, these girls smiled and giggled. They walked arm in arm and batted their flirty eyelashes. They were far from offended by our lack of sophistication. They actually seemed flattered. As we sped down this rugged Siberian road, my understanding of women hit a confusing cul-de-sac.

After another hour or so, Sergei spotted something on the horizon that pleased him. He squinted, then started to nod. "*Da*," he said with a smile as he slowed down. We came to a stop at a lonesome *shashlik* stand on the side of the road. A pillar of blue smoke rose up into the midday air from the metal grill.

"I'll be right back," Sergei said as he climbed out. "Gotta check if this is dog meat."

He returned holding three sticks, each weighed down with a dozen chunks of overcooked meat. The smell of grilled animal flesh filled the Kamaz. Sergei divvied out kabobs to Sasha and me.

"*Deech*," he said proudly as he took his first bite.

"I don't know that word. What is 'deech,' a dog breed?"

He laughed and shook his head slowly. "It's the meat a hunter brings back from a hunt."

"Sergei, you wouldn't like it in America," I said. "American roads are walled in by restaurants. The trick isn't to find food when you're hungry. It's a matter of resisting the temptation to eat when you're not."

Sergei looked over at me as if he had a lunatic in his truck. "Sounds horrible."

"I'm serious," I said. "You're a hunter, right?"

He nodded. "So?"

"What do you hunt for?"

"Deer in the early winter. Rabbits mid-winter. Ducks in the fall. By the way, duck season opens in two weeks. Keep your eyes open for them. I want to see where they're hiding this year."

"You hunt rabbits in the middle of the Siberian winter?" I asked rhetorically. "Why would you risk frost bite or worse just for *deech*? Especially when you can simply walk to the store and buy beef? I can't believe rabbit meat tastes that much better than beef."

Now Sergei didn't think that I was crazy. He thought I was an idiot.

"It's not the meat that's important. It's the process. Deech tastes better because you had to work for it. The hunt—that's the important thing," he explained in between drags on his cigarette and bites of shashlik.

"Exactly!" I shouted. "Even if they sold rabbit in the store, you wouldn't buy it. You'd continue to hunt, even when it's thirty degrees below zero. Right?"

Sergei grumbled, "Of course."

"Well, that's why you wouldn't like it in America. And that's why I'm living in Siberia. Here, everyday life is like going hunting. You're not sure if you're going to come back with any deech, but when you do, it tastes so much better than all the stuff offered to you when you're not even hungry."

Sergei's annoyed expression curved into a smile of recognition as he finally understood why I gave up scented toilet paper, pizza delivered hot to my door, and stores with shelves that strain under the weight of toys and toasters.

Blocking what little traffic there was, a herd of cows lazily crossed the road.

"Siberian traffic jam," Sergei said as he tossed a cigarette butt out of the window.

"*Tikho* (quiet). *Po gromshe* (louder)," Sasha said, leaving us confused about what he wanted until he made repeated motions with his thumb and index finger for Sergei to turn up the radio.

Sergei obliged.

A man's voice invaded our truck:

Surrounding the parliament building, the crowd that began forming early this morning continues to grow. Many are carrying red flags. Some are openly carrying weapons. Rutskoy made a speech calling for loyalty. He denounced President Yeltsin's actions and promised to restore order to the country.

"Bastard!" Sasha cried.

"Who, Rutskoy?" I asked.

"No, Yeltsin. Why did he only denounce the Supreme Soviet? He should have arrested all those goddamn deputies, locked those criminals up where they can't do any more harm to the country."

"He waited too long," Sergei said. "Now it's going to take violence to disperse that crowd and restore order. People are going to get hurt."

"What about the constitution, guys? The president can't go around arresting the legislative branch whenever he disagrees with them," I said, playing devil's advocate.

"That's fine in America where democracy is two hundred years old," Sasha said. "Our democracy isn't even two years old. Those bastards in the Supreme Soviet weren't elected. They're the same swine that raped this country for the past seventy years. They're not completely out of power yet and they've got a pretty damn good chance of retaking it. You heard how big that mob is. Screw the constitution if it means those assholes get to keep their jobs." He paused for a moment to take one of Sergei's cigarettes.

150

Then he suddenly erupted, "Yeltsin, you asshole! This could lead to a civil war."

"There won't be a civil war," Sergei said without much conviction. "Nobody wants to go back to the way it was."

"You don't think so?" Sasha asked, obviously not persuaded. "Then who are all those people carrying red flags threatening to restore order? No, Seryog. There are still a lot of people who would rather have their damn order and give up their freedom and responsibility." Sasha let out a laugh, an exasperated laugh. "This is just great. I'm on my way to move my parents out of a country where they can't find any peace because they're not Kazakhs, but I may be bringing them back into a country in the middle of a civil war. They already lived through World War II. They shouldn't have to endure that kind of suffering twice in one lifetime. It's not right."

Sergei put his arm out the window and waved to an oncoming Kamaz identical to ours except that its cab section was army green. The green Kamaz stopped, and the driver and his copilot got out. They crossed the road over to us. Standing in front of our truck, we all shook hands like campaigning politicians.

"Hey, brother, you coming from down there?" Sergei asked while simultaneously scanning a nearby pond for ducks.

Apparently understanding what Sergei meant, the other driver said, "Yeah. Got a *blyat* (fucking) bed full of apples from Alma Ata. What are you moving?"

"Potatoes," Sergei said as he pulled a box of Marlboro cigarettes from his shirt pocket. "Listen, brother, what can you tell me about the border?"

"Oh, *blyat*, you wouldn't believe it," the Kamaz driver said, his eyes locked on Sergei's red and white cigarette box. "Their country is even more *khuyovaya* (another, even more colorful expletive) than ours and they're putting up a huge building on the *yoboni v rot* (more of the same) border. Customs house, *blyat*; border control, *na khui*; and a bunch of other *govno*. Do they really think they're going to live better without us, *na khui*? Kazakhs don't do anything quickly, but that building is going up quicker than a teenager's *khui* during an American porno movie."

"They're a bunch of nomads and thieves," Sergei said, taking his eyes off the distant pond. He spit on the road and rubbed his loogie into the asphalt with his giant boot. With a deft flick of his wrist he got one cigarette to poke out of the little hole in the top of the box. Holding it out to the other driver, Sergei asked, "They give you any trouble at the border?"

With a quick nod of gratitude, the driver took the cigarette. Then he said with a sneer, "Don't worry about the *blyat* border. Grease a couple of their palms and, *pizdetz*, they'll let you in. They may be *yoboni* thieves and *vanyuchi* nomads, but they're not too proud to accept bribes, *na khui*. It's once you get in that the real *govno* starts. The farther south you go, the worse it gets. The GAI will *trakhat* you whenever they can. *Kozli!* Once they see your Russian license plate, they start to drool. They offer to exchange money. They say it with a smile on their dark faces, as if they're doing you a *blyat* favor. Our rubles are worth twice as much as their *pizdetski* rubles, but they exchange one for one. It looks like the *suki* are simply helping you out, but they're robbing you blind. And there is nothing you can do. If you don't exchange at least fifty thousand rubles, *na khui*, they find something wrong with your documents and fine you for a hundred thousand. And they demand that you pay the fine in Russian rubles. *Pizdets*. They're a bunch of greedy *ublyudki*. Their whole *blyat* country is one big heap of *govno*."

"We've got ten kilograms of chocolates," Sergei said. "They're weak when it comes to alcohol and sweets. They can't resist." Sergei held out the cigarette box to the copilot who quickly took a slender white cylinder of Western tobacco. He twitched a quick smile of gratitude at Sergei.

Sasha took the opportunity to bum another cigarette from Sergei.

"Yeah," the other driver laughed bitterly. "Those *khui, blyat* darkies probably will take chocolate instead of money. That's not the worst, though. Whatever you do, don't travel at night. Last night we got hit by some *blyat* bandits just south of Semipalatinsk. Half a million rubles they sucked out of us. *Pizdetz!*" he shouted, then spit over his shoulder, in the direction of Kazakhstan. "What are you going to do when they've got guns, haggle? It makes our *khuyovaya* country look like a *pizdovie* paradise."

Sergei held out his lighter as everybody leaned in one at a time to light his cigarette. The other Kamaz driver looked at me with suspicion. I was the only one without a cigarette in my mouth.

"He's American," Sergei said.

"*Ne khuya.*" The driver changed his expression from suspicion to surprise.

"He says that life's too comfortable in America," Sergei answered the unasked question.

"*Pizdets.* No problem with that here. Not for a long *blyat* time," the driver laughed. "Nope. Not for a long time, *na khui.*"

We all shook hands again and went our separate ways.

An hour later we stopped at a gas station. After passing a fistful of money into the sliding tray connected to a booth encased in metal bars, Sergei came back to the truck and started pumping volatile liquid into our bathtub-sized fuel tank.

I jumped down to stretch my legs. "How much gas can you fit into that tank anyway?"

"Over six hundred liters," Sergei said with obvious pride. "I welded this tank together myself. With the reserve tank on the other side, we can drive almost three thousand kilometers without stopping."

"That's half way across America," I said in disbelief.

"This isn't America," Sergei reminded me. "Here you can drive for days and not find a gas station, and when you find one, it may not have any gas."

"Shouldn't you put out your cigarette?" I said, looking down at a puddle of fuel by his feet.

Sergei pulled the cigarette out of his mouth and calmly examined the burning red tip. Looking at me, he held the cigarette between his thumb and forefinger. I watched with terror as he spread his thick digits. The burning cigarette fell, hot side down, into the puddle of fuel. It went out with a *tstssts* and a tiny puff of blue smoke.

"What the hell?" I said, feeling the adrenaline rush.

"Don't worry." He laughed in my pale face. "Diesel doesn't ignite except under pressure."

As my pulse was slowing back to normal, two young men in dirty army uniforms walked up to us. While looking over his shoulder suspiciously, one of them reached into his coat. As he pulled his hand out, I caught a glimpse of the black barrel pointed at Sergei. My heart heaved again. Without looking into Sergei's eyes, the young soldier asked, "Give us fifteen thousand rubles!"

"Get out of here, you parasites. Get back to your base," Sergei barked at them.

The second soldier joined in, "Come on, you know you could use it. You'll never find one cheaper."

"You little shits stole this from one of the trucks on your base, didn't you? What are you going to do when it's time to defend the motherland and all the trucks and tanks are missing steering wheels?"

I looked down at the pistol in the soldier's hand. It wasn't a gun at all. It was the fat blinker lever from a Kamaz.

"Lighten up, *muzhik*," the first soldier said, holding out his hand like a traffic cop.

"Don't tell me to lighten up, you little thieves," Sergei said angrily.

At that, the second soldier chimed in. "Go to hell, man. And take your damn motherland with you."

They both laughed as they walked off in the direction of another parked Kamaz. One yelled over his shoulder, "We're just trying to make some money. It's called the free market, man. Have you heard of it?"

22
South of the Border

We reached the bottom of Russia, the top of Kazakhstan. Sergei bribed a Kazakh border guard with a handful of chocolate, and we continued our way south. We were entering the great steppe, virtually featureless and practically limitless. It reminded me of the great American prairie, the Dakotas, where the wide-open expanse lures you in while the bleak emptiness repels you.

As we approached Semipalatinsk, I expected the Kazakh city to be dramatically different from the oppressively homogeneous Soviet cities all over Siberia. It was different, but only by degree. It was dirtier and even more monotonous. If Siberian cities were run down, then this city was broken down. It looked like a ghost town, except for one detail: people still lived in the shabby houses that leaned to one side or the other.

"So what did they do here? Is this another dying mining town?" I asked.

"They blew up nuclear bombs," Sasha informed me with grave seriousness. "This is the site for almost all Soviet nuclear weapons testing. They used to detonate bombs outside of town as often as several times a day."

Sergei added, "The city is still radioactive."

"What do you guys say we don't stop here for the night?" I asked.

"Not a chance. Not even to get something to eat. The food here is radioactive," Sergei warned.

I was glad to see the city fade away in the rearview mirror, but I also had an uneasy feeling in my gut. It seemed as if we were going the wrong way on a one way street. There was no traffic going in our direction, only a steady flow of vehicles fleeing into the city. What could be scarier than a radioactive city?

The words of the driver of the green Kamaz came back to me: "Don't drive at night. The bandits hit us just south of Semipalatinsk."

But his weren't the only words that worried me. There was also the news from Moscow.

The crowd has turned on the mayor's building. Armed with automatic weapons, they forced their way into the building.

We listened numbly to the radio as violence spread like a runaway virus across Russia's capital. All we had to do was turn off the radio and the horrible sounds of what seemed like Russia's next civil war would be silent, but not forgotten.

In the growing darkness and deathlike stillness of the uninhabited Kazakh prairie, we continued along a road that was as straight as it appeared on the map, and the map could have been a page from a geometry textbook. Sergei turned on the headlights.

Like a lone phosphorescent fish at the bottom of the ocean, the Kamaz's headlights created a tiny bubble of visibility. The world shrank into the fifty feet of straight road ahead of us. Nothing moved. Not the stars. Not the horizon. Nothing. I looked over at the speedometer every so often to make sure that we were actually moving. It felt like we were driving on a treadmill in outer space.

The mayor's building has been overtaken. The gunfire has ceased except for an occasional salute into the air. The crowd continues to grow. So far there has been no response by Yeltsin, who is rumored to have been flown into the safety of the Kremlin by helicopter.

Rage simmered just below the surface. Sergei gripped the steering wheel as if he were preparing to rip it from its base. With arms folded tightly, Sasha fixed his gaze on the road like a bull fixes his gaze on a red cape.

The crowd has broken into two groups. There were cries to take the Ostankino tower. It appears that some are heading back to the white house while the others are making their way to Ostankino to take control of radio and TV waves.

"Where are the riot police? What the hell is Yeltsin waiting for?" I asked, confused by the lack of resistance.

"The riot police? Sanya, that's not a crowd of teenagers with sticks and rocks. That's an armed mob. It's going to take the army to deal with them." Sasha paused. "That's assuming that the army is going to support Yeltsin, which is a pretty big assumption. Rutskoy is a military hero from Afghanistan. Yeltsin is a drunk politician from Sverdlovsk."

"If the army doesn't support Yeltsin, then it's already over, isn't it?" I asked, terrified by my own question.

"Yes, if the army is unified. But if the army splits in its support between Rutskoy and Yeltsin, then…" Unable to finish his sentence, Sasha just shook his head.

Sergei looked over at Sasha with horror, then back at the road.

Headlights appeared suddenly in the rearview mirror. My stomach tightened with fear. It seemed surreal, being held up for a million rubles by armed bandits on this desolate Kazakh road while Russia's future was being decided in the streets of Moscow. I watched with a strange detachment as the headlights gained on us.

The quaky breath of fear could clearly be heard in the voice of the radio announcer.

I can hear shots outside Ostankino. We can hear them below. My God, they're attacking us! I can see a fire burning near the entrance of the building. I've just received word that armored divisions are mobilizing toward the city.

The headlights in the rearview mirror continued to gain on us.

They have entered the building. I can hear gunshots on the floors below.

The sound of faint gunfire came from the radio speakers. It was hard to believe that those silly pops and cracks could come from something so deadly. They were not at all like the impressive eruptions of sawed-off shotguns and bullet-spraying machine guns that are ubiquitous in American action movies.

The headlights were right behind us now. The lights reflecting in the rearview mirror lit up Sergei's face. My mirror went dark as the car began to pass us.

I can hear gunshots on our floor. I don't know how much longer we'll be able to broadcast.

My gut was in a knot and my heart frantically bounced around in my ribcage like a wild animal desperate to get out. We helplessly listened as the angry mob battled its way toward its goal, to silence our frightened broadcaster. I wanted to yell, "Run! Get out of there!" but I clung to his voice, praying that he wouldn't leave us.

The car passed us. In the back seat, two big shaven heads sat atop massive shoulders. The car signaled right, then merged back into our lane directly in front of us. Its red lights shrank away into the distance.

I may have to… There was a pounding noise. *I don't…* More shouting. *They're here in the…* A second, barely audible voice interrupted him.

Say tha..y.u.….temp..a..ly..g..ng..off the air.

The familiar voice of our broadcaster lost its hysteria and became calm, almost serene. *Due to circumstances beyond our control, we are going off the air.*

There was a *click* followed by deafening silence.

The car in front of us disappeared over the horizon.

Sasha and Sergei vomited obscenities. Sasha slammed his fist against the dashboard. Sergei leaned on the horn for almost a minute. Eventually they tired and silence returned. The engine's constant rumble was the only sound in our world. We searched the radio for other stations. We picked up a station playing traditional Kazakh folk music. I was suddenly aware of being in a foreign country. I had been living in Russia, a foreign country, for some time now, but here, now was the first time things felt really *foreign*.

Sergei lit up a cigarette, crushed the empty cigarette box in his fist and tossed it out the window. "Those last words were spoken by someone with a gun pointed in his face. I wonder if they shot him after he went off the air."

I felt sick.

A bluish glow spread across the sky. The moon rose up, pouring crude-oil shadows over the backsides of rolling foothills.

Suddenly, a voice came on the radio. It was a voice so familiar and yet so completely out of place I thought I was hallucinating. The voice was singing, *Like a virgin / Like a vir-er-er-er-gin. Oooow!*

The song ended and, with the DJ's first words in Russian, a sense of renewed hope filled the truck. But, like having crossed the desert for a drink of water only to reach the salty ocean, the voice of the DJ provided no relief. He said nothing about the critical battle raging in the streets of Moscow.

We'll be right back with a song dedicated to Tanya from her secret admirer in school 129.

"This was probably recorded earlier. This can't be a live broadcast," Sasha said. "I remember how during the coup in 1991, instead of news, they showed symphony concerts on all the TV channels. Now there's progress for you." Sasha laughed. "In just two years, we've gone from Mozart to Madonna as background music for our political upheavals."

Eventually the people at the "Youth Channel" began to realize that all was not well in Moscow. They also learned that they were the only radio station still on the air.

Sergei pulled the truck off the road and drove across the grassland toward a wall of scrawny trees just outside a still village. Sasha and I spent the night listening to Sergei's constant snoring and the Youth Channel's occasional news blurbs. It was as if the world was coming to an end and MTV was the only station left to broadcast the mayhem.

The army managed to surround and contain the rebellious crowd and isolated them within the legislature building, the same building where a defiant Yeltsin had stood up to the leaders of the 1991 Soviet coup, bringing about their fall and the fall of the entire Soviet Union. Sasha was confident that Yeltsin would win this standoff as well.

"He can burn down the white house with those bastards in it, for all I care," he said. "Good riddance."

The early morning light revealed that the landscape was no longer flat. Glistening dew coated the smooth, golden domes of the foothills that looked like the sweaty bald heads of buried giants.

We headed south again. In a deep valley, a herd of horses galloped across the fenceless range. Like smoke from a distant brush fire, a pale orange dust-cloud kicked up by the hundreds of pounding hooves rose into the expansive, clear sky. The horses weren't trotting. They were galloping. They weren't running from anything. They were just running, because they could. It was breathtaking.

By midday, the world had gone flat again.

We came to a stop at a simple structure made from concrete slabs. The concrete cube stood like a lone die dropped from heaven onto the flat surface of this colossal board game. Rectangles had been carved out of the concrete slabs to create doorless doorways that led into the cube.

As I walked toward the cube Sergei tossed a roll of toilet paper to me. The insides of the structure were in keeping with the architectural flair of the outside. The floor was a concrete slab with a jagged hole in the center.

"Just like in America." Sasha said.

"Yep," I concurred. "You don't have to touch anything in order to flush."

"Actually, this service stop is even better than the ones in America. They've got a washing machine out here."

When I exited the cube, he pointed to a large rock beside a small stream. I laughed as I tossed him the toilet paper. "Don't fall in."

Moving south again, we watched a mysterious black thread that seemed to connect heaven and earth. We drove toward this odd phenomenon for the better part of an hour. Its source turned out to be a burning tire on the side of the road. The black smoke flowed straight upward, forever.

Sasha nudged me and pointed ahead on the right side of the road. At first I thought it was a grotesquely mutated horse—maybe from all the nuclear fallout. Then I laughed in amazement. It was a camel. A *camel!* Three days ago I had been in Siberia.

The narrow road became a divided highway, yet still lacked significant traffic. An occasional passenger car punctuated the modest flow of trucks pushing north into the expansive steppe. A plane, still a tiny speck in the sky, no longer drew its snow-white line across the heavens as it gradually descended through the thickening atmosphere toward the unseen city beyond the horizon.

It was evening when we found ourselves driving the crowded, chaotic streets of Alma Ata in search of Sasha's in-laws.

"Sasha, is that you?" a woman's voice called out from behind a steel door.

"Yes, Valentina Vasilievna," Sasha answered with a smile and a roll of his eyes, letting us know that Valentina Vasilievna was his *tyosha* (mother-in-law).

A short, white-haired woman with giant glasses distorting her face waved for us to come in. As she hugged Sasha, a loud voice came from the room at the end of the narrow hallway. "Sasha? Is that Sasha? He made it. Ha, ha, ha. *Molodets* (atta boy)," the voice blared. The unseen television in the far room made the walls ripple and glow.

I envisioned the owner of the powerful voice to be burly and bearded, like Luciano Pavarotti or Paul Bunyan. The large shadow of a man appeared on the wall. When he appeared in the doorway, I was reminded of how Toto pulled the curtain back to reveal that the Wizard of Oz was just a man. This man, Sasha's father-in-law, Lyuda's dad, resembled the mayor of Munchkinland more than he did an opera singer or lumberjack.

"Victor Mikhailovich," Sasha said as his *tyaist* (father-in-law) approached.

Victor Mikhailovich shook Sasha's hand vigorously. "All the way across Kazakhstan in a Kamaz during a revolution. Brave. Ha-a-a-a-a-a."

Sergei and I looked at each other, trying to understand what was so funny.

Victor Mikhailovich's machine-gun laughter seemed to come like hiccups, without warning and without reason.

"Ha-a-a-a-a-a. And who do we have here? *Zyat* (son-in-law), it's time for introductions."

Sasha obliged. "This is Sergei, our driver."

Victor Mikhailovich, using both hands, pumped Sergei's meaty paw up and down.

"And this is our American," Sasha said.

Victor Mikhailovich's eyes snapped open as if someone had dropped an ice cube down his back.

"*Our* American? Ha-a-a-a-a-a-a."

"Alexander," I said, sticking my hand out.

With both of his little hands, he shook my hand with such enthusiasm that, if I had been wearing glasses, they would have toppled off my face. Victor Mikhailovich could have shaken swimming goggles off my head.

"American, huh?" Victor Mikhailovich's loud voice filled the apartment. "Your friends at CNN have taken over my television. They're showing the spectacle going on in Moscow. It's all in English. I don't understand a thing. *Sprechen sie Deutsch?* Ha-a-a-a-a-a-a-a-a."

"What's going on?" Sasha asked, quickly slipping out of his shoes and heading for the glowing room.

Talk about luck! CNN in English. Now I could find out what was really happening. I slipped off my shoes and followed Sasha and his father-in-law.

Before I even reached the end of the corridor, Victor Mikhailovich's loud voice erupted as if he'd spotted a UFO. "Oh! Oh! Look at that. Oh! They've got tanks on the bridge. I'd hate to be in that building now. Fools. Ha-a-a-a-a-a-a. What did they expect, a welcoming party? Ha-a-a-a-a-a-a!"

I entered the room to see Sasha's face lit up in the flickering glare of the TV. He looked like someone watching his house burn to the ground. I looked down at the TV screen. My mouth dropped open as I saw the horrifying images of tanks firing into the windows of the parliament building. Even though we had heard on the radio about the fighting, I wasn't prepared for the images. I was used to the executive and legislative branches of government fighting each other with words, vetoes, and overrides, not tanks, automatic weapons, and soldiers.

"Looks like you're gonna get your wish, Sasha," I said. "Yeltsin seems intent on killing the legislature."

Sasha nodded, slapped his hands together several times as if to shake off some dirt, and said, "Well, that's it. It's either democracy or dictatorship from here on out. Either way, we're better off than before."

Selling Potatoes to the Father of Apples

Over a breakfast of potatoes and eggs smothered in Bulgarian ketchup, we discussed with Victor Mikhailovich where we could sell our eight tons of potatoes. Victor Mikhailovich gave us the insider's scoop on the local market. "The street value of a kilogram of potatoes these days is about four thousand rubles. That's if you're selling them by the bucket straight out of the back of your truck. But, if you do that, you'll have to deal with the local mafia. We could try to sell the whole truckload at the bazaar. But that's controlled by the Kazakhs. You have to remember that Russians are second-class citizens here now."

Sasha smiled. "I'm not Russian. Maybe they'll cut me a break because I'm Tatar."

Victor Mikhailovich erupted with laughter. "Ha-a-a-a-a. You're cunning like a Tatar. That's for sure."

Immediately after breakfast, Victor disappeared. Sasha, Sergei, and I headed outside. I looked around the courtyard. Large Kazakh women walked with shopping nets full of sausage, cheese, and bottles of milk. Old Kazakh men with war medals pinned to their faded civilian clothes sat arguing with each other on benches. Victor drove up in a custom-painted gray UAZ. I thought I could hear his laughter over the windy whine of the engine.

Sasha smiled as he watched his father-in-law behind the wheel. "He has three daughters. After his third daughter was born, he bought that jeep. Lyuda says he loves it like the son he always wanted."

We divided up, Sasha and his father-in-law led the way in the Uazik, while Sergei and I (and the potatoes) followed in the Kamaz.

After twenty-five minutes of nerve-wracking stop-and-go driving—the *go* part being far more nerve-wracking than the *stop* part—we arrived at the bazaar. Hundreds of bodies swirled and mixed together in chaotic harmony.

We walked up to a concrete building and through the cargo entrance, which put us in a dim corridor. White and red carcasses were piled high atop rusty metal carts so numerous it was difficult to maneuver between them. The dank odor of raw animal flesh mixed with the sharp smell of the fermented bloodstains on the concrete floor. "Who's in charge here?" Victor Mikhailovich asked one of the Kazakh men. The man was idly resting on the handle of his overloaded meat gurney. Not lifting his head and barely lifting his wrist, he pointed with a blood-encrusted finger to a set of narrow steps leading up into darkness.

Victor Mikhailovich scooted up the steps with Sasha and me close on his heels. We entered into a small, smoke-filled room. A single light bulb hung from the ceiling at shoulder height. A group of sturdy, swarthy men stopped what they were doing, which looked like counting bundles of money, and looked up at us with a combination of surprise and suspicion.

Sasha turned to me, "Go wait in the truck with Sergei. Victor Mikhailovich and I will handle this." Without a word of protest, I headed down the steps. I got back to the truck and waited quietly with Sergei until curiosity got the best of me.

"I'm going to take a look around the market," I told Sergei.

"Give me your wallet," Sergei said in a matter-of-fact voice.

"What for?"

"Because I'll give it back, which is more than the person who snatches it from your pocket will do."

"Fair enough," I said as I tossed my wallet to him. "Here, catch." I tossed my passport as well.

I approached the narrow gap in the rusty metal fence and found myself caught up in the powerful current of human bodies. Even if I changed my mind now, it was too late. The current carried me through the gate like a leaf down a drainage ditch. Once I was inside, the current lost its direction, becoming unpredictable surges and random ebbs. My foot kicked something solid. I looked down to see an old Kazakh woman glaring up at me with cloudy eyes. I saw a bucket of apples turned over in front of her.

I bent down and quickly put all the apples back into the bucket. I tried to apologize. She would have none of it. She insisted that I buy the apples. I didn't need a bucket of apples. So I offered her one thousand Russian rubles for two apples.

She held the strange bill close to her face.

Before I could explain, a woman sitting next to her said something in Kazakh. The old woman nodded her head and quickly stashed the bill into her little purse.

"Catch," I said, tossing one of the apples to Sergei as I climbed back into the Kamaz.

"That didn't take long." Sergei tossed my wallet and passport to me.

"I can't see a damn thing in there. One of the rare times when being taller than everyone else means having a worse view."

"I know. I saw you from here." Sergei laughed a little as he polished his apple on his dusty shirtsleeve. He looked at his apple. "Alma Ata—the father of apples. In Kazakh, *alma* means 'father' and *ata* means 'apple.' Maybe its the other way around; *alma* means 'apple' and *ata* means 'father.' In any case, Alma Ata means 'the father of apples.'"

Sergei and I relished the fruit that, by American standards, was puny and bruised. Sergei used his teeth to clean the sweet white meat off the apple until only a stem and a few seeds were left in his palm. To throw away the hourglass-shaped apple core that Americans consider garbage would shock and disgust most Siberians.

"Here they come," I said, pointing.

Sasha's father-in-law, as always, was doing all the talking.

"They didn't sell them," Sergei declared confidently.

"How can you tell?"

"Sasha's too relaxed. If they had sold the potatoes, he'd be worried about how to collect the money."

Still listening to his father-in-law, Sasha made eye contact with me and shook his head.

"Isn't there a restaurant or something around here that uses potatoes? Maybe we could sell to them," I said.

"Well, I have a friend—" Victor Mikhailovich stopped to correct himself "—actually, he's a friend of a friend, but I know him and he knows me. Anyway, he's got this little operation where he makes fried flakes from potatoes."

"Eureka! Potato chips!" I cried.

We drove for almost an hour along dirt roads through residential areas filled with squat cottages, barefoot children, stray dogs, and the occasional goat with its horns tied by a long rope to a rickety fence.

Eventually, we reached a fenced-off area that was full of what looked like bunkers. Sergei and I sat and waited as Victor and Sasha disappeared behind a weather-beaten door. After ten minutes, Sasha came out alone with a strained expression on his face.

"Sold?" I asked Sergei.

"Yep."

Sasha came up to the truck and told us to drive around to the large scales near the entrance. "We're going to weigh the truck full, and then again empty. They'll pay us for the difference," he explained.

"How much?" Sergei asked.

"Three thousand per kilogram. We'll probably only double our money," Sasha said with sincere disappointment.

"Let's have Sergei be in the truck when they weigh us the first time and not the second time," I suggested, trying to imagine what three thousand rubles multiplied by Sergei's weight would equal.

"Now you're thinking like a Russian businessman," Sasha said, patting me on the head as if he were my father and I had just gotten my first base hit in little league baseball.

After the Kamaz was weighed (without Sergei), a small army of stout Kazakh and Russian women wearing white uniforms and scarves on their heads filed out of the dark building. They looked like muscle-bound nurses. Each carried a pitchfork with rubber caps over the sharp tongs.

Victor Mikhailovich, stretching his arm up to put his hand on my shoulder, introduced me to a middle-aged Russian man in a black leather jacket. "This is *our* American. Ha-a-a-a-a-a."

I shook the man's hand.

"Genady," he said with a poker face.

"Alexander." I smiled.

"Do you have Russian roots?" He asked, still shaking my hand. "No."

"But you speak Russian like a native and your name is Russian," he said, ceasing to shake my hand, but not releasing it.

"Actually it's a Greek name. But I don't have Greek roots either."

"He's a Viking," Sasha cracked.

"Swedish?" Genady asked.

"Norwegian."

"You look very Russian," Genady persisted. "Are you sure you don't have any Russian blood?"

I nodded.

Genady let go of my hand.

He then gave us a tour of his factory. As he talked, it became clear that he thought that he had invented the potato chip. Maybe he had. He was ambivalent when I told him that Americans eat potato chips, lots and lots of them. Maybe he wasn't the first person to invent potato chips, but if this invention had a history in America, then maybe it had a future in Kazakhstan. He complained that the local Kazakh population hadn't acquired a taste for them yet. I advised him to sell his chips in the same places that sell beer.

He promised to give it a try.

As we were getting into our vehicles, Genady walked up with a box in his hand. It was filled with about fifty small bags of his potato chips.

"There are two kilograms here. They're fresh." He handed them to me.

"Take that out of the money you owe us," Sasha said.

"No." Genady shook his head and waved his arms like an umpire calling a base runner safe. "I wouldn't think of it. It's a present."

"If you want your business to expand, you can't give away your profits," I said.

His innate Russian generosity in direct conflict with his dream of a fruitful business, Genady paused for a moment. "I'll sell them to you at cost, without any profit," he finally said, having found a suitable compromise.

"Deal," Sasha agreed.

24
Moonshine and Garlic

"Let's go to the dacha. You can wash your Kamaz out there," Victor Mikhailovich said to Sergei. "There's no point in going home. With all that crap going on in Moscow, they've stopped showing *Simplemente Maria*."

Apparently, it wasn't just women who were addicted to that Mexican soap opera.

The dirt road narrowed as we entered the encampment of dachas. Each tiny plot, separated and totally enclosed by rickety metal fences, was flush up against the adjacent plot. There was no sensation of being in the great outdoors, no wide-open spaces. It was, however, green here and smelled of clean air, not car exhaust. We stopped in front of a metal gate. Victor unlocked the padlock and swung the gate open. The driveway was exactly the length of the jeep. The gate shut inches behind the spare tire that was attached to the back of the UAZ.

"What's this?" I asked, looking down into a two-meter deep concrete pit in the dacha's front yard.

"It's a swimming pool. Ha-a," Victor Mikhailovich boasted. "There's nothing better in the summer than a banya, followed by a dip in the pool."

I could no more swim in this over-sized bathtub than I could take a car for a joy ride in a garage.

While Victor Mikhailovich rummaged around in the kitchen, he told Sasha and me to sit at the "table," an old desk in the corner of the room. Out the window and through a bush, we caught glimpses of Sergei splashing buckets of water over his truck and scrubbing the dust off with a broom. The dust came cascading down the sides of the Kamaz in gray mudslides.

When Victor Mikhailovich returned, he had a bottle in one hand and a garlic bulb in the other. He slammed the bottle down boldly and tossed the garlic on the table, where it rolled around erratically like a rodent exercise ball with an indecisive mouse inside. He slammed his fist down on the garlic bulb, separating the cloves. He dealt each of us a clove.

"Give Sergei a holler," Victor Mikhailovich ordered.

"He's pretty good about not touching alcohol when he's going to be behind the wheel," Sasha said. "He's a professional driver. "

"You guys aren't leaving until tomorrow," Victor said.

Sasha shrugged his shoulders. "I know. He still won't drink. He doesn't want a hangover when he's behind the wheel. He takes his job seriously."

"Holler anyway." Victor Mikhailovich pointed to the window.

"Okay, but I warned you." Sasha leaned out the window and yelled, "Hey, Seryoga! How about some vodka?"

"No!"

"I'll pour you a glass. You can drink it when you're finished out there."

"I'm not going to drink anything."

"Oops," Sasha said. "Too late, it's already poured. Sorry, Seryog; now you've got to drink it."

Sergei shook his head and mumbled something under his voice.

"See, I told you," Sasha said with a satisfied smirk on his face.

Victor Mikhailovich pulled three glasses—drinking glasses, not shot glasses—from the drawer and placed them on the table. When all three glasses were half full, Victor slammed the bottle down again on the desk, sending a spit of clear liquid out the top of the bottleneck.

"To the meeting on the Elbe," Victor Mikhailovich said. He was looking right at me.

"In every joke there is a grain of truth," Sasha recited a proverb from the seemingly inexhaustible supply of Russian proverbs.

"No, Sasha. In every joke there is a grain of a joke," Victor Mikhailovich corrected his son-in-law. "The rest is truth."

We clinked our glasses together and tossed down the clear liquid. It took three gulps to empty my glass. The liquid burned its way down my throat. We each chased the vodka down by biting off half a clove of garlic. It felt like I had a nine-volt battery in my mouth.

"AAAAAGGGghhh!" Victor growled with satisfaction. He looked at me, then laughed.

Tears were leaking out of my eyes.

"Haven't you ever tasted *samogon* before?"

"We call it moonshine," I gasped. "I was just expecting vodka." I never thought the day would come when I considered vodka to be a relatively weak drink.

Victor laughed with pride. "This moonshine is around fifty-five percent alcohol."

"Isn't alcohol flammable at that concentration?" I asked, looking into my empty glass as if to see the rainbow swirls of gasoline in the bottom.

"Nope, you need sixty percent before smoking and drinking becomes life-threatening," Sasha informed us.

Victor Mikhailovich poured another round of liquid liver remover. "We have to finish the other halves of our garlic cloves."

"Aahhhhh!" Victor Mikhailovich sighed with satisfaction after the second glass.

"You look happy," Sasha said.

"Why shouldn't I be happy? I've done all three things a man ought to do in his life."

"What three things?" I asked, wondering if I had done any.

Victor Mikhailovich turned to me with a smile, "Build a house, have a son, and plant a tree."

Sasha gave him a polite, but questioning look.

Victor Mikhailovich laughed. "Okay, I haven't built a house, but this dacha is pretty damn close. And I don't have a son, but I have three daughters. Besides, I've planted more than half a dozen trees."

"You built this yourself?" I asked, looking around the room with new appreciation.

"Of course." Victor Mikhailovich looked at me with surprise. "Who else would have built it?"

I shrugged my shoulders.

Victor Mikhailovich indulged himself in romantic nostalgia. "Building this dacha was the best job I ever had. Each nail I pounded filled me with happiness. Sure it was harder than just paying someone else to build it for me, but it was worth it. Digging holes for someone else, now that's hard work that isn't worth a damn."

"You guys know the joke about the two guys digging holes?" Sasha asked. Without waiting for our answers, Sasha began his anecdote. "On his way to buy some vodka, Ivan notices two guys working with shovels. He stops to watch them. One is digging holes and the other is filling them in. Confused, Ivan walks up to them and asks, 'Hey! What are you guys doing? Why are you digging holes and then filling them back in again? The first man stops digging his hole and looks up with an annoyed expression. 'We plant trees for the government. I dig the holes. Mikhail plants the trees. And Genady fills in the holes. Unfortunately, Mikhail is sick today. Do you mind? Genady and I have a lot of work to do.'"

Sergei walked in just as Sasha finished his joke. "Victor Mikhailovich, where can I wash up?"

Victor Mikhailovich launched to his feet. He looked at all of us, pointed his index finger at the ceiling, turned on his heel, and disappeared out the door. Sergei shrugged his shoulders and followed him.

"Sash, you've got quite a father-in-law," I said.

We were both overwhelmed with another wave of luxurious, lazy laughter. Tears streamed from my eyes.

Sasha said almost apologetically, "I think all that crap in Moscow has got him on edge, even more than usual. That's where all that laughter is coming from."

"I was like that on my first date, back in my freshman year in high school. I was a zit-faced nervous breakdown in a tie. And she was calm and lovely."

Interweaving his fingers into a cradle for his head, Sasha sat back and listened.

I took the cue and continued to reminisce. "To keep the embarrassing silence to a minimum, I made jokes that weren't funny and laughed like a horse. I pointed out ordinary things as if they were remarkable and asked questions to which both she and I already knew the answers."

"Quite the lady's man," Sasha said.

"No doubt. By the middle of dinner she had had enough. She turned to me, put her small, soft hand over my large, shaky paw, and said, 'Relax, Al. Don't spaz out on me.'"

Sasha laughed through his nose. "Good for her!"

"After that, I suddenly felt a sense of relief. I apologized, looking directly into her lovely brown eyes. The rest of the evening was fantastic. We danced, laughed, and had a great time. Later, when I dropped her off, she even said, 'Thanks, Al. I had a wonderful evening.'"

"You should have thanked her," Sasha said as he bobbed his eyebrows up and down.

"I know." My smile faded as I was overcome with a pain in my stomach. It wasn't the moonshine. It was a pain I carried around with me all the time. Like an ulcer, it hurt a little bit all the time, but acted up every once in a while, when I let myself remember. "She killed herself during our senior year."

Sasha groaned. His shoulders sank and his eyes closed.

"But, you know," I said, taking a deep breath in an attempt to regain my composure, "she lived more in eighteen years than a lot of people do in eighty. She taught me that you have to live deliberately. It's not about how long you live, but how well you live."

Sasha peeled the skin off the last garlic clove, cut it in two and gave me half. He poured the remaining Russian moonshine into two glasses. After handing me one, he raised his glass.

"To life."

Lenin Street in downtown Novosibirsk

Lyuda, baby Alina, and Sasha

Sasha dressed for a Siberian stroll

A row of trees in winter, scenery from an early morning commute

Pooper (a.k.a. Scout) keeping his paws warm on the stovetop

A snow-covered road outside of town

Siberian traffic jam. We were stopped a dozen times each day by livestock crossing the road. In Siberia, it was usually cattle. In Kazakhstan, it was more often horses.

On the road to Kazakhstan—on one of Siberia's vast, featureless plains

*The Kamaz, with Sergei at the wheel, shows surprisingly
little damage the morning after hitting a horse.*

Guardians of the road. These solitary plaster animals stood sentry alongside the road every twenty miles or so.

*The author with Lyuda's father, Victor Mikhailovich,
standing on a rock in front of his dacha*

*Siberian Okies. From a lifetime of possessions
in the back of the Kamaz, Sasha extracts
a gas can to fill up Kamil's Car.*

*Kamil on the threshold of his
verdant dacha moments
before he left it forever*

Saying good-bye. Baba Masha, Sasha, and Kamil at the grave of Sasha's grandmother, Baba Masha's mother.

Bundles of cash. This is the money Baba Masha and Kamil received for their apartment. It was worth less than $5,000.

Baba Masha serving another meal

Sasha's extended family—Stasik, Nuria, Ahsya—poses in the living room.

Groundbreaking in Siburbia

Movie house marquee on Ilicha Street in Akademgorodok

Snow brings out the inner child in everyone, even the children.

Car camping on Olkhon, the largest island in Lake Baikal

Pulling Up Roots

In the morning, after a few swigs of Sasha's sudsy hangover medicine, we pointed our Kamaz east and drove toward Sasha's childhood hometown, Kentau. Along the desolate road, the GAI (Government Automobile Inspectors) stopped us every thirty minutes or less. They shook us down for bribes of chocolate and money. I posed as an American journalist doing a photo essay on Kazakhstan. Instead of chocolate or money, some of the GAI just wanted their pictures taken. Some wanted their pictures taken *and* some chocolate *and* some money.

We made a minor detour into Kyrgyzia, hoping the shakedowns would be less frequent there. They weren't. We arrived in Kentau in the late evening.

We stepped out of the Kamaz and stretched our stiff backs and legs in the crisp air of a tree-sheltered courtyard. Even in the faint evening light, I could see that the trees were still fully adorned with thick green foliage. By now, the trees in Novosibirsk were bare and snow was on everybody's mind, if not on the ground.

Sasha took a deep breath and yelled. "Come on. Mama's waiting."

"I'm just going to go to sleep in the Kamaz anyway," Sergei said. "I'll meet your folks tomorrow."

"Nonsense," Sasha said with a smile. "Come on. Mom will be offended if you don't come in and eat something."

"I'm not hungry," Sergei persisted. "I'm tired."

Sasha's smile vanished. "Mom won't be the only one offended."

"All right," Sergei gave in. "But after ten minutes I'm coming right back out here to get some sleep."

Sasha trotted toward the door. We followed him up the stairs to the dark second-floor landing. Sasha rang the doorbell and simultaneously made an identical buzzing sound with his voice. There was a metallic clicking sound as the lock began to turn.

In the seconds before the door opened, a cascade of images of what Sasha's mom might look like flowed through my mind. Because Sasha was a descendant of the Tatar-Mongols, I envisioned his mother as a lady-version of Attila the Hun—leaves and grass in her long black hair, battle scars on her face, and a bloody axe in her hand. I remembered that Sasha was a Muslim. I discarded the image of Madame Hun and envisioned a shapeless figure hidden in a black burka. Looking at Sasha's sky-blue eyes and earth-brown hair, I imagined his mother as a tall Swedish woman with long blonde hair and rosy cheeks, then as a short, bosomy Italian woman with the temper of a volcano.

The door opened. Nobody was there. I saw coats hanging on wall hooks at chest level. My eyes dropped down to see a tiny woman in a simple gray robe. Her steely gray eyes inspected her son. Several gold-capped teeth peeked out from her smile. Her skin was as white as paper and her long salt-and-pepper hair was wrapped up in a tight ball. Straight, disciplined wrinkles covered her face. Sasha rushed in and kissed both of her cheeks with respect and then embraced her with tenderness.

"Kiss your father," she commanded, opening the door all the way to reveal the silhouette of a man standing in the darkness behind her. Sasha let go of his mother and moved to the dark figure. He kissed the man's cheeks three times and embraced him.

"*Zakhodite* (enter)," the little woman instructed Sergei and me. We obeyed. Her iron smile conveyed both sincerity and severity. She introduced herself as "Baba Masha." There was a moment of confusion as to whether we should kiss her cheeks in greeting or not. We ended up nodding respectfully, awkwardly.

"Eat," she said after placing on the kitchen table three large bowls filled with liquid too thick to be soup but too thin to be stew. Floating on the surface of the steaming liquid, dozens of grease dots, like tiny magnifying glasses, distorted the shape and size of the submerged vegetables and meat.

When we finished eating, we were sent to bed.

The next morning, as I brushed my teeth in the tiny bathroom, I looked in the mirror that hung on the wall so low that the one-eyed reflection of my belly button was all that stared back at me. Sasha probably stood on his tiptoes to look into this mirror while brushing his baby teeth. Underneath the bathtub, I noticed a familiar blue box. It was Iranian BARF. Just then, the door opened. At the level of the doorknob, Baba Masha's head poked in.

"I washed your clothes this morning. Take a shower. Your clothes will be dry by the time you're done. Breakfast will be ready soon, so don't drag your feet." She placed a towel on the doorknob and shut the door behind her.

Back in the bedroom, I found my clothes draped over a chair back. My jeans felt cool and crisp. My shirt smelled like fresh air.

"Thanks for the clean clothes," I said to Baba Masha as I walked into the kitchen.

Wearing her steely smile, she turned only for a moment from her doings at the stove. "No need. I wake up every morning at five. I need something to do. I can't stand to be idle. If I'm idle, I get to thinking. And thinking makes me sad."

I rubbed my hand over the dry sleeves of my shirt. "How did you dry them so quickly?"

"Desert air. I hang the clothes out on the balcony in the morning before the dust gets stirred up." She turned her attention back to the stove. "Sit down. Sasha just went out to wake up Sergei."

This woman of modest proportions made a breakfast of decidedly immodest proportions. With her little hands, she carried each plate overloaded with food from the stove to the table. When I looked down at the plate, I was overwhelmed by the quantity of eggs, vegetables, and meat before me that I was expected to pack away. Before long, however, I was wiping my plate clean with a slice of bread. I savored the yolk-saturated slice like the cherry after a banana split.

Sated, I pushed my plate forward and sat back.

"More?" Baba Masha asked, rising to her feet.

"Thanks. No. That," I pointed to the empty plate, "was wonderful, but any more and I'm afraid I'll be useless today."

"Nonsense. Those who eat well, work well," Baba Masha said. "That's how people used to choose their hired hands, by watching them eat. If you can't put much food in your mouth with a table fork, you probably can't stack much hay with a pitchfork."

"In that case, I guess I will have seconds."

After I finished seconds and refused thirds, Baba Masha seemed neither impressed nor disappointed as she took my plate and put it in the sink.

Sasha yawned and rubbed his eyes.

Baba Masha laughed. "Still tired, son? Don't want to wake up?" She laughed again. "I used to try everything to get him to wake up for school. Once I told him that a neighbor found a ruble just lying in the street. If he woke up, maybe he'd find a ruble too. 'So what?' my little Sasha said as he hid his face in the pillow."

"Mama," Sasha said, slightly embarrassed.

Undeterred, his mom kept on telling her story. "The man found the ruble because he was up and about at the crack of dawn, not lying about in bed," Baba Masha said, looking at her son as if he were again five years old. "But that story didn't work on you, did it?"

We all looked at Sasha.

He shrugged his shoulders. "I figured the guy who lost the ruble must have gotten up even earlier."

"Five years old," Baba Masha marveled, shaking her head. "He was a clever little rascal. He wouldn't even let us talk to him in Tatar. He'd lock himself in the bathroom and scream, 'Mom, talk to me in Russian. I don't want to speak Tatar.' Now you regret not knowing your mother tongue, don't you?"

Sasha nodded dutifully.

"I'm going to teach Alina to understand Tatar. I don't care if she locks herself in the bathroom." Baba Masha set the table for tea. On my third cup of tea and milk, Kamil entered the room like a whisper.

"*Poyekhali* (let's go)," is all he said.

Within minutes, Kentau was receding away from us as we cruised along a road so desolate that the long highway across the steppe we had traveled several days earlier now seemed hospitable in comparison. Despite the fact that there were no natural obstacles to avoid—no trees, bushes, or even patches of tall grass—the asphalt road swayed and swiveled left and right periodically, seemingly at random. It looked like God had stretched a gigantic piece of yarn until it slipped from his fingers and fluttered tensionless to the ground. Kamil swiveled down the curvy road. Sergei kept the Kamaz steady, going in a straight line by ignoring the tradition of sticking to the right side. There were no other cars on the road. He just let the road wiggle underneath us.

When we came to a lone road jutting out at a ninety-degree angle, Kamil's little orange car slowed down, turned, and accelerated down the dusty trail. Sergei followed. My eyes drifted down the dehydrated path until they came across what seemed to be a mirage. On the horizon, like a fuzzy green patch of fungus on a piece of bone-dry bread, a green oasis interrupted the arid desert.

"What is that?" I asked Sergei, breaking Baba Masha's food-induced silence.

"Dachas," Sergei burped.

The boundary was sudden and dramatic. The desert remained a tribute to the absence of life right up to the last inch before we entered this defiant fortress of foliage. My arms grew goose bumps as the temperature suddenly dropped in the cool shade of trees. Dense greenery hid dozens of dachas. An occasional window, door, or chimney came into view for an instant only to vanish again behind the camouflage of fruit trees, grapevines, and flower-freckled bushes.

Sasha popped out of the car and opened a metal gate covered by sprawling vines. Kamil drove into a leafy cave. I jumped down from the Kamaz onto the gravel road, kicking up a cloud of white dust around my feet. It felt like we were in the Garden of Eden; the parched road reminded me that with just one misstep, I could be back under the deadly desert sun.

Sergei and I walked through the gate to find the orange car already empty, both of its doors left wide open. On both sides and above the car was a bower of grapevines straining to hold up bunches of succulent fruit. I picked a few grapes and tossed them into my dry, dusty mouth. When I bit down, they popped, filling my mouth with sweet juice.

Looming trees, crawling vines, and loitering bushes embraced the small cottage. Inside, Sasha and his dad passionately argued.

"Let's take this bookshelf," Sasha said, already moving his hands over it in search of a good handgrip. I ducked through the low doorway, grabbed the other side of the bookshelf, and prepared to heave.

"No, sonny," Kamil sang in his high-pitched voice. "We have to get the carpets from the attic first."

"Why?" Sasha said without releasing his grip on the bookshelf.

"If we start taking things out that are closest to the door, we'll be messing up the places we just cleared. No, sonny. We start with the attic and work our way toward the door, cleaning up behind us as we go," Kamil explained his version of the obvious.

"But, Pop," Sasha said, "if we start from the attic, we are constantly going to be running into everything on the way to the door. Let's clear things out from the door and work our way to the attic. That way the path will always be clear."

At this point I wasn't sure whose plan was better, but I didn't really care, either. I released my grip from the bookshelf and rested my elbows on top, waiting for the critical decision as to how we were going to empty this cottage of its contents. Actually, in the previous weeks Kamil had already done most of the work. He had removed everything except the things too large to fit in his orange car. The bookshelves were empty of books. The bare kitchen cabinets were stacked on each other on the kitchen floor. The bed frame, leaning against the wall, had no mattress.

Still explaining the advantages of his method, Kamil climbed up the steep steps to the attic, assuming his son was behind him. Sasha, while continuing to argue with his dad, motioned for Sergei and me to take the bookshelf out to the Kamaz. We laughed quietly as we headed out the door with the bookshelf.

When we returned, Sasha and Kamil were in the attic arguing. They couldn't agree on who should go down the ladder first.

"Pop, that's stupid. I'm going first. What if the carpet slips? I don't want you to get crushed," Sasha said.

"No, sonny. I've already lived my life," Kamil insisted. "You've got a wife and daughter to look after."

"You've still got Mom to look after. I'm going first," Sasha passionately declared.

I had no idea that moving carpets was such a heroic endeavor that it required a man to lay down his life. Meanwhile, Sergei and I carried out bookshelves and kitchen cabinets. After ten minutes of work and forty minutes of arguing, the dacha was empty. A small pile of belongings rested in the Kamaz's cargo section.

Sasha took me on a tour of the robust garden. Despite the fact that Kamil and Baba Masha had already collected and canned this year's harvest, the generous garden continued to bear plentiful fruit and vegetables. There are no off switches for gardens, except, of course, winter. As Sasha and I walked along the neatly arranged rows, we bent down, wiped the dirt off of ripe raspberries and tomatoes and ate them there and then.

Kamil shuffled carefully and slowly through the cottage, as if collecting any memories he had forgotten, then shut and locked the door. As he headed for the car, he stopped to pull up some weeds from the gray soil around a plant bursting with ripe strawberries. He meticulously pulled up every weed until he was satisfied that the plant's roots wouldn't have to compete for precious water. He then grabbed a bucket and gently poured water around the single plant until the soil was black and sparkling. Leaving the plant well cared for but ignoring its grateful offering of dangling fruit, Kamil threw the bucket into the trunk of his car and started the engine.

Sasha and I took up our respective places in the passenger seats of each vehicle. We exited the shady green oasis, and headed back toward Kentau under the deadly rays of the desert sun.

As we pulled up to the courtyard in front of the apartment just before noon, I noticed a small group of young men squatting in the shade. Men don't sit in Central Asia; they squat. Discussing something of importance, men will squat down and sketch in the dust with sticks. Clusters of waiting Kazakhs ignore the dusty benches at bus stops and squat like gargoyles. Elbows resting on their knees, hands dangling from their extended limbs, and heads drooping forward, some old Kazakhs can even sleep while squatting.

"Dad's car is going to turn over one hundred thousand kilometers on the drive back to Novosibirsk." Sasha pointed with his thumb over his shoulder back to the little orange car.

"I didn't know Russian cars were built to last that long. Especially with the roads being what they are."

"They're not. But Dad takes such good care of his car, I bet it'll go another hundred thousand."

"In America, if your car takes you 99,999 miles, you are supposed to push it the last mile. But most people get distracted and notice when the odometer reads 100,002."

Just then, one of the squatting men called out, "Sasssha!"

Squinting his eyes, Sasha looked over at the crowd.

"Sasssha, it's me," a skinny shadow of a man stood up from the squatting pack.

"Yura? Hey, Yura. Uuuuaaaagghhh!" Sasha yawped as he recognized his childhood buddy, and quickly walked over to hug him. When Sasha released his embrace, Yuri began to fall over. Sasha quickly reached out and caught him.

"Sasshhaa."

"What?"

Pause.

"Sassshaaa," Yuri repeated, his head moving around as if he were following the path of a fly in front of his face.

"Yes, Yura. I'm listening," Sasha said, moving his head back and forth in an attempt to maintain eye contact with Yuri.

"Sasshha. Har you listenn-nen-ening?"

"Yes. I'm listening." Sasha laughed.

"Sasshaa," Yuri repeated emphatically. Then he seemed to forget what he wanted to say.

"How are you, Yura? What's new?" Sasha decided to take the burden of asking hard-to-remember questions away from the emaciated, inebriated remains of his childhood friend.

"Me? How'm I?" After a long, long pause, he finally answered, "Ah. Ssame old, same ol'. Heh, heh." He flicked his jugular with his middle finger. A scattering of laughs came from the group of squatting men. They, too, were completely stupefied and senseless with alcohol.

With the patience of a monk, Sasha waited for something intelligible to come out of Yuri. Before that happened, however, Baba Masha called out from the kitchen window, "Son, come home. It's time for lunch."

At the sound of Baba Masha's voice, Yuri snapped straight. He quickly wobbled backwards under the cover of a tall bush in an obvious and futile attempt to hide from Sasha's mom.

"Yuri, I see you. Shame on you! Shame on you! You're drunk again. Oh, Lord. Shame on you! Leave my son alone." She pulled her head back in and closed the kitchen window.

"Sober up, Yura, and then we'll catch up," Sasha said to his friend as he eased him back down into the circle of wobbling squatters.

We sat down for another feast, followed by tea and conversation.

"They said my father was an enemy of the people because he was too successful as the director of the collective farm. That's how it was then." Baba Masha said, shaking her head. "He didn't have much, but someone decided that it was too much, especially for a Tatar. So they took it all away. All of it! His job, his home, his wife and family. They put him in prison, then exiled him to Sakhalin."

Although lost deep in her own memories and the memories that her mother passed down to her, Baba Masha periodically poured hot tea into our cups.

"Stalin decided to send all the Tatars to Kazakhstan. So Mama packed all our important possessions and we got on a train going to Kentau. When we arrived, our luggage was gone. It turns out it was never even loaded onto the train." Her hands mechanically swept up the few crumbs on the table. "We arrived in Kentau with only the clothes on our back. And those clothes were my father's shirts that mom had cut up and sewn into little pants and dresses. We had no money, no food. Nothing. I remember going to sleep hungry night after night. Our school had one textbook for all forty kids. We'd each get ten minutes to read from the book, and then we had to go home. Out of spite, that winter was bitter cold. Minus forty for days on end."

Just when I thought it couldn't get any worse, Baba Masha said, "Then the war began." She laughed. Her sad laughter seemed as odd as do tears of joy.

"Mama, because she had children and no husband, was eligible to receive some of the American aid. She came home one night with a bag full of things. She gave me a wool dress that I wore every-day for years until the color was gone and then I wore it for another year until I could no longer squeeze into it. Mom also pulled three cans of beans in tomato sauce out of the bag of American aid. She made soup from the beans. We had dinner that night. Dinner! We had forgotten what a real meal was like. We sat around the table. I can still taste it like it was yesterday. It was the best soup I've ever had in my life. I can still taste it," Baba Masha repeated. "We were all so hungry." The muscles in her face tightened, folding her cheeks and forehead along well-defined wrinkles. "Mama told us not to be greedy, but I ate quickly so I wouldn't have to share. It was so good. I can still taste it. Sooo good, I can still taste it...." Her arthritis-warped fingers dabbed her lips as she savored the memory of the soup she had eaten more than fifty years ago.

Suddenly Baba Masha opened her eyes and looked at me as if I had offended her. "Now America sends us those awful television shows. Why are you sending that stuff over here? It's all violence and sex."

The economist in me wanted to answer, "Supply and demand. Americans produce crap, but Russians watch it. It takes two to tango." But I only shrugged my shoulders and said nothing.

Kamil walked into the room. "*Poshli* (let's go)."

Everything we could pick up went into the back of the truck. We packed up the belongings of a lifetime. Sasha and I carried dressers, bed frames, tables, sofas, and cupboards. I went down the steps first so that our height difference balanced out. Baba Masha packed the contents of the most vital room in the house, the kitchen. Sacks of flour, rice, and sugar went in the truck. Then came boxes filled with knives, cutting boards, pots, and pans. Then the chairs and the table went. We wrestled with the refrigerator. Finally, we pried the stove away from its spot, leaving an unpainted square in the floor. With a bucket and a rag, Baba Masha washed the kitchen floor. Then she shut the kitchen door like the lid of a coffin.

There were dark squares on the sun-faded walls where family pictures used to hang. Baba Masha had cleared out all the closets and scrubbed the walls and floors sterile.

Everything was in the truck, everything but four mattresses, four blankets, and four pillows. We would sleep in the apartment one last time, then leave in the morning.

"It's time to visit your cousin," Baba Masha instructed her son.

26
Behind Father's Wake

The night air was cold. The wind kicked up dust swirls that danced like banshees under the dim streetlights. Sasha and I hurried through the eerie, empty streets as if we were sneaking through a graveyard. I was relieved when Sasha darted into the stairwell of an anonymous apartment building. I followed close on his heels, whisking my hands back and forth through my hair to free the dust.

After a single knock from Sasha's hand, the door opened to reveal an oddly beautiful woman. Her face was empty; she was a true stoic. Her long, sandy-brown hair was pulled back into a thick ponytail. Her big eyes were the color of molasses. When she recognized Sasha under his stubble, a soft smile curved a rainbow of life back into her face, but it lasted only a moment.

They embraced without words. Sasha introduced me to his cousin Nuria, whose name was as strangely beautiful as she was herself. She gave me a tired, but pleasant smile. Her face quickly returned back to its stoic emptiness.

"*Kto tam* (who's there)? *Kto tam? Kto tam?*" A child's voice called out like a parrot. I could hear the soft thumping sound of little stocking feet scampering across a carpeted floor. A moment later, a boy's face wearing a curious and surprisingly serious expression popped through from under Nuria's arm.

"*Kto tam?*" he said again.

"Stasik, don't you recognize your *dyadya* Sasha?" the woman asked in a soft, tired voice.

With the jerky eye movements of an android, the little boy examined Sasha's smiling face. "Yes," he said without emotion.

"And who is that?" He pointed at me.

"That's *dyadya* Shura," the woman said with her hand on the boy's head.

The boy looked at me neither warmly nor coldly.

I smiled.

He didn't.

He pulled his head back behind his mother, then disappeared into the apartment. His stocking feet thumped across the carpet in the unseen room beyond.

"Come in," Nuria said, holding out her hand and bowing her head.

We took off our shoes in the dimly lit corridor and followed Nuria into the living room. The little boy was seated at a small table in the corner. He was completely absorbed in some kind of work.

"Stasik makes miniature figures out of clay. Everything from soldiers to rocket ships. He's quite good. He has his father's gift for creativity," Nuria said, then let out a sigh.

"Does he paint, too?" Sasha asked.

Apparently not hearing Sasha's question, Nuria continued to look at little Stasik.

"Where's Ahsya?" Sasha asked.

"She's in her room listening to music." Nuria snapped out of her trance. "I'll get her. She'll be so glad to see you."

"No, I want to surprise her," Sasha said with a devious smile on his face.

Without looking up, little Stasik said in his parrot voice, "She has her headphones on. She can't hear anything except, of course, the telephone."

Sasha sneaked down the short corridor and slowly opened the door, poking his head in. There was a loud scream, followed by a girl's delighted voice. "Uncle Sasha!"

Nuria invited me to sit on the couch while she went to the kitchen to prepare something for us to eat.

Sensing what Nuria was up to, Sasha yelled from Ahsya's room, "Nuria, we already ate. Mama fed us. Don't make anything for us."

"Nonsense," Nuria answered and continued into the kitchen.

Paintings of Nuria and some rather morbid landscapes scaled the walls. I could hear the voices of Ahsya and Sasha chatting and laughing down the corridor. Little Stasik, oblivious to my existence, was still hunkered over his latest creation.

"What are you making?" I asked.

"Waterloo," he shot back in a matter-of-fact voice.

"Can I see?"

"I don't see why not," he said, turning a surprised look at me for a moment, then spun back to his work.

I was astonished by what I saw over his little shoulder. On a wooden slate no larger than a shoe box cover, this ten-year-old boy had created a battlefield reenactment of Waterloo, complete with cannons next to little pyramids of cannonballs, soldiers carrying bayonet-tipped muskets, and corpses of men and horses.

"That's really good," I said.

Stasik looked up at me with his non-childlike eyes. A flicker of a smile came over his face and was gone so quickly that I was convinced it was just my imagination.

"I don't like these soldiers. Their hats are wrong," he said, and with one destructive motion, he flattened half a platoon of soldiers that must have taken him hours to create.

"They looked okay to me."

"I'll remake them better," he said as he scraped up the glob of squashed soldiers.

"You're mom said you can make anything out of clay."

"Da," Stasik said without a hint of pride.

"Can you make a car?" I asked.

"What kind?"

"Uh, I don't know."

"Formula One cars are hardest," he informed me. "Here, let me show you." Like a tiny Leonardo da Vinci looking for the sculpture to be freed from a stone, Stasik held the glob of dead soldiers in his little hands and examined it, looking for the car hidden within. In quick, confident motions, he rolled, twisted, and pinched the clay with his fingers. Five minutes later, he held a Formula One racer in his hand, complete with front and rear spoilers, four wheels, steering wheel, exhaust pipe and driver with helmet.

"Here," he handed it to me.

"Another masterpiece," I said. "And you said Formula One cars are hard to make. You must be able to make other cars with your eyes closed."

A boyish smile snapped across his face; this time it lasted long enough for me to see it and know that it wasn't just my imagination.

"You can keep that car if you like. I can make another for myself," Stasik explained.

"Thanks. And I have a car for you, too," I said, remembering the Matchbox car I brought along for just such an occasion. "Wait a second while I get it."

I retrieved the toy car from the pocket of my leather jacket. It was still in its clear plastic and cardboard packaging. I walked back into the room with it hidden behind my back. Stasik turned his back on his little battlefield and watched me with curiosity and a hint, just a hint, of childlike anticipation.

"Here. It's not a Formula One, but it is a race car," I said as I pulled it from behind me and held it out to him.

The colorful design on the cardboard panel caused his eyes to open wide then squint with intense scrutiny. He was quickly on his feet, standing in front of me, his eyes fixed on the car like a cat's on a strand of yarn. Almost involuntarily his hands reached out to hold the bottom corners of the cardboard panel as if to keep it from getting away. We both held on to it for a moment. Then I gently let go.

Stasik revealed that he was indeed a boy and not a robot. His open mouth stretched into an ear-to-ear grin. He slowly backed up to his chair and sat down, his butt almost missing the seat.

"Open it," I encouraged him.

Still speechless, Stasik placed it on the table in front of him. He examined the toy that had been made in a factory in China, transported across the Pacific Ocean to America, then over the Atlantic in my suitcase to Moscow, then to Novosibirsk, and finally hauled by Kamaz here to Kentau. I could see that this little car couldn't have found a more appreciative owner if it had traveled twice the distance.

"Go ahead, open it," I repeated.

"How?"

"Just tear it open," I said, reaching my hand down to show him.

"No." He pulled the car protectively to his chest to prevent me from tearing open the plastic and cardboard casing. Stasik spun around to his table and grabbed what looked like a clay-covered fingernail file. Like a surgeon with a scalpel he carefully separated the cardboard panel from the plastic casing. Once he finished his incision, he delicately extricated the car and carefully placed the packaging down on the table as if it were a diamond tiara.

Turning the car over and over, he inspected it thoroughly. He gasped with excitement when he noticed the indented shapes of the muffler, exhaust system, and both front and rear axles cast into the metal on the bottom of the car. This encouraged him to look for more details that only this master of miniature could fully appreciate. He joyfully showed me that the doors had handles carved into them. Even the plastic windshield, much to Stasik's delight, had the shape of a rearview mirror in the center.

He hadn't once placed it on the table or floor to take it for a test drive. He looked in through the driver's side window. "There is a steering wheel in there."

"What? Let me see," I said.

After a moment of hesitation, he handed the little car to me. I opened the door to get a better look.

Stasik screamed.

In a flash, he grabbed the car from my hands and ran toward the kitchen, "MOM! THE DOORS OPEN! THE DOORS OPEN!"

Nuria, hearing her son's screams, rushed from the kitchen with a spatula in her hand. They crashed into each other in the doorway.

"Oooff. Slow down. What's wrong, Stas?" Nuria asked, getting down on her knees to put her hands on her son's shoulders.

"The doors open! The doors open! Look!" he said, opening the passenger side door with a giggle.

"Oh, Lord. Don't scare me like that," she said. "Where did you get that?"

Already walking back in my direction, Stasik answered, "Dyadya Shura gave it to me."

I looked at Nuria and nodded.

She returned a soft smile, got up, and headed back to the kitchen. I sat back down on the couch. Stasik sat down next to me. He giggled every time he opened and closed the doors.

Sasha and a tall, smiling young girl walked into the room. She was the awkwardly beautiful, early pubescent reflection of her mother.

"Sanya, this is Ahsya," Sasha began the introductions, "Ahsya, this is Alexander. You can call him *dyadya* Shura."

"Are you really from America?" Ahsya asked me to make sure that her real dyadya had not been playing another one of his jokes on her.

"I'm afraid so," I said.

"Why did you leave America to come here?"

"Honey, it's not polite to be so curious," Nuria's voice came from the kitchen.

"*Mom*," Ahsya whined her rebellious displeasure.

"I don't mind," I said. "Because, Ahsya, life is more interesting for me here than in America."

"God. This place is so boring. You're crazy."

"Ahsya!" Nuria rebuked her daughter.

"Well, it's true. You'd have to be crazy to leave America for this place," Ahsya declared. Suddenly embarrassed, she put her hands over her mouth and looked at me, "Oh, I'm sorry, Dyadya Shura. I didn't mean it like that. I don't think *you* are crazy. It's just that..."

"Look, Ahsya, the doors open," Stasik showed his sister his new car.

"Cool. Very cool, Stas," his sister said with polite interest.

"How about we take some pictures?" I asked.

Ahsya's eyes lit up.

"Good idea, Sanya. Get that fancy camera of yours," Sasha said, giving me a smile and a nod.

"Mom! Come in here. We're going to take pictures," Ahsya cried with excitement.

"Oh lord, and I'm such a mess," Nuria said. Without even looking, I knew that she was fixing her hair in the kitchen just like Ahsya was doing in front of the little mirror hanging on the wall.

"Mamechka, can I wear some of your lipstick?" Ahsya pleaded. "Please?"

A sharp "Nyet" came from the kitchen. "You're too young."

"But Mama," Ahsya whined, "I'm already fourteen."

"I know how old you are. I'm your mother. You already have earrings. That's enough."

"Look, there are handles on the insides of the doors," Stasik said, holding the car up for me to inspect.

"You notice everything, Stas," I said, messing up his hair with my hand. I sat on the couch and pulled the camera out from its case. Stasik rested his elbow on my leg.

"Stas, don't disturb Dyadya Shura. He has to get his camera ready," Ahsya nagged, her eyes locked onto my camera with the same intensity that her brother had for his toy car.

"It's ready to go. I've got seven more shots on this roll. Who's first?" I asked, as if there was any doubt.

After a moment of polite restraint, Ahsya cried, "Dyadya Shura, take a picture of just me."

"Daughter!" Mother banged a spoon against a pot.

"Mother!" Daughter stomped her foot.

Ahsya then turned to me. "I'll sit here in this chair. Is that okay? What about the light? Isn't it too dark in here?"

"Nope." I pushed the yellow button on the camera. The flash bulb popped up like a jack-in-the-box. Ahsya let out a delighted squeal.

I took two pictures of Ahsya. She claimed that she had closed her eyes in the first one. Then I took a couple family photos of the trio and one with Sasha and his relatives. Sasha insisted that I be in at least one picture. I handed Sasha the camera and sat on the couch. Stasik hopped onto my lap. Sasha aimed the camera at us. Nuria aimed her stoic gaze at the camera. Ahsya tried to make her girlish grin look as mature as possible and Stasik held his toy car up with both doors open for the camera to see.

With one frame left on the roll, I set the camera on the table, lined it up and pressed the delay button. I ran to the couch and squeezed in with everyone, frozen with excitement and anticipation. We all held our breaths. *Click.* Everybody let out a burst of relieved laughter, everyone except Nuria.

Nuria got up and called us into the kitchen where we sat around the small table. Stasik sat on my lap, driving his car between the plates and cups like a grand-prix racer through narrow city streets, until his mother tenderly asked him to drive somewhere else.

When Sasha pulled out one of his many remaining bottles of Terminator Vodka, I expected Nuria to protest. She didn't. When Sasha poured three shot glasses, I expected Nuria to refuse hers. She didn't. After Sasha's toast to everyone's health, I expected Nuria to politely take a sip. Instead, Nuria sighed and tossed the whole shot down.

"What about me, Mama? Can I try?" Ahsya asked.

"*No!*"

"Let her have a sip," Sasha said, giving Nuria a wink.

Nuria looked at her cousin for a few seconds. A tiny smile cracked her granite face.

Sasha poured a quarter shot glass of vodka for Ahsya and then refilled our three glasses to the rim.

"If you're going to drink, Ahsenka, you have to say a toast." Sasha raised his glass and looked at Ahsya. "Come on. The toast is yours."

"To Mama," Ahsya said with unexpected diplomacy.

Nuria didn't smile or drink. Sasha and I tossed ours back, then watched as Ahsya cautiously drank hers as if it were scalding tea. She held it in her mouth with a pained expression on her face. Her eyes squinted shut.

As she swallowed, Ahsya opened her eyes wide and frantically waved her hands in front of her mouth. She coughed sharply. Tears welled up in her eyes. "Fooooo! That's awful! Why do you drink this stuff? I'm never drinking vodka again." She washed it down with an entire glass of red juice.

Sasha turned to Nuria and gave her a second wink. Nuria smiled and even let a tiny laugh escape. She shook her head and squeezed Sasha's hand in gratitude. Sasha leaned over and kissed his cousin on the forehead.

We munched on salads of tomatoes, cucumbers, and herbs.

When the phone rang, Ahsya jumped to attention and darted to answer it.

"Some boy has been calling her for the past few weeks. She stays at home all day after school hoping he'll call," Ahsya's mother explained.

"*Dyevushki* (girls)," Stasik said, rolling his eyes as he drove his car up my arm and down my back.

Ahsya returned after a minute with a disappointed look on her face, "That was Baba Masha. She wants you guys to go home. She says it's getting late."

We drank one for the road. In strong contrast to our arrival, Stasik was smiling like a boy and waving good-bye to us. Ahsya sent us off with a smile. Nuria, too, perhaps from the vodka, had a slight glimmer of cheer in her face. But the empty, stoic expression that greeted us just over an hour ago was making a strong comeback. When the door shut, I was overwhelmed with sadness.

As Sasha and I stepped out into the dark streets, I grabbed him by the arm and asked, "Where is Nuria's husband? Their dad?"

"He died this spring of stomach cancer."

27
Wounded Eternity

We woke in the numb hours that separate late night from early morning, rolled up the blankets and mattresses, and quietly abandoned the apartment. There were no tears. This family found warmth, safety, and occasional joy within the protecting walls of this apartment for decades. But after Kamil shut the door behind him, the apartment was forgotten. The past was irrelevant. The future was uncertain. Only the challenges of the present mattered.

The Kamaz coughed to life, grumbled erratically for a few seconds, and then growled its readiness to move. Like train passengers hearing the whistle of the locomotive, Sasha and I ran to take our places in the Kamaz. Directly behind the Kamaz, Kamil's car looked like a baby elephant following its enormous mother. We drove out of the courtyard into the empty streets. Within minutes, we were surrounded by black desert. Kentau, once a thriving mining town, now, since the free market had caused the inefficient mine to close down, was doomed. Sasha's parents had spent almost all of their lives here. Now they were fleeing to the relative prosperity of Siberia.

We reached Victor Mikhailovich's apartment in the evening.

Baba Masha tried to help out in the kitchen, but she was sent back to the table to *enjoy* herself. Unaccustomed to enjoying herself, she uneasily took a seat as if it were a dentist's chair. There were only two toasts, one from Sasha's father and one from his father-in-law; both toasts were about the blessings of family. Prolonged nods of approval followed each toast, then the awkward silence resumed.

"I got through to Lyuda on the telephone yesterday," Victor Mikhailovich suddenly said.

Everyone turned to him with desperate interest.

"Sasha, she expects you to try and call her tomorrow." Victor looked at his son-in-law. "She's worried. I told her everything was okay. But she wants you to call anyway."

Sasha nodded.

"Victor Mikhailovich, how is our granddaughter?" Kamil asked with a smile.

Victor Mikhailovich put his fork down as a big smile stretched across his face. "Ohhh. Little Alinechka even talked with me for a minute before she got too shy. She calls me *dyedushka* Vitya."

Everybody laughed and looked at Sasha. He was wearing a proud smile.

Victor Mikhailovich suddenly looked at his watch, got up from the table, and flicked on the television. The chaos in Moscow must have resolved itself because CNN was gone. *Simplamente Maria* had recaptured her regular time slot. All heads turned to the glowing box.

I looked at Sasha across the table. He shrugged his shoulders, then poured vodka into two shot glasses.

Sergei put a third glass directly in front of Sasha. Sasha looked at him with confusion. Sergei nodded and pointed to the shot glass. "We're not leaving until the day after tomorrow, right?"

"That's right. Tomorrow we have to get mama on an airplane and pick up the rest of the potato money from Genady," Sasha said.

"Then fill 'er up," Sergei said with a nod.

Sasha smiled and poured the vodka into the third glass. Instead of a toast, Sasha just winked.

Victor Mikhailovich heckled and laughed as he watched the Mexican soap opera with Russian voice-overs. Sasha's mother and mother-in-law took turns gasping in disgust and sighing with delight. Kamil watched with a contented smile. Sasha, Sergei, and I ate our plates clean and refilled them again with spicy carrot salad, heaps of mashed potatoes, and pucks of meat. Occasional vodka shots punctuated the boredom.

"Want a beer?" Sasha asked as he put the empty vodka bottle on the floor. "There are some bottles left in the Kamaz."

Sergei got up and went out with us.

Even though it was late in the evening, the courtyard was full of life. A man had his head under the hood of his car. Another man stood next to him, pointing a flashlight into the automobile's open mouth. Two old men on a bench loudly slurred the words to songs that caused them to alternate between laughing, swearing, and sobbing. In a dark corner, a group of young men talked in hushed voices; their cigarettes danced around in the dark like fireflies glowing brightly whenever one of them took a drag. In the center of the courtyard, two boys fed trash into a small fire.

After opening a bottle on the metal step of the Kamaz, Sasha passed it around. We each took a few swigs before passing it on. We emptied the bottle before it had made two cycles. Sasha flicked the remaining foam out of the bottle with a snap of his wrist and then tossed the empty bottle into nearby bushes.

"We got any more potato chips?" I asked.

Sasha's eyes lit up. "Beer and potato chips, just like in America."

"They're in a box behind my seat," Sergei said.

After Sasha retrieved the box of potato chips, he opened another bottle of beer and passed it around. The bag of chips followed the bottle around the circle.

A young couple walked by arm in arm. The girl's high-heeled shoes ground the thick layer of Soviet-city grit into the concrete sidewalk.

A woman's voice called out, "Ksssss, ksssss, ksssss, kssss. *Domoi* (home). Ksssss, kssss, ksssss."

Scurrying out from bushes and shadows, a dozen cats converged just underneath the woman's window. The woman held a towel out the window. The cats jumped up and sank their claws into the towel. The woman pulled the towel up and the cats, like fish in a net, came with it, two and three at a time. After the woman hauled in the last cat, she shut the window. Minutes later, the apartment went dark.

"Evening," a voice came from out of the darkness. We turned to see a Kazakh man approach. He was wearing a dirty shirt and frayed pants. A streak of grease ran across his forehead. A cigarette dangled precariously from his lower lip. After wiping his hand on his pant leg, he reached out to shake our hands.

"You don't have a wrench I could borrow, do ya? I've been working on that damn car all day. Just a few things to tighten up and I'll be done."

I looked over at the car in the far corner. The man with the flashlight stood alone.

"How'd you get things loosened without a wrench?" Sergei asked.

"Had to swear a lot," the man said.

Sergei asked, "What's wrong with it?"

"Nothing anymore; carburetor was running lean. Car kept dying on me whenever I came to a stop," the Kazakh explained.

"So, don't stop," Sergei said.

The Kazakh puffed a smoky laugh through his nose, "Can't help it. Fixed the brakes last week. Stopping is all that car does well."

Sergei nodded, then asked, "Spare a cigarette?"

With the back of his greasy hand, the Kazakh pushed up a box of cigarettes in his breast pocket. Grabbing the box with the other hand, he held it out to Sergei.

Sergei grabbed a cigarette and put it in his mouth.

"What kind of wrench do you need?" Sergei asked as he put on his canvas jacket. From underneath his seat, Sergei pulled out a leather pouch that clinked with metal contents. He walked with the man over to the car.

The waning moon, just a sliver now, floated above the concrete apartment building.

"It looks like a Muslim tombstone, and they look like corpses," Sasha said, looking in the window on the first floor of the apartment building. The television cast a blue glow over his extended family. They wore cold stares on their numb faces.

Sergei returned and put his leather pouch back under his seat. "Fixed?" I asked.

Sergei nodded.

"He didn't privatize any of your tools, did he?" Sasha asked.

"That's why I went over there to *help*."

"Come on. The show should be ending soon," Sasha said, tossing the fifth empty bottle into the bushes.

When we entered the apartment, the soap opera was over and, as always, everybody was in a foul mood. The glamour of a Mexican soap opera may have provided a temporary escape from the monotonous struggle of ordinary life in the former Soviet Union, but when the show was over, the return to reality was as pleasant as is the return to sobriety for an alcoholic. Being the only representative of the Western Hemisphere, I had to bear the brunt of their bad moods.

"Why do you make these shows, anyway?" Baba Masha complained. "They aren't anything like real life. Not a bit."

"That's the point," I said. "It's an escape from reality."

"What's the point of art if it doesn't imitate reality?" Victor Mikhailovich threw his hands into the air, disgusted.

"I wouldn't exactly classify a Mexican soap opera as art."

The next day, while Sasha and Victor took Baba Masha to the airport and collected the remaining money from Genady, Sergei grew noticeably anxious. He went over the Kamaz half a dozen times, kicking tires, checking cables, tightening bolts. When he couldn't find anything broken, he simply looked harder.

28
Nightmare

The next morning, Victor Mikhailovich escorted us out of town. We said our good-byes on the shoulder of the road leading north.

"Thanks, Victor Mikhailovich. Thanks for your hospitality," I said, then suddenly remembered a Russian proverb. "A home is beautiful not by comforts, but by hospitality. You have a beautiful home."

Victor Mikhailovich grabbed my hand, shook it, then pulled me down and kissed my cheeks.

As we began to pick up speed, I reset my internal clock. It was time to forget about minutes and hours. Only distance had meaning now. I removed the watch from my wrist and slipped it into the pocket of my leather jacket.

We were back on the asphalt river that ran through the dry steppe north to Siberia. The buildings clinging to the sandy shoulder gradually disappeared. The horizon stretched out in all directions.

"American truck drivers are really rich, aren't they?" Sergei asked after several hundred kilometers of silence.

"I've never heard of a millionaire who made his fortune driving a truck."

"But those big trucks can haul more in one trip than I can in four. American truck drivers don't have to waste a lot of time repairing their trucks or looking for cargo. Besides, they don't have to pay bribes to the GAI or other bandits. How can they not make fortunes?"

"I don't know, Seryoga. Maybe they do make a lot of money. But those big rigs are pretty expensive."

"How expensive?" Sergei asked, trying to determine how much his eighteen-wheel dream would cost.

"About one hundred thousand dollars," I said, holding my shoes out the window to dump out the sand from the last bathroom break.

"So, let me get this straight. In order to get rich, I have to be rich," Sergei said with disgust. "Where does the first one hundred thousand come from?" Sergei sucked on his cigarette.

The little orange car raced by us.

"What the hell has gotten into Kamil?" Sergei asked, sitting up and grabbing the steering wheel with both hands.

The red brake lights went on and the orange car started coming back toward us. Sergei hit the brakes.

"What the hell?"

We came to a stop.

Sasha got out. He started walking back toward us with an odd expression on his face. Once he reached the back of the car, he turned. He put his hands on the trunk.

"What does he need in there?" Sergei asked, reaching his hand out the window to tap the gray ashes off the end of his cigarette.

We both watched with interest.

Sasha began to push the car.

"Oh, shit." Sergei said, reaching for the handle on his door.

As I saw Sasha dig in for traction, I began to laugh. "Nothing's wrong."

"Then what is he doing pushing the car?" Sergei's door was already open and he had one leg dangling down.

I savored the rare occasion when I knew something that Sergei didn't, then answered just before he jumped down. "He's just thanking the car for the first hundred thousand kilometers."

A white concrete statue of a horse stood on the side of the road.

"What is with those white animal figures?" I asked Sergei. "Every hundred kilometers or so, there is a statue of a goat or a deer or a horse. What's up with that?"

"The nomads here think they guard the road," Sergei said as he shifted gears, accelerating after Sasha's sentimental pit stop.

"Guard the road from what?"

Sergei didn't answer.

"Sergei, are you happy?" I asked.

"What kind of question is that?"

"A simple question."

After taking his time to light up a cigarette, he finally said, "A friend of mine moved to Germany a few years ago. He came back for a visit this summer." Sergei took a deep drag and blew it out. "You know what he said?"

I waited.

"He said that Russians are the happiest people on the planet—Russians have no idea how poor they are. He said 'Russians' and not 'we.' He wasn't a Russian anymore. He knew how poor we are. He wasn't happy anymore."

The sun set several hundred kilometers later. Sergei stopped the Kamaz across the road from a dark, one-story building that looked abandoned. In front of us was the Soviet version of a service station: a pair of concrete planks on top of concrete pillars with concrete ramps on either end. Do-it-yourselfers (a prerequisite for being a Russian truck driver) maneuvered their vehicles up onto these planks to get a look at the underside of their ailing vehicles.

Out here there were no lights, no dark silhouettes of church steeples or water towers, not even a row of telephone poles. The land was a perfect plane, as featureless as the ocean after dusk. I could hear the occasional whinnies from a herd of horses in the distance. Although there was no wind, it was noticeably cool. We had been driving due north all day. We were driving toward winter; every hundred kilometers saw the thermometers dip a few degrees. I zipped up my leather jacket. Impatient stars were already piercing through the day's retreating glow. High in the sky, thin horsetail clouds bled deep red from the last light of the sun now far below the horizon.

I grabbed Sasha's arm. "Let's go for a walk."

The dry grass crunched under our feet. We walked in no particular direction. There were no fences to stop us.

When we turned around, I could barely see the tiny black silhouette of the Kamaz in the violet western sky.

"Ooooooooaoaaaaagghhhh!" Sasha whispered a reverent yawp as if we were in a mosque.

Surrounded by nothing, we stood for a moment of placeless, timeless awe.

"It's funny," I whispered. "Lots of people are scared by places like this. What are they afraid of?"

"The scariest thing about solitude," Sasha said with the certainty of someone who had grown up in a desert town, "is that you have to live with yourself."

"Not something you have to worry about anymore," I said. "Where are you going to put your parents anyway?"

"In the cottage," Sasha said, referring to the four brick walls he'd bought in the suburbs.

"Really? That place doesn't have any heat or water yet. Or does it?"

"Nope. It still doesn't have anything yet," Sasha said. "It's still just a shell, but if things keep going well for us..." Sasha superstitiously spit three times over his shoulder so as not to jinx our good fortune, "I'll be able to afford finishing it. Hopefully they'll be able to move in by next summer."

"And until then?"

"They'll live with us in the apartment," Sasha declared with a sigh. The gravity of his predicament was starting to weigh on him. "Lyuda won't like it. I think she'd rather I got a second wife instead of bringing my mother to live in our apartment. According to Muslim law, I'm allowed to have up to four wives, but I have to keep them in different houses. Fortunately, Muslim law doesn't forbid me from having my mother and wife live under the same roof."

"Allah probably didn't forbid it because he didn't think anybody would be crazy enough to try it."

"Probably." Sasha laughed. "Hopefully it will just be for the winter."

Just one winter, I thought—one, long, dark, Siberian winter. I felt sorry for my friend. I also felt glad about my job again. It wasn't as fun as it was in the beginning. But now I knew that any profits Sasha got out of our business would go toward promoting domestic tranquillity. If anybody needed a house in the suburbs, it was Sasha. I was glad to be able to help.

When we walked back to the truck, we heard an unfamiliar voice.

"Sure. That's what the generator is for. I don't turn it on much anymore. They stopped delivering diesel. Not enough money, they tell me. I turn the generator on once a day, when they show *Simplamente Maria.*"

Having heard the title of his favorite soap opera, Kamil suddenly perked up. "Did Juan Carlos finally ask Maria to marry him?"

Sasha and I walked around the Kamaz to find a wrinkled man standing with Sergei and Kamil.

"No," the wrinkled man said with disappointment. Then he looked suddenly anxious, "I think he is going to do it tonight. What if she says no? Last night she saw Juan Carlos dancing with his sister-in-law."

Kamil jumped in, "But Maria doesn't know that that woman was his sister-in-law. She thought that he loved her."

"He's going to ask her tonight," the wrinkled man repeated.

"Tonight? Do you think so?" Kamil seemed genuinely alarmed.

"Dad. We're not going to stay and watch Maria," Sasha warned as we joined the circle of men. We shook the old man's hand.

"I know. I know," Kamil said quietly, almost to himself. "I just hope your mother is watching in Novosibirsk."

Sasha laughed. "Don't worry, Lyuda wouldn't miss it for anything. I'm sure all three generations will be planted in front of the television tonight."

Sergei bartered some of the diesel fuel in his mammoth gas tank for the use of the man's acetylene torch. The wrinkled man got to run the generator so he could watch his soap opera, Sergei was able to repair the Kamaz's brakes which, he said, felt a little soft. The free market strikes again.

We drove on for another fifty clicks on the odometer.

Up in the distance, I could see the rear end of a horse slowly walking across the road and out into the darkness on the other side. Years of driving on roads spotted with deer have taught me to fear running into large animals. But that was not a lone buck deer. It was a horse. I had never seen a lone horse in Kazakhstan. They were always in herds.

My heart surged in anticipation as I turned my head to the right. The head of a mare came out of the night, crossing our path.

"*Smotri* (look out)," I said calmly, trying not to startle Sergei into a violent swerve.

Sergei made no correction in steering, nor did he slow down. The mare, seemingly oblivious to the several tons of steel coming at her with deadly speed, continued to saunter onto the road. The head of the horse was now connected to a body. Unless we changed our course…

"*Smotri!*" I said, this time loudly.

As the distance between us and the suicidal horse dwindled, my perception of speed became terrific. The horse was now directly in front of me. Its color went from dark brown, to light brown, to a brilliant tan in the beams of the fast approaching headlights. Sergei hadn't reacted at all. He was looking out his side window. We were going to hit.

"*SMOTRI!*" I yelled, as the horse disappeared under the dashboard.

In an instant, the window filled with cracks, warm liquid splattered onto my face, and my door flung open. Sergei slammed on the recently repaired brakes. They worked all too well, hurling me against the dashboard.

We came to a complete stop in the middle of the road. All was silent, except for the engine's steady growl.

I jumped down out of my already open door and walked into the headlights to see if I was covered in horse blood. I was covered in water. I sniffed my sleeve. It smelled like window cleaner. The windshield fluid reservoir, located down by my feet, must have exploded on impact.

Sasha and Kamil stopped right behind us. I walked back toward them. The air reeked of shit. I paused for a moment. *I hadn't been that scared*, I thought to myself.

Sasha got out of the car and asked what happened.

"We hit a horse. I'm going to make sure that it's dead."

"If it isn't, put it out of its misery. Cut its throat with your knife. But stay away from its hooves. I'll go check on Sergei," Sasha said, heading for the tempest of foul language coming from the front of the Kamaz.

In the total darkness, I stumbled into the horse's carcass about fifty feet behind the Kamaz. Eventually, after my eyes adjusted to the darkness, I could make out the horse's shape. In the glow of the distant vehicles' taillights, the tan horse glowed red, the red of someone's cheek with a flashlight in his mouth. I felt the mammal's neck. It was warm, but I couldn't find a pulse. I didn't really know where to find it. So I put my hand in front of its nose to feel for any breathing. Nothing. I snapped my knife closed and put it back in my pocket.

"What were you thinking? How could you not have seen us?" I scolded the carcass.

The sound of hooves clopping across the road in the darkness reminded me that I was not alone. I wasn't sure whether horses are vindictive animals, but I decided not to find out. I quickly walked back to the truck.

Sergei was still fuming. He walked into the darkness screaming obscenities. His anger was further fueled by the irony of successfully repairing the brakes but failing to use them.

"Poor, Seryoga," Sasha quietly said. "Driving is his life. He had a perfect driving record...till now. This has got to hurt."

After a long while, Sergei cooled down enough to start going over the damage to the Kamaz. This didn't raise his spirits. With each new discovery, Sergei erupted with more obscenities. A broken headlight, a severely cracked windshield and a mangled radiator cage scarred the Kamaz's face. My door exploded open when the horse's impact deformed the cabin, making the door a square peg in its own frame. The engine, fortunately, seemed unharmed. Sergei suddenly became dead calm when he discovered that the battery, mounted on the backside of the cab, was split open at the bottom.

Little drops of acid fell into a large puddle below the battery's cracked shell.

The entire side of the Kamaz was covered with horse manure and partially digested grass. Apparently, we hit the head and barrel chest of the horse, folding his rear end around the front corner of the Kamaz. All of the grass that the horse had consumed over the past few days was forced out the usual exit hole with unusual speed, caking the side of the truck with foul goo.

"We saw your brake lights go on, and suddenly we were skidding on a slippery layer of shit. I didn't even see the horse's body," Sasha recalled, chuckling a little. "By the way, Sanya, did you find him?"

"Yeah. Dead. Very dead."

"Damn shame," Sergei said, "It wasn't his fault. Why don't these damn nomads put up some fences!"

"Sergei, can the Kamaz keep moving?" Sasha asked.

"I don't know. Maybe. I can't turn off the engine until we get back to Novosibirsk. With a dry battery, I'll never get it started again."

"Come on, then. Let's get going. There's nothing we can do here."

As we got back into our vehicles, I noticed a concrete statue of a horse guarding the road, but from what?

The Kamaz was wounded, but not fatally. It could still go forward at half speed. It wasn't the engine that slowed us. The engine was willing; the body wasn't. If Sergei drove any faster than 70 kilometers an hour, the cracked windshield and deformed cabin began to rattle and shake, threatening to fall to pieces entirely.

Sergei was determined not to let any of his driving buddies back in Siberia find out about the accident. When the sun had climbed above the horizon the next morning, while the rest of us ate hard-boiled eggs and tea on the side of the road, Sergei examined his damaged truck. The rage had faded. He had become very pragmatic, making a list of the parts he'd need. The quest for parts became his primary mission. Getting back to Novosibirsk was now of secondary importance. We stopped at almost every gas station (fortunately, there weren't that many) so that Sergei could buy spare parts from the other truck drivers. By the time we got to the Russian border, Sergei had repaired the most obvious damage. Both head-lights worked again. We had a new fender. The passenger side door still wouldn't latch shut on its own, but he managed to tie it shut with some rope. Ever-colder air whistled through the loose seal as we made slow progress north. For two days we limped along, breath-ing the fumes of the other trucks and cars that passed us by as if we were standing still.

We crossed the bridge over the Berd River just after sunrise, two weeks to the day after we had crossed it on our way south. Minutes later we turned onto a side road that led to our little town nestled in the birch forest. Sergei parked the Kamaz outside Sasha's apartment building. Kamil pulled up alongside the Kamaz and shut off his engine. Sasha stepped out of the little car with a sleep-wrinkled face. "Sibir," he said as he zipped up his jacket. There were patches of snow in the building's shadow.

Soon the apartment building's door swung open as Lyuda came bursting out. Apparently, a few days with her mother-in-law had made Lyuda appreciate her husband more. At least it did in the short run. Alina came out the door screaming with delight. It seems that grandma had been conducting too many Tatar lessons for Alina's comfort. Alina, too, was giddy to see Sasha. Sasha caught his wife as she jumped into his arms. His daughter crashed into his legs and hugged them tightly.

"Alina, don't run," Baba Masha yelled down from seventh-floor window. "You'll fall and hurt yourself."

Kamil smiled as he put his hand on his granddaughter's head and rustled her hair. With the other hand he waved up to his wife.

"Come on up for tea," Lyuda said to everyone while she clung to her husband with both hands.

"I'm going home to my family," Sergei said.

Instead of feeling the relief of being home, I felt lonely. Coming home is what makes a journey complete, makes it worthwhile. But my homecoming felt empty. I had nobody to come home to.

29
Cosmetic Changes

My recent homecoming compelled me to commit the most common, most pathetic mistake of the lonely guy; I called my ex-girlfriend. Katya seemed neither angry nor pleased to hear from me. Typical. Her emotional even keel, something that would have driven me crazy if we were still going out, now gave me encouragement. Since she didn't seem to have the urge to verbally lash me for breaking up with her, I decided to ask her to lunch. She accepted. When I hung up the phone, I felt ambivalent, a kind of nauseous relief.

I met her at her new job in the gift shop of the hotel Sibir, the most luxurious hotel in town. She gave me a nod of recognition when I walked in. I tried not to betray the contradictory swill of emotions inside me. Being in her presence made me weak. And the weakness made me want to be with her all the more.

We ate at the hotel's restaurant. She looked lovelier than ever in her baggy black sweater with little purple beads sewn into the reflective fabric. It was a tacky little number, but it made her cream-colored face shine brightly. Her dark brown eyes were as enigmatic as ever. God, she was beautiful. It was all I could do to not ask her to take me back. She talked about work and about her parents, who, by the way, said hi. Not only was Katya not angry with me, her parents also seemed to harbor no animosity toward me.

I made it through lunch without giving in to my weaker instincts. I wasn't going to go back. It was over, and rightfully so. Katya, the woman I had worshiped from afar for years, simply wasn't the girl for me. Just because I was lonely didn't change that. It was over. We were over. I kissed Katya on the cheek after our lunch date and left. I felt relieved. I felt single.

I suddenly found myself looking at the women around me in a new light. I knew that all Siberian women were not desperate gold diggers. Surely there was one out there who would see past my passport and find something lovable. But just as I was reassessing the qualities of Siberian women, these very same women were reassessing their own deficiencies. Glossy women's magazines from America appeared in the windows of the neighborhood newspaper kiosks. The first few magazines were in English and several months out of date. An enterprising entrepreneur was probably making a handsome profit buying for pennies unsold magazines headed for the recycling plants in America, shipping them to Russia, and selling them for the equivalent of about one dollar. Demand was high for these handheld windows onto the world of Western beauty.

The combination of high demand and low supply always manifests itself in high profits. And high profits always encourage imitation, which leads to increased supply. Sure enough, recognizing the potential profit to be made selling images of supermodels to Russian women, Western glamour magazines soon opened offices in Moscow and began printing Russian versions of their glossy periodicals.

As I sat drinking tea one evening at Sasha's, Lyuda thumbed through the pages of the latest Russian version of *Cosmopolitan*. She treated it like a book, to be read from cover to cover, one page at a time. She didn't skim or flip past anything, not even the advertisements. The advertisements were enjoyed purely for their entertainment value since most of the products they pushed were unavailable in the Siberian market. With each turn of the page, Lyuda would ask me about whether women in America liked this kind of facial cream or shampoo, this brand of mascara or lipstick. I fielded her questions with the aplomb of Dan Quayle at a press conference. "Oh, I don't know. Er, ah, yeah. Well, maybe. I guess so. Sure."

But the advertisements were soon not just for entertainment value. The advent of *Cosmopolitan*'s Russian version marked the opening of the floodgates of consumer products directed toward the

Russian woman. There was one product that quickly saturated the entire Russian market, including Siberia: Tampax tampons. They became so ubiquitous that a joke was quickly coined, a joke that Sasha loved to tell.

"Masha, have you tried Tampax?" Masha's girlfriend asks. Masha replies somewhat apathetically, "Yeah, but I prefer Snickers."

Playboy was next to come out with a Russian version of its magazine, including pictures of Russian girls posing in exotic locations. Seeing their own countrywomen sprawled naked across fuzzy green billiard tables or on white sandy beaches seemed to inspire a powerful combination of hope and envy in Siberian women. Siberian women bought up the copies of *Playboy* before Siberian men even got a chance. The cigar and whiskey ads were lost on these women who learned the art of flipping from photo spread to photo spread, admiring the clothes that quickly fell off the lovely and still silicone-free bodies of the Russian models.

Slowly but surely, the myriad images of skinny women on the pages of these magazines inculcated these Siberian women with the often contradictory Western ideal of both thin and buxom beauty. It was a look that was nearly impossible for American women to emulate without surgery or eating disorders. Just as Russian women were getting the news that skinny was sexy, another import from the West arrived: fatty snack foods.

Colorful bags filled with air and potato chips of every flavor—dill, chives, BBQ, vinegar, and even pork—soon hung like drying laundry on ropes behind the windows of the kiosks. These greasy snacks, combined with the ever-increasing amounts of chocolate, both foreign and domestic, started to expand the Siberian woman's figure, and not in the most flattering places.

Our company was starting to feel a little bloated too. We fired the two secretaries who talked all day but only to each other and never to any of our customers or clients. We hired Irina as our new *referent*. On her first day of work, she promptly kicked Sasha and me out of our own offices and locked herself in. All day, odd sounds came from behind the door.

"Are you okay?" we asked after an especially loud clatter.

"Go away," is all she said.

When she finally let us back in at the end of the day, we didn't recognize the place. Actually, I recognized it. It was an office—a place of business, and not just a busy mess.

"Looks matter," she said. "If the office doesn't look professional, then it isn't professional." She made it clear that she was our teacher and we were her students. It was all we could do to not say "yes'm" after her every comment.

So that we could attend to matters of importance, Irina screened calls with unerring judgment. She made sure that we signed all necessary documents before we left for the day. In short, she became indispensable. We paid her twice as much as we paid the previous two secretaries combined, and she was worth every ruble.

One day after we were left stranded in the city because both of our Russian cars broke down, Sasha picked up the phone and called a former classmate, now living in St. Petersburg. Sasha's classmate sold used Swedish cars. Within two weeks, we were driving, or rather, being driven around Novosibirsk in, a Saab 9000 Turbo.

Zhenya had been complaining that the chocolate business was taking money away from the language program, and he was right. So, to square the chocolate department's debt before the language department, Sasha gave the two broken Russian cars to Zhenya. This infuriated Zhenya, who threatened to take the language program away altogether. He threatened to secede. For the most part, Sasha ignored Zhenya and his threats. The chocolate business generated ten times as much revenue as the language program. If the language program and all its employees split off, it would simplify things, and not significantly hurt the bottom line.

Along with all these changes, I noticed a subtler, but far more significant change—rather than chasing the opportunities, the opportunities now chased us. They just fell into our laps. Strange people came to our submarine with get-rich-quick schemes. It was our job to sort through them and choose which ones actually had potential. It seemed as if every scientist in the cash-poor research institutes all around town was trying to turn his particular and often peculiar knowledge into something marketable. We were bombarded with bizarre proposals, everything from selling Siberian snake venom to marketing a pen that wrote in different colors depending on how hard you pressed it to the paper. I considered most of the ideas to be absurd. But I held out hope of finding something that could find a market abroad. I wanted to balance out our import business with some exports.

Sasha, however, was more intrigued by another potential import. There was equipment available in Holland—or so promised the brochure brought in by a young Russian entrepreneur—that could mix paint to perfectly match any color. The young man said that with Siberians buying more and more Western cars, there would be a rising demand for custom-mixed paint to cover up the inevitable scratches and dings received on the wild Siberian roads. Sasha nodded as the man made his pitch. Our Saab did have several dings on its blue hood that hadn't been there last week. After a little deliberation, we ordered the equipment.

Another idea that just wouldn't go away, despite Sasha's best efforts, was his wife's beauty salon. Sasha dragged his heels as long as possible. He was convinced that it would be a financial fiasco. Then we took a fateful trip to Moscow. Lyuda had made some phone calls and managed to get an appointment with a French company that was rapidly expanding its cosmetics business in Russia. Sasha gave his approval for Lyuda to fly to Moscow to see if she could become the French company's regional representative. Lyuda was afraid that she'd blow the deal because she lacked business experience. She insisted that Sasha go with her. Sasha was afraid that his Russian business experience wouldn't be of any use with a French perfume company. He insisted that I go with him, not that I had any more experience with the French. Actually, Sasha was convinced that there wasn't any deal to blow, with or without experience. I, too, had my doubts. But we had to meet with Dmitri about future cocoa shipments anyway. So we all three flew to Moscow.

The meeting with the French company's representative was at the fanciest hotel in Moscow—but of course. The representative for the company, a French woman in her forties who spoke Russian with a thick French accent, boasted about the sales volume of just one of her Moscow stores. Sasha let out a skeptical laugh after hearing the huge figure. It rivaled our chocolate sales. Lyuda gave him a venomous glare, cutting Sasha's laughter off cold. After the meeting, Sasha and Lyuda argued for hours. Sasha remained skeptical that perfume and makeup could be such big business.

"I don't think it's going to work," Sasha said.

"I think you don't want it to work," Lyuda said. "You don't want your wife to work."

As much to save their marriage as to investigate a possible business opportunity, Sasha suggested we do some crude market analysis. We went to the very Moscow store that the French woman claimed sold such unbelievable amounts of beauty products. Sasha stood at the door and counted how many women came in each minute. I stood by the cash register and counted up the sales figures that lit up in little green lights. By our calculations, the French woman hadn't exaggerated. If anything, she had understated cash flow. There was a constant flow of women walking in the door, and more often than not, they left with something in a bright green plastic bag. Women forfeited wads of rubles willingly, eagerly, in exchange for some liquid, crème, powder, or spray.

Sasha was converted.

Within a month, the salon, located on Tereshkova Street, was open. We called it "Valentina" after Valentina Tereshkova, the world's first woman in space. The Chinese furniture, rugs, and mirrors proved to be of very poor quality, but they looked very Western. The decor, in itself, drew half of the clientele. The other half came for the verbal pampering they got from the sales women who were always, always, always polite. We paid them to be polite, and customers paid us to be served by these polite sales women.

In addition to cosmetics and perfume, the salon sold imported latex gloves for keeping a woman's newly manicured hands soft while she washed dishes, scrubbed floors, and peeled potatoes. Apparently no Russian woman was too beautiful for housework. One of the better-selling items took up only a tiny corner of the display case: condoms. Eight different varieties of condoms. Frequent customers received a few pieces of chocolate from the Novosibirsk Chocolate Factory.

This was little-luxury heaven.

As our business enterprises grew in scale and scope, it became harder and harder to remain in the attic of the university building. We had installed large radiators (at our own expense) to make the cold winter days bearable, but the corridor remained frigid. The blistering heat of summer, short as it was, forced us to install air conditioners in every room. I assumed that the market for air conditioners in Siberia was as weak as humidifiers in Seattle, but Sasha managed to find plenty of Polish air conditioners in the city. I had long ago learned not to underestimate both the diversity and absurdity of the Siberian market.

Another problem with the submarine was its limited space, not just vertical. For every unnecessary employee that we fired, we hired two more people who quickly became essential. People were crawling over each other. We didn't have enough telephones for everyone. And the crowds of foreign students learning Russian in Zhenya's language program created the atmosphere of an international youth hostel, not an international business.

Things became especially cramped whenever we had an office party, and Siberians had a one-word secret for how to party: often. There were plenty of excuses to celebrate, some good, some not so good. We celebrated them all. There were at least six official holidays when, instead of staying home from work, everybody went to work to have a food and alcohol orgy. In addition, birthdays had to be recognized with half-day feasts. Our submarine had a crew of more than thirty, which meant that hardly a week went by without an office party. Most parties ran late into the evening with plenty of singing, drinking, and other inappropriate office behavior. These were the days when I loved working in Siberia. The days that followed each mini Mardi Gras, however, made me want to have a regular American desk job, safe in a cubicle. During each party, our office shrank. What had been awkwardly cramped to work in became impossibly small to party in.

Zhenya provided the final straw to break the camel's back.

Ever since the debt-for-cars swap—a deal he understandably felt had been in our favor—he had been pursuing his secessionist plan. He told the rector of the university about our cocoa business, especially about the enormous amounts of money we were making. Proving that the Soviet culture of envy was far from dead, the rector decided that it was time for another redistribution of wealth. "After all," he said, "the rent I charge you for that outstanding office area is ridiculously low." The language program had a symbiotic relationship with the university—the university lent authority to the program and the program brought in foreign students, and money. They fed each other. What was symbiotic for Zhenya was parasitic for us. Being affiliated with the university brought us no gain. The chocolate factory directors weren't exactly impressed that our offices were in a university. They were producers, not professors. Sasha refused to pay more rent.

Rather than let Zhenya secede, we decided to beat him to the punch. It was time for us to leave the submarine.

We found an office building that was under construction. Actually, the construction had stopped due to insufficient funds. If we paid in advance, the owner of the unfinished building explained, we could rent the first two floors of the building, still only an empty shell. The floor plan looked perfect. There were twelve rooms, a six-car garage, and, best of all, ten-foot high ceilings. The clincher was that it had a conference hall that would serve as an excellent place to receive our respected guests and an even better place to have parties. We agreed and paid the advance. Construction resumed.

Another construction project began about the same time. With all their belongings locked into the basement of the brick house in the Siberian suburbs, Kamil and Baba Masha split up for the first time in decades. Kamil locked himself into the shell of the house;

he would work through the winter building stairs, putting up doors, and installing radiators. We had delivered as much building material as possible to Kamil before snow made the road impassable.

"Aren't you worried about him all alone out there?" I asked as we drove away in the Kamaz after making the last delivery of saws, wood, nails, and propane tanks.

"No," Sasha said. "You forget, my dad was a miner. He worked underground all his life. This will be a cinch for him. He's got a propane heater, electricity, and, most important, plenty of work to keep him busy. He'd die in a matter of days if he had nothing to do."

"What about food?"

"He's got enough food to last ten winters. Remember all those sacks of rice, and jars of fruits and vegetables that we loaded up in Kentau? That's all in the cellar. If anything, we're going to be coming to him for food. Just in case, I gave him some money. It's a twenty-minute walk to the *electrichka* (commuter train) and then one stop to Berdsk. He'll be able to buy bread, milk, and cheese there. If he wants, he can take the train to our village and visit us. But I don't expect we'll see him until springtime."

It was still fall in America, but winter had descended on Novosibirsk. I celebrated Thanksgiving by cooking two large geese that I bought from a burly woman at the city market. The entire American ghetto gathered at Sarah's. Twenty expats and their Russian friends crammed into the apartment that evening. As we ate the juicy goose meat, mashed potatoes and gravy, and canned wild mushrooms (courtesy of the Russians), the obvious parallels between us and the Mayflower Pilgrims were impossible to ignore. In a foreign land full of hardship and promise, we were glad to have friends.

We were thankful.

30 Weekend in Germany

Hyperinflation made a fool out of anyone who held money for even short periods of time. Money didn't burn holes in your pocket, but, sooner rather than later, money in your pocket did burn up. Legal tender went in and worthless ashes came out. Money in the bank, even if it was earning two, three, four, or even five hundred percent annual interest, met the same fate. If it didn't vanish overnight in one of the dozens of banks that were going belly-up like overfed goldfish, then it smoldered in a bank account, the impressive interest rates earning back only a portion of what was lost each week to rampant inflation. There was only one kind of money worth holding: other people's money.

Borrow today's rubles and pay debts with tomorrow's significantly less valuable rubles. While Americans were learning to surf the Net, Russians were learning to surf on debt. It was the only way not to get soaked by wave after wave of hyperinflation. Companies with huge accounts payables on their balance sheets were often in better financial shape than the companies with huge accounts receivables.

Frugality had become folly and borrowing was now a virtue. Accordingly, we spent much of our time trying to owe, rather than being owed. The only things that we still paid for in advance were the condoms and latex gloves. So, we decided that I should fly to Germany to renegotiate our relationship with our supplier. Getting to Germany—not separated from Siberia by a large body of water or a mighty mountain range, just incomprehensible distance—required two long flights. Or so I thought.

We had recently hired a woman, Lena, to become the in-house travel agent. Her primary task was to send the influential Siberians to Thailand, Turkey, Egypt, England, and, for the lucky few, America. When she wasn't sending executives, bankers, and "protectors" abroad, she put together tour packages for anybody willing and able to travel. When I told Lena that I needed to fly to Germany, she immediately went to work making phone calls. Within an hour, she wore a smug smile.

Lena had found a charter flight from Novosibirsk directly to Hanover, Germany. The German government, it turned out, chartered flights to repatriate the German war prisoners (and all of their descendants) that had been exiled to Siberia to be forgotten. The chartered planes were Russian, owned by a Russian company. If there were any extra seats on a flight, the Russian company auctioned them off and pocketed the profit. Lena managed to get me a ticket for $125. It wasn't exactly first-class flying, but I didn't have to switch planes in Moscow, and that alone was worth ten times the ticket price.

As I boarded the plane dressed in my business suit, I couldn't have looked more out of place with all of the haggard immigrant families. Rather than treat me with suspicion, however, these "Germans" treated me to one of the most festive flights I've ever been on. With their life possessions reduced to one suitcase per person, they remained generous almost to a fault, force-feeding me apples, sausage, bread, and salted fish, all pulled from purses, pockets, and even the inside of an old man's hat.

These merry Russian refugees sang songs and told jokes as they flew to their new lives as Germans. I couldn't help but suspect that this was the last happy day of their lives. They were about to learn just how poor they were.

I met Monika, the glove company's manager of sales for Eastern Europe and, almost as an afterthought, Russia. Monika had flown up from Munich to meet me, the mysterious American who kept buying enormous amounts of latex gloves for a Siberian town called Novosomethingorother. Monika had a cigarette-stained smile and a genuine laugh. I guessed that she was probably in her late forties, early fifties. After getting over the shock of how young I was, she said, "Zo, how do you like Siberia?" She didn't say it with any hint of sarcasm. "It must be great," she added, looking me straight in the eyes.

She knew. She understood.

I wasn't crazy. Or, if I was crazy, at least I wasn't alone in my insanity. There were others, like Sarah, and now Monika, who knew that comfort wasn't exempt from the law of supply and demand— the more comfort, the lower its value.

Monika and I talked for nearly an hour about the numerous joys of daily life in formerly communist countries. She really did understand. She had chosen to work in Russia and Eastern Europe because she understood. We eventually got down to discussing business: future orders, payment terms, transportation logistics, etc. She accepted my proposal to change payment terms for future glove and condom shipments. She granted us a ninety-day grace period from the day of shipment.

"I hope it will help you increase your sales volumes," she said.

"It certainly won't hurt."

"If you can increase volumes by another ten percent or so, I'll be able to justify a trip out to Siberia."

"I think we can manage that," I said.

"Good." She smiled. "I zo want to see the taiga."

That taken care of, she got up, shook my hand, and said that she had to catch her flight back to Munich. I said that I had to catch my flight back to Siberia.

At the airport, a man at the security checkpoint stopped me when he saw the X-ray image of my laptop inside my briefcase.

"Take it out," he insisted.

"Why?" I asked.

"It might be a bomb," said the man in the diarrhea-colored uniform. "Turn it on and I'll let you go."

"I can't," I said. "The batteries are dead."

"Then plug it in and turn it on." He pointed to an outlet in the wall.

I held up the power cord. It had angled American prongs on the end, not the round European prongs. I had left the adapter in Russia.

The security officer shook his head. "*Nein.*"

Just then, the Russian flight crew was passing through the security checkpoint. They pulled hand-dollies loaded with cartons of cigarettes, electronic toys, and blue jeans.

"What's the problem," the pilot asked me in Russian.

"They think my computer is a bomb," I replied in Russian.

The security officer gave the pilot a proud smile, as if to say, "Look how well I'm protecting you."

"Danka, Felix." The Russian pilot said as he grabbed my computer away from the security guard, whose nametag read "Holger."

"If I keep this computer in the cockpit until after takeoff, they can't do anything," the pilot explained a security loophole. "With your permission?"

"Of course," I said.

The pilot placed my computer atop his mountain of merchandise and walked onto the plane.

Holger mumbled something to himself and waved me on. I was tempted to stick out my tongue.

I flew back to Novosibirsk aboard an empty plane—no German refugees heading to Siberia. An hour into the flight, the pilot came back and gave me my computer.

"Germans," he said, rolling his eyes. "Too orderly for their own damn good."

I laughed in agreement.

"You want the lights on or off?" he asked. I wasn't even in first class and I got to decide whether the whole plane had the cabin lights on or off. Cool.

"Off," I said. "I'm going to try and get some sleep."

"Yeah," the pilot said. "Me too."

I did a double take.

"Just kidding." He laughed as he walked back to the cockpit.

Even though I could sprawl across an entire row of seats—any row on the plane—I couldn't fall asleep. So I just looked out the window as Europe scrolled behind and Siberia opened up ahead. The city lights below thinned out with each passing hour. Still two hours away from Novosibirsk, it was difficult to tell whether we were flying over the open ocean or the limitless taiga. Those isolated lights below could have easily been mistaken for ships at sea, rather than the remote villages that they were. From ten thousand meters up, the geographic magnitude of their isolation was awesome. Good thing they had Mexican soap operas to keep them company.

Soon after getting back to my blissfully chaotic Siberia, I had to go on another business trip, this one to America.

The Director of the Novosibirsk Chocolate Factory had taken a particular liking to our new Saab. He never got tired of complimenting us on how well it handled, how smooth it rode over potholes, and, most of all, how much he would like to have something like it for himself. Eventually, after a few weeks of elevated prices for chocolate, Sasha and I took the hint.

We decided to take the Director to America again—this time to buy a car. Sasha decided that it would be an opportunity lost to go to America for just one car. Sasha wanted to buy another company car, a minivan to haul our growing company ranks to and from the city. Sasha invited his neighbor to come along after learning that he was looking to buy a new car. The Director invited the factory's chief accountant; she, too, wanted a car. Once again, a quick trip for the Director had ballooned into a group outing.

And just like the last American adventure, we spent most of the time in a rented minivan. The last trip went north to south, from Niagara Falls to Miami Beach. This trip went west to east, from the Mall of America to Manhattan. Along the way, we bought three cars, five fur coats, dozens of rings and assorted jewelry, designer clothes, and everything else on the lists compiled by the Siberian wives back home, and all of it with cash.

From a roadside motel in Indiana, Sasha called his wife. Lyuda said that things weren't going well for the salon. A new beauty salon and cosmetics store opened in the city practically every day. The competition was eating away at Lyuda's customer base. The street her salon was located on gave it a clever name, but it didn't bring in enough foot traffic. The debts were mounting quickly. Sasha told her that there were two choices: move the store or close it. Lyuda said that the rent for stores on busy streets was too high.

"Then let's shut it down before we lose any more money," he said. "I'm sorry, Lyudonya."

When Sasha hung up the phone, he turned to me and said, "She blames me. That's why you should never mix business with your marriage. I was stupid to have agreed to open that salon in the first place. Well, maybe now she'll decide it's time for her to stop goofing around with business and time to have a son."

Although the closure of the beauty salon indicated that not all little luxuries would find buyers in Siberia, it seemed that the Siberians on this trip would find every luxury in America to buy. The money they spent made sales clerks drop their jaws. All in cash, of course.

By the time we got back, I would have been glad never to see another supermarket, mega mall, or factory outlet. I didn't need most of the stuff for sale in America. And when I was in Siberia, there was no temptation to buy things I didn't need. The ubiquitous commercials couldn't fill me with feelings of inadequacy at not having the latest model of SUV. The temptation to shop with reckless abandon was negligible in Siberia. The temptation to live with reckless abandon, however, was overwhelming. It was a temptation I welcomed and gave into regularly.

Sadly, there were other temptations placed before the Russians that they had little experience in resisting. This inexperience was exploited with devastating efficiency.

31 Russian Pyramids

For seven decades, the Soviets edited the Russian language, censoring and exorcising words with a paranoid political agenda. Now the country had a chance to heal, and so did the language. But there was to be no convalescence.

The problem now wasn't a drought of old words; it was a flood of new words. The flow of foreign words into everyday life set many Russians adrift in unfamiliar waters. Reading the newspaper or watching television made the average Russian scratch his head in confusion. Some of the words sounded almost as foreign to me as they did to the Russians—*marketing* (the g was pronounced), *bucks* (pronounced like *box*, but referring to dollars).

But the first new word to really affect everyone was *voucher*.

In order to privatize what was left of the former worker's paradise, a couple of hot-shot Western economists told the Russian government to give every Russian citizen a voucher with a face value of ten thousand rubles (around twenty dollars). Russians were supposed to invest these vouchers into former state-owned enterprises. Voila! Instant capitalist Russia.

Lenin needed a revolution to wrest private property from the Russians, and it took a bloody civil war in order for his party to hang onto it. Yeltsin was giving all the property back without spilling blood.

It was ironic. It looked like capitalism was finally going to make good on communism's promise to redistribute the wealth equally. From babushka to biznesman, everybody would own some equity. Everybody would have a stake in the economy, an equal, ten-thousand ruble stake. Or would they?

For several generations, people were told that profit was a crime and property was theft. Could an empire dedicated to overthrowing the imperialist conspiracy of capitalism suddenly become a nation of stockholders and portfolio managers? The economist in me hoped that it could. But I had lived in Siberia long enough for my American optimism to be tainted with Russian pessimism. I hoped for the best, but expected the worst.

What happened was difficult to stomach, if not so difficult to predict.

Because the vouchers were issued several months before any state enterprises were put on the auctioning block, people had to do a most unnatural thing during times of hyperinflation. They had to wait.

What the majority saw as a problem, a minority saw as an opportunity. A group of entrepreneurs realized that there was money to be made. They hired an army of muscle-bound thugs to buy up vouchers for between five and six thousand rubles each. WILL BUY VOUCHERS read the signs on the muscular men that hung out on every crowded street corner in Novosibirsk, and all the other cities in Russia.

People were glad to sell their ten-thousand-ruble vouchers for six thousand or even less because rumors were circulating (I wonder who started the rumors) that the vouchers would be worthless within months, maybe weeks. These vouchers, however, were the one piece of government-issued paper that wouldn't lose value. Their quantity was fixed—one per citizen. I understood that, and so did the people buying them up. But most other people reasoned that it was better to get cash now, rather than hold on to a voucher backed by the same government that had brought about this cursed hyperinflation, the very thing that had wiped out people's savings in the first place. Besides, who wants to buy stocks in a clunky Soviet enterprise? Future monopolists and robber barons, that's who.

The hungry sold their vouchers for food. The alcoholics sold their vouchers for booze. Sweet-tooths sold their stake in Russia's future for chocolate today. The majority used its tiny income from voucher sales for instant gratification. And they were the lucky ones.

At least they got a little gratification. The unlucky ones were those who cashed in their vouchers in order to invest in one of the many sensational pyramid scams.

Even if there wasn't much temptation to buy things, the temptation of money ran deep and, when exploited, ran wild.

Whereas the Egyptians built pyramids that lasted more than four thousand years (so far), the Russians built their pyramids to last less than four thousand hours. They were built upside-down, standing on their heads, doomed to collapse under their own weight. The Russian pyramids were designed by the few to steal from the many.

The pyramid scams lasted for several weeks. Television advertisements were as ubiquitous as political ads in New Hampshire in primary season. The ads were very different from everything else on Russian TV. They were slick, professional. They had a Western crispness to them.

The first wave of commercials seduced with sexy models and even sexier return rates. Men forked over cash at the many offices that had popped up overnight across this, the largest country on Earth. The husbands' money was quickly put to use enticing their wives. The next wave of ads had handsome celebrities, urging the women to rip open their mattresses and hand over their rainy-day money, money they had been hiding from their husbands. With Ma and Pa cashed out, the pyramid builders turned on Grandpa and Grandma. The most trusted face in Russia, the Mexican actress who played Maria in the soap opera *Simplemente Maria*, appeared in a commercial promoting one of the funds. In the commercial she sat in a chair while a man asked her questions. She seemed confused. Why shouldn't she be? The man spoke Russian. She replied in Spanish. The translation claimed that she recommended putting money into a particular fund. This was enough to get every babushka and *dedushka* to invest whatever they had.

The pyramid funds promised huge returns, and, for a while, delivered on these promises. Some people watched their investment accrue ten, twenty, and even thirty percent monthly. People invested whatever savings they had. Some even borrowed in order to invest in these miracle funds.

Nobody asked what these funds were investing in, where these miraculous returns were coming from. The answer, of course, was obvious. They weren't investing in anything except ignorance. These Russian fund managers were disciples of P.T. Barnum. They knew it was hard to go broke underestimating the intelligence of the Russian public.

Then, predictably, the pyramids all suddenly collapsed. The offices closed overnight. People who hadn't lost everything to inflation had the rest stolen in a nationally televised scam. The fund managers were mysteriously abroad when their funds collapsed, and it didn't look like they planned on coming back anytime soon. That "great sucking sound" that kept Ross Perot from sleeping at night wasn't American jobs going to Mexico; it was the sound of Russia's money going to Switzerland. The Russian government did nothing to warn the public. In fact, many of the commercials for these scam funds were broadcast on state-owned TV.

The new era of democracy and free enterprise was turning into a scandalous free-for-all. At first it was only Russians swindling fellow Russians. But profits always attract others. Soon enough, foreigners started to show up, trying to get their share of the action.

Soon after "voucher" became a four-letter word, *Herbalife* inserted itself into the Russian language. The company sold "health" products using the Tupperware system: no stores, no advertisements, just friends pressuring other friends in the comfort of their own homes. It was another type of pyramid scheme, except this scheme took advantage of the sellers more than it did the buyers. The scheme promised great rewards for those who sold vast amounts of a dietary supplement, a powder that, according to the colorful brochure, made you thin and healthy—only half of which was true. Sellers had to buy the product up front, then sell at prices determined by the company. The difference between purchase cost and sales price (what you and I understand as profit) went not to the person who had made the initial investment and final sale, but to the person who had recruited the seller.

What was the incentive for the seller?

A good question. At least I thought it was a good question to ask Lyuda, who had become a disciple of Herbalife. With a hungry look in her eye, she told me that she would receive a little money from sales, and a lot of money from the sales of her "converts." The religious language was used to distract people from the ass-backward economics of this scheme. By converting other people into joining the club, sellers like Lyuda were inviting other people to take her market share. They had mistaken the "share" part of *market share* for a verb, not a noun.

Whenever I started to chip away at Lyuda's faith in Herbalife, she would turn to the refuge of the company's bible: a multicolor brochure that extolled the advantages of being an Herbalife representative. A diagram in the shape of—that's right, you guessed it— a pyramid outlined how a lowly seller could rise up the hierarchy, gaining ever greater commissions, and earning impressive titles prefixed with words like Bronze, Silver, Gold, and Platinum.

As Lyuda recruited more and more people into the Herbalife family, she would receive the majority of their sales commissions, the fruits of other people's labor. This seemed only fair, since her sales commissions were being siphoned off by her *sponsor*, the person who had hooked her on this stuff in the first place. So now Siberians were not only hounded on the streets by missionaries eager to convert them into Baptists or Lutherans, they were now hounded in their own apartments by friends eager to convert them into Herbalifers or, at least, to buy some diet elixir.

The diet elixir, according to the brochure, was a specially designed blend of dried herbs and flower essences, but it looked like good old-fashioned sawdust. If you mixed the powder with water, drank the concoction (and nothing else), then you'd lose weight. No kidding.

Lyuda, unlike most drug dealers, made the mistake of using the stuff she sold. She was thin to begin with. When she stopped eating food except for a couple glasses of water with this super powder stirred in, her body began to whither. Her body went through its tiny reserve of fat in just a few days, then it began to cannibalize itself. She lost her energy, then her color, and finally her sanity. For a month, she was a venomous little bitch, snapping at the heels of anyone in her proximity. She slapped Alina for minor transgressions and lashed out at Sasha for things he did and didn't do. Under her eyes, black bags oozed lower and lower down her face. Her hair thinned. All the while, she talked about how wonderful she felt. "And it is all due to Herbalife," she would say in a weak, but positive voice, just like the sales manual had instructed her to do.

In this grotesque state, she didn't manage to convert many people to join the Church of Herbalife, and she didn't sell much of the life-enriching powder, either. But, as the diagram reminded her, she had to sell a certain amount in order to graduate to the next level, where the commissions would be bigger. So, she did the logical thing, she kept her sales levels up by buying her own product, lots of it. Her failure to sell anything or convert anybody exacerbated her feelings of emptiness brought about by genuine hunger. Her body finally collapsed. She was taken to the hospital where, against her will, she was forced to eat food again.

Then came the next scam. This one targeted everyone, including Sasha and me.

The Central Bank of Russia announced that the bottom had fallen out of the ruble. The cost of a dollar doubled. Overnight, our business went from being very profitable to hopelessly unprofitable. What was a generator of jobs and wealth yesterday was a bottomless pit that swallowed up money, jobs, and hope today. Worst of all, there was nothing we could do. We had overcome so many obstacles before, things that seemed fatal at the time. We had become hardened to bad news because we had always managed to prevail.

But the news of the ruble suddenly losing half of its value hit us hard. Just like that, all our imports had become twice as expensive. It meant that we were out of business. The next morning, however, we were back in business. The ruble had miraculously recovered.

(It took us a little longer to recover from our going-out-of-business drinking binge.) Sasha was convinced that some clever financial barons had pulled off another national scam, causing a major panic in the currency market, then cashing in on it.

Sasha's reaction to all of this confused me. I expected that someone who witnessed the premeditated looting of his country would feel anger—and that, in particular, someone who watched a profit-making scam lay waste to the mental, emotional, and physical health of his wife would be furious at the crooks who perpetrated these crimes.

Instead, Sasha seemed to admire the conductors of these orchestrated scams. "Kudos to them," Sasha said. "They made millions of dollars."

I had long regarded capitalism as a nuclear reactor that harnesses the power of greed into a controlled explosion of productive energy. But capitalism in Russia was beginning to resemble a specific nuclear reactor: Chernobyl. The power of greed in Russia was anything but controlled. There were no control rods to contain the chain reaction. Money dictated morality, rubles overshadowed responsibilities, and self-indulgence came before self-respect.

The profit motive in America yielded a banal landscape of comfortable materialism. The profit motive in Russia created a ruthless landscape that would have made Niccolò Machiavelli seem like a bleeding-heart liberal.

Maybe comfort wasn't as bad as I had originally assumed. Perhaps it was the lesser of two evils.

32
Turn of Fortune

Ever since we had begun working with Dmitri and Yuri, Sasha and I had become ambivalent about our work. We were making more money than before, but we had become more like employees than entrepreneurs. We were no longer building our Siberian chocolate empire. We were building a small part of somebody else's Russian chocolate empire. We had gone from being the head of a dog to the ass of a lion. Sasha and I complained and grumbled to each other about the situation because complaining was all we could do.

Then, suddenly, we got what we wanted—or, at least, what we thought we wanted. Our competition pulled out. Yuri and Dmitri had financially overextended themselves. Before anybody really knew what had happened, they were gone. The pipeline of cocoa beans suddenly dried up for the Siberian factories, and they came to us to keep them in business. Just like that, we had our empire back. We were again the head of the dog, a very big dog.

We were tempted to borrow money, huge quantities of money, in order to supply cocoa beans to all the factories within our reach. But we decided to avoid making the same mistake as Yuri and Dmitri. We were going to figure out what we could and couldn't do. Some factories were less reliable at paying their debts than others were. By declining to sell to these troublesome factories, we freed up our capital and time to focus on the more dependable, and therefore more profitable, factories. This was a basic rule of market economics: successful companies maximize profit, not cash flow. We would continue to sell cocoa beans to Novosibirsk and a few other factories, but we would have to let the rest of the empire go, at least for now. Best of all, the profit we were maximizing would be our own, not our employer's.

My professional life was falling into place. Unfortunately, my personal life remained pathetic. Sasha had a family and now a house on which to spend money. I, however, was alone. I had nobody to share my success with, and finding a soul mate, a lifetime lover, seemed unlikely in Siberia. Eleven months after I broke up with Katya, I learned that she was a mother. She had gotten pregnant by some guy from Krasnoyarsk. She didn't marry him because, as she put it, "I've got a little baby to take care of now. Why would I want to have to take care of a big baby, too?"

After this experience and a few other unsuccessful attempts at love, I was ready to give up, to become gay, or a monk, or maybe a gay monk. I don't know whether it was despite my growing indifference or because of it, but I suddenly got what I wanted most of all.

On April Fool's Day, Sarah invited me to go party-hopping on the university campus. She wanted to dance. Somewhat reluctantly, I agreed. I wasn't really in the mood to be patronized by beautiful students in miniskirts. But spending another lonely evening in my apartment watching pirated second-rate American movies with nasal voice-overs seemed even worse.

Most of the parties were in dorm number six, the math dorm— April 1 is Math Day, after all. The poorly lit halls were filled with students, some dancing, some singing, all of them drinking. We slipped into the room of one of Sarah's star pupils, Anwar, a gaunt little guy from Kyrgyzia. We found the usual table spread: cheese, pickles, and lots and lots of alcohol. Sarah added a bottle of champagne and I put out a box of chocolates. Even though there were only six people in it, the small room felt crowded. Anwar's towering girlfriend, annoyingly named Katya, sat next to him on the bed-turned-couch. His curly-haired roommate, Misha, sat nervously in a chair. There was a long-haired woman sitting to the right of Katya. She looked bored, or sick, or both. After a few glasses of champagne and bites of chocolate, Anwar turned on his Elektronika cassette player. Queen's "Bohemian

Rhapsody" filled the room. Anwar and Katya started dancing, her head swaying several inches above his. Sarah pulled Misha out of his chair and got him to cut a rug. She was old enough to be his mother. By the process of elimination, my dance card was set. The long-haired woman with the apathetic expression on her face was for me. I was tempted just to leave. Leave this party. Leave Siberia.

More to be polite than anything else, I asked her to dance.

"*Pochemu nyet* (why not)?" she said rather coldly. When she stood up, I was surprised at how little elevation she gained. She was tiny. Our size difference must have made us look like an odd couple. But, considering the other dancing pairs in the room, we fit right in.

Something about the absurdity of trying to dance with a woman half my size made me forget myself, my worries. She, too, seemed to find dancing with me both funny and fun. I slouched over, grabbed her arm, put my cheek on hers.

"Tango," she yelled.

The difference in our wingspans meant that when I extended my arm forward, her face didn't rest against my cheek, but rather lined up with my bicep. She let out a whoop of laughter as we stepped across the room. Her little legs couldn't keep up with my strides, so she just lifted them, trusting me to carry her like a bag of groceries. I carried her out into the hall and back in again, then dipped her with exaggerated gallantry.

"*Klyova* (cool)." She laughed. "Now let *me* try to dip *you*." She maneuvered into position, grabbed me, one hand on my lower back the other on my hand, and took a deep breath. She looked me in the eyes, as if waiting for me to call her bluff. I didn't. I wanted to see if she had the guts to drop a complete stranger on his back.

Surprisingly, she had the guts. Even more surprising, she also had the strength to keep me from hitting the floor. As I went back, she quickly realized that this wasn't a one-hand job. She let go of my hand and put a second hand on my back. Over the music I heard her grunt as she strained to hold up all of my two hundred pounds. She could hold me off the floor by herself, but she needed my help to get me vertical again.

Her face was red from the effort but she no longer looked bored.

"Let's go to *pyetyorka* (dorm five)," Anwar shouted.

In front of pyetyorka, a one-story building had been hastily converted into a dance club. From its windowless, cinderblock exterior, the dance club looked more like a bunker. If you shoved five thousand rubles into a hole cut in a metal wall, your hand came out stamped, which got you past the uniformed policeman gatekeeper. The inside was always filled with the mostly shaven heads of thugs and the mostly shaven legs of women. In this smoky room you could dance to a tasteless mix of techno pop, Russian rap, and American crap. But none of that seemed to matter. The little, long-haired woman and I were in our own silly world of carefree dancing. Sarah got bored and left with a crowd of bohemians to other parties. I stayed and danced with this little dynamo until we were both drenched with sweat.

I walked her back to her dorm and made a point not to kiss her. It would seem ridiculous after all the raunchy dancing we had done for the past few hours. A kiss would seem sarcastic rather than sincere. I asked her what her name was.

"Natasha," she said over her shoulder as she disappeared up the dorm's bare concrete stairs. I watched her bound up the next flight of steps in the window's reflection on the opposite wall.

Every day of the following week, I walked the halls of the university during my lunch breaks. I was searching for Natasha, even though I wasn't sure if I'd recognize her. I stared far too long at several long-haired university girls until they were thoroughly concerned and I was duly embarrassed. By Friday, I realized that I was going about my search all wrong. I shouldn't have been looking for little Natasha. I should be looking for Katya, her WNBA-sized girlfriend. Sure enough, while walking down the village's main street with an ice cream cone in my hand, I spotted a tall woman with short brunette hair from about two hundred yards away. Next to her walked a short woman with long, sandy brown hair. It was Natasha. I could hear her loud voice even at that distance.

After a few minutes of walking toward each other from opposite ends of the long, straight street, we stood face to face.

"*Nakonyets* (finally)," I said, looking straight at Natasha. "I've been looking for you all over."

"Why?" She was cold again.

"I had a great time dancing last weekend. I was hoping we'd be able to do it again sometime."

"Watch out." She pointed. My ice cream cone was melting onto my shoe.

"Don't worry; they're waterproof."

"That explains it," she said with an a-ha expression.

"Explains what?"

"I saw you yesterday from my dorm window. You were eating an apple as you walked down the sidewalk. You didn't go around the puddles. You just went right through them. I thought that you weren't normal when we danced, but when I saw you walking through the puddles, I knew for sure that you weren't normal." She looked up at her girlfriend. "I just thought it was because he's an American."

"You don't like Americans?"

"Nope." She blushed at her own bluntness. "As far as I'm concerned they're all a bunch of missionary wackos."

I nodded sympathetically, then said, "Well, I'm not a big fan of Russian women."

She nodded sympathetically. "*Ponyatno* (understandable)."

"So, now that we've agreed that we don't like each other, how about we go dancing tonight?"

"Yeah. I guess we could dance." She laughed and shook her head. "You're definitely not normal. I like that."

And again we danced like fools, boogying blissfully from one party to another. When the parties faded out one by one, we were still full of energy.

"That was too quick," she said. "I'm not tired. Let's go for a walk."

"It's three in the morning," I said.

"So?"

"So, nothing. Let's go."

We strolled through the woodsy campus in no particular direction. We had danced together two weekends in a row, at least six cumulative hours of carefree body gyrating, but this was the first time we talked.

"I love this place," she said as she tilted her head back to take in the night sky beyond the treetops.

"Me too," I said. But I didn't look up. I took a step back to get a good look at this little woman standing in the blue moon glow. She spread her arms straight out to her sides and turned the palms of her white gloves skyward as if receiving a blessing from above. I reached out and gently grabbed her hand. Still looking up at the stars she squeezed my hand.

We didn't let go.

She took a deep breath and let it out as a delicious sigh. We walked slowly on. We weren't hurrying toward any destination. We just walked. It didn't matter if we were here or there, so long as we were together.

"You're definitely not a missionary," she said as we stood in the middle of a soccer field after spotting a shooting star. "That much I can tell by the way you dance."

"Hey, now." I laughed. "You weren't exactly dancing like a nun."

She cocked her head to the side in mock indignation. She folded her arms and walked away from me with her chin proudly elevated. Just as I was getting ready to apologize, she spun around, ran straight at me, and jumped into my arms with a whoop. Giggling with excitement, one arm wrapped around my neck, the other dramatically raised like a gymnast having just successfully completed a triple back flip, she turned and looked into my eyes.

Although we had danced wildly, foolishly, and raunchily, this glance was the most intimate moment we had shared. Without the crowds and music, there was nowhere to hide our feelings. Fortunately, there was no need to hide them.

"Who *are* you?" she whispered into my ear as I held her in my arms.

"I was going to ask you the same question."

"Are you sure you're an American?" she asked, as if I'd been playing a practical joke on her.

"Last time I checked," I said. "You sure you're Russian?"

"That's what my passport says."

We walked around the village holding hands and talking, getting to know each other.

She said that she was from a small village in Kamchatka, six time zones to the east of Novosibirsk, two time zones east of Japan. She had been raised on salmon and caviar. She didn't eat meat, no chicken, no beef. Just fish. She loved fish. She also loved math. She had taken first place at a math competition in Kamchatka when she was fifteen, making her eligible to enroll in the University of Novosibirsk's prep school. She matriculated at seventeen into the university and became a math major. She was also a biathlete.

"So that's where you get your stamina," I said. "Skiing and shooting."

"Wow." She stopped in her tracks to give me a surprised smile. "I didn't think Americans knew any other sports besides basketball and hockey."

"I'm from Minnesota. Lots of cross-country skiing there."

"Is that how you got your stamina? I've never met anyone who could keep up with me on the dance floor."

"I swam competitively in high school and college."

"When the snow finally melts we should go running together. I need a partner to set a good pace."

"I'll do my best."

The sun started to lighten the eastern sky.

"Oops," she said. "You better walk me home. I've got to study for exams. I'd hate to flunk out with only one year till graduation."

Outside her door, I kissed her. It was a clumsy kiss. I missed her lips, mostly wetting her chin. It was an awkward ending to a wonderful night. Unfortunately, it got worse. She stood in front of her door, watching me back away down the corridor. When I reached the end, I waved to her and turned to make my exit. Maybe I was tired, in love, or both, but I turned the wrong way, right into a concrete wall.

"Are you okay?" Natasha asked with genuine concern, holding out her hand and taking a step toward me.

As I rubbed my shoulder and turned 180 degrees toward the door, I said, "Never felt better."

Progress

Just as we regained our status as the undeniable leaders of the Siberian cocoa bean market, we took possession of our new office. It was still unfinished. We needed to install wood floors, lights, telephones, windows, shades, carpets, desks, chairs, doors, and toilets. Since Kamil was still locked inside the cottage, we couldn't get him to do the work. And we didn't have any Chinese cooks to do the job either. So, we had to rely on Russian workers.

Usually with construction you have two choices: 1) you can do it quickly, or 2) you can do it right. The Soviet construction worker, according to Sasha, takes his time doing things wrong. We were looking at a few more months of finishing work. And even then, the place would feel far from finished. The wall paneling would likely bulge in places. Ceiling lights would dangle precariously by single screws. The windows would fit so poorly in the window frames that strong drafts would cause the window blinds to rustle like wind chimes. Some of the doors would scrape the carpets when opened. Other doors would have enough clearance for a mouse to flee under, if not a pursuing cat as well.

Sasha wanted the office to look better than that. He wanted it to look like a Western office. So we found a recently established company that sold Czech office furniture. The chairs had little black balls so you could roll across the room to grab a white phone with dozens of speed-dial buttons (phone sold separately). The desks had drawers that glided open on rollers. We bought bookshelves that matched the wardrobes, desk lamps that matched the sleek design of the desk, a conference table that stretched the length of our conference room, and a carpet to cover the entire floor space. The furniture did look Western, about as Western as K-mart office furniture. But judged on a relative scale—the scale that really mattered—both the quality and prices were much higher than anything else available on the local market. So we bought it.

"Now we need to find somebody to install the windows and doors," Sasha said.

The office furniture salesperson recommended a company that could do all the installation and finishing work that we needed. "They did this place." He waved his hand around the room. It was pretty impressive work. If we hadn't walked in through the dismal lobby, I would never guess that this furniture gallery was inside a Soviet-built research institute. The work crew would consist of only four guys, a quarter the size of the Soviet construction brigade that Sasha could have hired for a quarter of the price. It would take them one month to turn our brick-and-mortar office into a plaster-and-wallpaper office. The company boat captain, Ivan Ivanovich, equipped the bathrooms with the Chinese toilets, sinks, and fancy faucets left over from the hotel and beauty salon debacles. We hoped to move into the new office by late summer, early fall at the latest.

Victor, a muscular construction kingpin who had been on the last trip to America, invited Sasha and me to celebrate his birthday at a nearby *baza otdizkha* (relaxation base). When we got there, we found ourselves surrounded by former athletes turned businessmen. There was one athlete there who hadn't found another vocation. Alexander Karelin, the reigning world champion in Greco-Roman wrestling. He and Victor were longtime friends. When I was introduced to this formidable man, I realized why short guys tend to shake hands more firmly than big guys—fear. When Karelin looked me in the eye and took my hand, I was filled with fear, which made me squeeze his hand nervously.

"*Tikho* (easy)," he said in his deep voice as his pulled his hand away and shook it in mock pain. "I'm gonna need that to beat the Americans at the next Olympics."

Everybody laughed.

Karelin asked me why I was in Siberia. I told him my stump speech, that I enjoyed life in Siberia more than America. That America was too comfortable.

"I told you," Victor said. "He's one of us."

Karelin gave a nod of approval. "Did you know that Hollywood offered to cast me opposite Arnold. They wanted me to play an evil cyborg or Russian terrorist. Had to turn them down. Couldn't interrupt my training for the Olympics. Besides, I don't think I could stand to live in Hollywood. I went there a couple of times. Couldn't make heads or tails of Los Angeles. Is it even a city?"

"Sasha is the best wrestler in the world," Victor said with a chummy slap on his pal's enormous back. "But not much of a businessman. He could have made millions being Hollywood's bad guy."

Victor's playful slap would have knocked the wind out of a normal guy, but Karelin just smiled, unflinching.

"Vitya," the wrestler said, "this is *your* day. Let's not talk about me. Pour the vodka and let's toast to your health."

Victor beamed. "Fair enough, Sash."

The gravel yard in front of the secluded building quickly filled with high-end sport utility vehicles. As the fist-sized slabs of meat were pulled out of their marinade and skewered for *shashlik*, a blue Mercedes sedan followed by a Ford Scorpio drove up the dusty road and came to stop amid the SUVs. Six bejeweled Azerbaijani men in shiny suits got out. They flashed broad, gold-toothed smiles as they approached Victor.

There was a flurry of cheek kissing and hugging, but it was clearly deference and not affection that guided this ritual greeting.

There was vodka, of course. Rows and rows of bottles on side tables. There was also a keg of beer. A keg of beer, here in Siberia! I was astonished at how something so common at a Wisconsin dorm party, now, here, seemed as exotic as a rhinoceros head. Equally exotic, the table was adorned with fresh fruit: oranges, bananas, and grapes. Victor grabbed a bunch of grapes and looked at me.

"Just like in America, uh?"

I nodded, duly impressed.

After a few courses and half a dozen toasts, people got up to walk around. Upstairs, Nikolai, Victor's equally muscle-bound partner, challenged one of the Azerbaijani men to a game of billiards.

"Sanya," he turned to me, "do you know how to play this game?"

"Yeah, sure." I started to explain the rules.

"Ah, forget the rules," he said, then turned to his opponent. "Let's just play a hundred dollars per ball. You sink a ball, the other guy owes a hundred bucks."

The swarthy man agreed with a stoic nod.

"You want to play the winner, Sanya?" Nikolai asked.

When I saw Nikolai grab the wooden cue as if it were a shovel, I was tempted to say yes. I'd played pool in my friend's basement hundreds of times. I could really clean up. Then I realized that if I won, I'd be taking money from somebody who I didn't want to piss off. If I lost, well, I'd be out a thousand dollars. "I'll pass, thanks."

"Suit yourself," Nikolai said with a smile and a shrug. "If you don't have the money with you, I can lend it to you."

All heads in the room turned to look at me, as if I had committed a huge gaffe by not bringing several thousand dollars in cash to the party.

"That's alright," I said. "This really isn't my game."

"Me neither. I've never played before."

In fact, nobody had played before. The balls went flying off the table with amazing speed, becoming deadly projectiles. Karelin walked in, blocking out the light from the corridor as he stood in the doorway.

"Sasha's on my team," Nikolai said handing his cue to the wrestler. "Hundred bucks a ball."

"But I've never played before," Karelin said.

"Just shoot. Be sure to hit it hard. It's more likely to go in, eventually."

I got up and left the room before Karelin took his shot. I didn't want to be anywhere nearby when Arnold's cyborg nemesis took his first shot. As I walked back toward the dinner table I heard the sound of a ball hitting something, hitting it hard.

Nikolai laughed, then said, "Ne *khuya*, Sasha. You made a hole." A chorus of laughter erupted then went silent as I turned the corner.

Victor came up to me with two cups of beer in his muscular hands. He handed me one. "We make it ourselves at our own brewery. We bought German equipment a few months back. We put a little Altai honey in there for a slightly sweet taste. Try it."

I did. "This is good," I said. "I'm not just saying that because it's your birthday. This is really good."

He smiled. "I'm going to start selling this beer at my gas stations. You know, like in America."

"You've got your own gas stations?"

"Yep. I opened three new ones around town this last month. They're pretty crude right now, just a couple of pumps inside forty-foot cargo containers. If they turn out to be profitable, I'll build bigger ones. I prefer building stuff. I'm a builder. Kolya and I just do all this other stuff to make a little money to tide us over until things improve. Most people are too poor right now to afford new houses. That's what we really want to do, build houses. By the way, if you ever want me to build a house for you, just let me know. I'd be glad to do it. I know most of the houses we build are crap, but we're buying new equipment and learning new techniques all the time. Pretty soon we'll be making houses better than in America."

"I don't doubt it, Vitya."

Sasha was still at the table drinking shots with one of the Azerbaijani men. I saw Sasha shiver as he swallowed the last shot. He was approaching his limit. He would probably force a few more shots down, then start to fall asleep in his chair.

"I think it's time for us to go," I said, pointing in Sasha's direction.

Victor nodded. "*Da*."

After I'd eased a tipsy Sasha into the Saab, Victor walked up and gave me two jugs of his honey-sweetened beer.

Victor was proof enough for this economist that, although the GDP for Russia said that the economy as a whole was shrinking, there was some development, some form of progress. The Siberian economy was already more complex than just little luxuries. And when the GDP finally did rebound and begin to climb upward, spreading the wealth to a greater percentage of the population, I had no doubt that Victor would be building entire neighborhoods of brick homes.

The next day, I wanted to see Natasha. I made the hike to dorm number six. She wasn't there, but her roommate told me to look for her in the library. Sure enough, I found her with her head buried in a textbook. I tapped her on the shoulder.

She turned and looked up at me with her green eyes. She greeted me with a smile, then it disappeared.

"Big test coming up?" I asked.

"Yeah, in two months. Usually about the same time as when the lilacs bloom. I'm getting started now so that I can enjoy the lilacs instead of being locked up in here with all the procrastinators who reek of hangover."

"How about a study break? The sun is out and the mosquitoes aren't."

She tapped her forehead with the eraser of her pencil a couple of times. "Okay," she finally said, "but only for an hour."

"Fair enough."

"What are you studying?" I asked as I held open the door leading outside.

"It's kind of hard to explain," she said without looking at me.

"Try," I said.

"Differential equations on linear tension. I'm trying to figure out the ideal tension a sail's fabric should have in order to maximize energy capture."

"Yikes," I said with a shake of my head.

"I told you," she said. "So, where do you want to go?"

"Can I take you to lunch?"

"Sure," she said with a nod.

Along the way to the restaurant a blue Mercedes came to a stop alongside us. Victor stepped out. He was wearing sweatpants and a T-shirt.

"Sanya, *privet*," he said as he jumped out. We shook hands. He was popping sunflower seeds into his mouth and spitting out the shells. His shirt was littered with sharp-edged shells stuck in the fabric. "*Gulyaesh?*" he asked, using the verb that could mean strolling or having casual sex.

Natasha took a few steps backward.

I nodded and looked into the car. A stocky little boy with Victor's square jaw and a girl with long hair in pigtails sat in the back seat. I recognized Victor's wife from the party last night sitting in the front seat. I waved. "Taking the family for a Sunday drive?"

He nodded and asked about Sasha, whether he had gotten home okay.

"I dropped him off. Lyuda wasn't pleased about his condition."

Victor laughed and shook his head. "Well, okay, we're off." He shook my hand again and drove off.

As I watched the Mercedes accelerate down Illich and turn right on Morskoy, I wondered whether the Azerbaijanis had given it to him as a present or if he'd won it playing billiards.

"Friend of yours?" Natasha said with a surprised expression on her face.

"Sort of," I said. "I showed him around America this past winter."

"*Strashno* (scary)," she said.

"He's pretty intense," I admitted. "You should see his friends. Then you'd really be scared."

Natasha looked at me with a suspicious eye. "You really aren't normal, are you? What kind of American hangs out with Siberian thugs who drive around in Mercedes?"

"Just trying to experience Siberian life at its most colorful."

She mumbled something under her voice as she shook her head. She was obviously not amused. I had realized pretty early on during our all-night walk that Natasha had an emotional exoskeleton. Whatever she was feeling at any given moment was clearly visible on her face and in her body language. She was an open book for anyone who cared to read it. I could tell that something was bothering her, and it wasn't my association with Victor.

"What's the matter?" I asked.

She took a deep breath in obvious preparation to say something very serious.

I got a lump in my throat. How could she be breaking up with me? We weren't even going out yet.

"When were you planning on telling me?" she asked. It wasn't a question so much as it was an accusation.

"Tell you what?" I searched my brain for something, anything.

"About Katya," she said. "More importantly, about her baby."

I felt a pulse of panic, but it passed almost instantly. If Natasha was going to be an open book to me, I figured she deserved the same in return. I smiled as I told Natasha the truth. "Katya's baby is a girl. Her name is Alla. And," I paused, "she is not mine." I wiped the smile off my face and looked Natasha in the eyes. "If she were mine, I wouldn't be standing here with you. I'd probably be changing diapers right now."

Natasha's furrowed brow smoothed. "That's what I thought," she said, her lips curling at the edges to produce a relieved smile. "I just wanted to hear it from you."

"How do you know so much about my past?" I asked with genuine interest.

She gave me a look as if I'd asked a very stupid question, then she kissed me on the cheek so that I knew that it was an endearingly stupid question. Smirking, she waved her arm in a slow, grand motion, inviting me to look around. Then she said one word: "*Derevnye* (village)."

34
Domestic Bliss

C miulim, rai dazhe v shelashe ("with your lover, paradise can be found even in a thatch hut"). My one-room apartment became a thatch hut; it became three hundred and fifty square feet of paradise.

I invited Natasha to my apartment for a celebratory meal of wild mushroom soup in honor of the 5—equivalent in the American grading system to an A—she'd received on a recent paper. We ate the Siberian soup with Turkish bread and German wine on the tiny balcony of my apartment. The meal segued into a marathon conversation that wandered freely from math, economics, philosophy, and religion to family, friends, camping, and sports. For the second time in as many meetings, we stayed up all night talking. When the sun came up, it was Monday morning. I had to go to work and she had to go to class.

I changed into my work clothes and gave her a sweater to protect her from the crisp morning air. As we walked back to her dorm, we ran into Sasha walking Alina to preschool. Sasha looked at my sweater hanging on Natasha like a tarp. He gave me a sly nod that made Natasha blush crimson. Natasha and I had done nothing more than hold hands. In fact, we were still holding hands.

"That's Dyadya Xander's sweater," Alina said in an accusatory voice.

Natasha squatted down in order to poke Alina in the belly button. "He let me wear it so I wouldn't get cold. Isn't he a nice boy?"

"Mm, hmm," Alina agreed meekly. She clearly wasn't sure about this unfamiliar, long-haired lady holding my hand.

"My name is Natasha. What's yours?"

"Alina," she whispered tentatively.

"Alina Ballerina?" Natasha asked.

Alina giggled, quickly coming out of her bashful shell. "Do you want to see my Barbie doll? My daddy bought it in America."

"Of course," Natasha said without hesitation. "Wow. Look at all that pretty hair."

As Natasha and Alina became fast friends, Sasha told me about the latest crisis at work. The logical and inevitable breakup of the company into its two distinct parts—commercial and educational—was becoming a clash of personalities. The submarine had long ago been bisected down the long corridor: the language program residing on one side and the commercial department on the other. Accounting, answerable to both, was behind the padded, red door on the commercial side of the corridor. This irked Zhenya to no end. He seemed to feel that its location symbolized the disproportionate influence Sasha had on the half-dozen lady accountants. The copy and fax room was on the language program's side, which also seemed to annoy Zhenya. He perceived it as an incursion into his space. The imminent departure of the commercial department to its own building on the outskirts of the village didn't soothe tensions a bit. If anything, it exacerbated them.

Like a couple in the midst of a bitter divorce, Zhenya and Sasha couldn't have a civilized conversation without it descending into heated arguments about who would get what. Every table, chair, and even stapler became a point of contention. When Sasha was convinced that Zhenya was secretly removing things from the office in the evenings, he hired an armed guard to watch over the property.

"He's as conniving as a Chinese businessman. I can't stand his ugly face anymore," Sasha said with venom. "The sooner we move out of the submarine and into our new building the better."

Even though I was directly involved, I couldn't get excited about any of it. I was too damn happy to be angry. It was springtime, we were making money, and, most important of all, I was falling in love.

I remember the specific moment when I knew that I had fallen hard for Natasha. She suggested that we go for a picnic at the botanical garden, a mile's walk through the woods. We had packed a blanket, a loaf of bread, some cheese, and a few potatoes. The potatoes were raw, but we figured we could start a little fire and roast them. Instead, when we found ourselves in a meadow, one of the potatoes became a ball. We tossed it back and forth. She would catch the potato with both hands and let out an enthusiastic whoop as she threw it.

"I throw like a girl," she complained. "Show me how to throw like a guy."

With the potato in my hand, I slowly went through the over-hand motion as if I were an outfielder throwing the ball to home plate. Wearing a serious expression, she mimicked my motions.

"Okay. I've got it," she declared confidently. "Toss it to me."

I did, but in my attempt to show her a flawless overhand throw, my toss was too hard. The potato sailed high. Natasha started backpedaling in order to get underneath it. She wasn't going fast enough; the trajectory of the potato was still beyond her. She pivoted her body around and started sprinting with her short, muscular legs. Like a wide receiver, she looked over her shoulder and put her hands out in front to catch the projectile. The spud was still sailing long. She leaned forward. The potato bounced off of her fingertips and fell to the ground, as did Natasha. She slid across the ground, leaving a line of black soil in her wake where her knee had ripped up the thin layer of spring grass.

"Are you okay?" I asked as she got to her feet.

"Yes," she laughed. "Did you see that? I almost caught it." The knee of her blue jeans was black. She shrugged her shoulders after seeing the stain, picked up the potato and tossed it to me. Her toss still looked a little girly, but it sailed all the way to me and made a loud smack when it hit my palm.

That was the moment I fell in love—when she laid herself out in order to catch a potato. She was more distressed about missing the catch than at ruining her jeans—and jeans, even Polish jeans, were still considered a fabulous luxury in Siberia then. I was charmed by her enthusiasm.

Within a week, her toothbrush stood with mine in a cup above my bathroom sink and my toilet seat was perpetually down.

She physically moved into my apartment as quickly as she had emotionally taken up residence in my heart. As surprising as the speed of our coupling was the effortlessness of it. It didn't feel like an invasion, but rather, it felt like a reunion. I felt like I'd known her and loved her all my life. Best of all, she made it clear that she was just as tickled to be with me. Whenever I started to turn the key to the apartment after a long day at work, I would hear a cheer from behind the door and then her footsteps as she scampered to meet me. I was harassed with kisses and hugs as I struggled to take off my shoes in the narrow corridor.

After our morning runs through the woods, we'd eat breakfast and coordinate our lunch hours so that we could meet at home and make love. Satisfied, but still hungry, we'd buy food from the babushkas on our walk back to campus.

"I thought you went home to eat lunch," Sasha said to me one day when he saw me eating bread, scallions, and cheese at my desk. I just gave him a dumb, contented smile and offered him a scallion.

"No, thanks," he said. "Lyuda made me borscht for lunch. I'm stuffed."

Natasha would often pick me up from work at the end of the day so that we could walk home together. As we gathered food from the stores, kiosks, and babushkas, we divided the labor according to our abilities. She haggled and I hauled. We cooked together in the tiny kitchen, which used to feel cramped but now felt cozy.

During her week of final exams, while all the other students were cramming for their test, Natasha and I walked around the village in the evenings savoring the heavenly aroma of lilac bushes in bloom. Natasha not only stopped to smell the flowers, she demanded that I lift her up so that she could bury her nose in the fragrant purple blossoms. When I let her down, her eyes were often glazed over or shut altogether. She just smiled blissfully and reveled in springtime ecstasy.

When she finished her last exam, I gave her a bouquet of yellow narcissus and suggested we go for a celebratory swim in the recently thawed Ob Sea. We jumped into the water and flailed about frantically, hooting and hollering like lunatics. As we sat on a log putting on our clothes, she turned to me with a grimace.

"You stink like dead fish."

"I thought that was you," I said. "I was just being polite by not saying anything."

She smelled her wrist. "Foooo. It is me."

I smelled my forearm. "It's me, too. We both stink like dead fish."

We ran home to wash off. When we got home, however, the hot water was gone. Every summer, the village's hot water supply was turned off for two to three months for "maintenance." Reeking of rotten fish, we heated up water on the stove. We then took turns pouring the water over each other from three-liter jugs while standing in the bathtub. It was one of the most satisfying showers I'd ever had.

A few days later, I took Natasha to the airport. She flew to Kamchatka to be with her parents for the summer. After only a month of living with Natasha, the prospect of three months alone in my bachelor pad depressed me. Whenever I came home to my apartment, there was no cheer from the other side of the door. My hut was empty. I almost found myself wishing Siberia's brief summer to be over.

Almost.

35 The Castle

After winter finally pulled back its white carpet, we drove the Saab within sight of Sasha's brick house before getting stuck in mud. We slogged by foot the remaining quarter mile through the muck.

After knocking on the steel door, we heard the sounds of several locks unhooking, sliding back, and twisting open. A troop of kittens scrambled and stumbled over each other through the doorway and into the fresh air. The fuzzy felines squinted and blinked their eyes at the bright sunshine. Licking herself leisurely, a black-and-white cat sat in a cardboard box tucked into the corridor's dark corner. Kamil also stepped out into the sunlight, and only then did he stick out his hand. (It's considered rude to shake hands through a doorway.) I shook the old man's leathery hand. He turned to Sasha. They respectfully shook hands man-to-man, then lovingly embraced as father and son. Sasha handed over a bag full of milk, cheese, bread, and a few bottles of Russian beer—pretty meager compensation for a winter of work.

Over the past five months, Kamil had managed to turn the inside of a brick shell into something that strongly resembled a house, if not quite a home. Wooden floors covered the concrete surfaces. Sturdy wooden staircases connected the floors. Kamil had built fifteen doorframes. If he hadn't run out of wood, he would have built the doors as well. Instead, temporary doors made out of blankets hung in the new doorframes.

Sasha told his dad to take a break, to come visit his granddaughter and daughter-in-law, not to mention his own wife, back in the village. Kamil refused. He couldn't leave; there was too much work left to do. He gave his son a list of materials that he needed.

Running a growing company in Siberia is more than a full-time job. Finding, buying, and transporting building materials for a Siberian house is also more than a full-time job. Sasha tried to do both.

In between our credit negotiations at various banks and confidential conversations at the chocolate factory, we took detours in search of home supplies that were sold behind unmarked doors in narrow alleys. Sasha bought door hinges at a camera shop that had no cameras. He bought floor tiles at a toyless toy store, and curtains at a bookstore that sold everything but books. He hired a local artisan to build six handcrafted doors for the inside of the house. The porcelain toilets and sinks came from the Chinese hotel leftovers. Sasha was like a bowerbird, frantically gathering twigs and sticks to build an attractive nest for his mate. Sasha obviously wanted Lyuda to nest in the big house. Maybe then she might get pregnant again and he'd finally have a son.

Pretty doors and shiny floor tiles were nice, Kamil told his son, but the house needed a furnace. Neither Lyuda nor Baba Masha would move into the house if it had no heat.

Back at Sasha's apartment, Baba Masha had planted seedlings in dozens of empty Hungarian juice boxes that she had cut in half. Every horizontal surface supported the boxes of tender seedlings, extending themselves slowly upward. Baba Masha moved them from room to room, chasing the sunlight throughout the day. And Baba Masha wasn't alone in her vigilance. Every third window of the village's apartment buildings glowed all night long with the cold light of fluorescent bulbs suspended over trays of future fruits and vegetables.

Over the next few days, at the end of the workday, we took at least one trip to the cottage with a trunk load of Baba Masha's plants. The cottage's attic/greenhouse filled up as the apartment's windowsills freed up. When the last tray of seedlings went into the car, Baba Masha got in as well. She moved out of the apartment, leaving her son, daughter-in-law, and granddaughter to rejoin her husband after seven months of separation.

Lyuda wasn't sad to see her go. Loving your mother-in-law can be difficult. But living with her in a two-room apartment during a Siberian winter can be a monumental challenge, a challenge Lyuda wasn't up for. There were no ugly incidents, just a constant friction that produced no warmth, just chilly silence.

Sasha bought a used stove from one of our distributors who owed us money for a few tons of chocolate. We cancelled his debt in exchange for a steel furnace. Getting the stove from the Kamaz into the basement was an ordeal. Although gravity was on our side, we had to avoid letting gravity take the stove through a wall or shatter a doorframe. We managed to push, shimmy, pry, ram, and drag the one-ton hunk of metal across the floor to the edge of the stairs leading to the basement. With ropes to pull from above and wooden planks to push from below, we gently lowered the massive furnace down the stairs, Sasha and Kamil arguing passionately all the while about who should lay down his life in order to get the job done. In the end, there were no casualties except a few crushed fingernails, stubbed toes, and sore backs.

Sasha called Victor to find out where he could buy a ton of coal. The dump truck arrived later that same day. We shoveled the pile of black rock into the pit in the garage.

The cottage had heat—not a trivial matter in Siberia. Ironically, the stove was fired up for the first time when the temperature outside reached eighty-two degrees. After fixing the half-dozen leaks in the radiators and pipes, we fled the house for the relative coolness outside. Kamil grabbed a spade and started tilling the soil surrounding the house. Baba Masha walked behind him, poking her growing seedlings into the soft earth. Alina watered each plant individually from a plastic toy watering can. When the house cooled down enough, Baba Masha went inside to prepare dinner. Kamil built a swing for his granddaughter.

The following weekend, Sasha bought a puppy with enormous paws. It was a *Kavkaskaya* (Caucasian) Shepherd. Although it looked like a tiny St. Bernard and was every bit as friendly, this little puppy, Sasha promised, would grow into a fierce monster. This is what he wanted—a bloodthirsty guard dog to protect his family and estate when he wasn't around. For a while, however, it was cute and clumsy. I got down on my hands and knees and played with little Rex. When the cat's kittens were weaned, Kamil gave them away to neighbors who had mice problems. The female cat turned her maternal instincts on the puppy, even though Rex was already twice her size. Sasha was afraid that between my playing and frolicking with it and the cat licking and snuggling with it, the dog would become soft, friendly, and useless. It was a fear that proved entirely unwarranted. Rex grew into a savage beast. He barked and spit with rage at anybody he didn't recognize. Fortunately, Rex remained friendly to me. He preferred to lick my hands rather than rip off my flesh. If he tried to play too rough with the cat, she'd swipe his monstrous snout with her tiny paw. It looked like certain suicide for the cat, but Rex always put his tail between his legs and groveled before the alpha cat.

In addition to a ferocious beast on a long, iron chain, Sasha had iron bars put up on all the windows and even enclosed the two balconies. Sasha subscribed to the adage that a man's home is his castle. I suggested he build a moat filled with alligators around the brick fortress. He looked at the ground next to his house, then he shook his head: "The alligators would freeze in the winter."

Instead, we built a chicken coop. The director of the chocolate factory gave Sasha the number of a friend who could sell him sixteen chickens. For a day, we alternated between chasing chickens that had escaped and repairing the holes in the fence through which they had escaped. By the end of the day, the chickens had no way out and we had no energy.

The next day, we went to the Berdsk market. There were a dozen piglets for sale in a car's open trunk. Middle-aged women stood holding puppies and kittens. Children stood several feet away and stared at the petrified baby animals. A few feet away, meat hung from hooks under a rusty, metal awning. A few old women sold a

green and purple chive called *cheremsha*. We asked a woman selling chickens where we could buy a rooster. She pointed with a
twitch of her head toward an old man standing alone. The man
held two roosters, one under each arm. A small bag was on top of
the birds' heads. He pulled off the bags so that we could look at the
birds. One of the roosters was a beautiful, colorful cock with an aris-
tocratic red crown atop his puny head. The other was smaller and
almost solid black.

Sasha bought the grand rooster and put it in the trunk of the
Saab. On the way out of the market, Sasha bought two loaves of
bread, a five-kilogram block of butter, three tubes of *kalbasa*, and
four bottles of milk.

When we dropped off the rooster and the provisions, Baba
Masha gave her form of gratitude—silence.

The following Tuesday, Sasha showed up at work with a long
face.

"What's the matter?" I asked.

"I went to the cottage last night," he said. "The chickens killed
the rooster."

"What?"

"They pecked him to death. I knew I should have bought that
ugly rooster," Sasha said with a laugh. "Have you heard the story of
Ivan and the ugly rooster?"

I shook my head.

Sasha grinned, asked Irina to hold all his calls, then sat back to
tell the story.

"Ivan woke up in the afternoon, as always, with a hangover. His
wife said the chickens needed a rooster. His wife gave him one hundred rubles and sent him off to the market. On the way, he bought
a bottle of vodka for fifty rubles and drank it. He staggered into the
market to find plenty of roosters for sale, but they all cost one hundred rubles. Then he saw a gypsy woman sitting with a rooster in
front of her. The rooster looked old and haggard. It only had one
eye and its beak was crooked. There were bald patches where the
feathers had fallen out. The gypsy told Ivan that he could have the

rooster for fifty rubles. Fifty rubles was a lot of money for a crippled old rooster. Ivan could get a perfectly good bottle of vodka for fifty rubles. The gypsy looked him in the eye and said that this was a special rooster. Ivan didn't believe her, but he was afraid of going home empty-handed. The only thing he feared more than sobriety was his wife's temper. He gave the gypsy woman his remaining fifty rubles.

"When he let the rooster loose in the chicken coop, he expected the chickens to descend on the haggard bird and peck him to death. Instead, the rooster shook the dust off himself, sending half of his remaining feathers to the ground as well. Then the rooster started vigorously fulfilling his male duties, going from one chicken to the next. He nailed every chicken in the coop in a matter of minutes, then he went around again for good measure.

"Ivan was amazed. The gypsy was right; this really was a special rooster. Just then, the rooster flew up and over the tall fence. He landed near the goose pond. The rooster started servicing the geese. When a large gander came over to defend his mate, the rooster mounted him too. This rooster was special, all right—a little too special. Feathers flew out of the pigeon house for ten minutes while the rooster had his way with the frightened little birds.

"Suddenly, the rooster emerged from the pigeon house and fell to the ground with a thud, leaving a puddle of feathers. It got to its feet and staggered a few steps then fell again. It got up, staggered, and fell again. It dragged itself by its featherless, bony wings. When it reached the middle of a field, it collapsed and didn't get up.

"Ivan ran out to the rooster. 'You can't die,' Ivan said. 'You're the best rooster I've ever had. You just can't die,' he pleaded. The rooster looked up with its one eye and said to Ivan, 'Get out of here, you fool. You'll scare away the vultures.'"

Kamil's chicken coop would have to remain roosterless for another week, but most of the neighboring houses seemed doomed to remain empty indefinitely.

With the exception of Sasha's castle, the neighborhood looked like Dresden after the war—row after row of empty brick shells. Some had two stories and no roof, some had just one story, some just a wall. In some places there was only a hole in the ground, now full of melted snow. There were pallets of bricks everywhere. But there was nobody around to stack them. It looked like the setting for a *Twilight Zone* episode—a half-built town abandoned overnight for some unknown reason. Had aliens abducted all the workers? Maybe some mysterious hysteria overtook them all, sending them scream-ing into the woods never to return. To many Russians, the real rea-son was no less mysterious. Wealth had vanished. There was no money to build these houses.

"But it takes bricks to build houses," Kamil said while digging an irrigation ditch for the garden, "and there are plenty of bricks just waiting to be stacked. Since when did money build houses?"

"Since people stopped building their own homes," I said as I pushed my shovel into the black soil. "Not everybody can build their own house. But, with enough money, anybody can have somebody else build it for him. Money is how you get other people to do things for you."

Even as I lectured Kamil on the market's ability to transform strangers into helpers, I couldn't help but think of the other side of the coin, namely, the tendency for market economics to turn friends into strangers. Who has time to hang out with friends when there is money to be earned to make house payments?

After an hour of earth moving, we watched with satisfaction as the water flowed from the giant steel tank down our canal. Sasha, watching with Alina from the balcony, let out a cheer when the water reached the distant pea patch. Within minutes, the wilted leaves began to fill with water, straighten up, and stretch toward the sun, not shirk away from it. My back hurt, my hands were pocked with tender, maroon blisters. I felt great.

Kamil and Baba Masha cultivated the garden plot into rectan-gular beds of thriving carrots, tomatoes, strawberries, raspberries, potatoes, peppers, onions, garlic, beans, and peas. The other half of the plot, Shura's side, went fallow, pushing up four-foot weeds into which Alina got lost and screamed until her papa came to res-cue her.

Holding his daughter, Sasha stood in the tall weeds. He looked at the empty half of the house. There were no iron bars on the windows, or glass, or even wooden frames. A gentle breeze blew cool, dank air out of the lifeless hull.

"Doesn't he have time?" I asked Sasha as I walked through the weeds. I stuck my tongue out at Alina, who went from whimpering to giggling.

"He has time," Sasha replied, wiping the tears from his daughter's cheeks with his thumb. "He just doesn't have any money."

Sasha explained that during the winter his friend's pantyhose business had slipped away from him, just like his gum business had. There were still plenty of his Italian pantyhose in the stores and kiosks, just like there was plenty of gum everywhere. Shura, however, was no longer ruling either empire. To expand the business, to conquer new territory, he had borrowed too much money at too high an interest rate. When he was unable to pay the interest on the loans, he avoided his creditors. When they found him, he got a warning: if he didn't pay up, he'd be in trouble. He didn't have the money to pay, so he moved to St. Petersburg, then to Italy. He left behind his wife and kids.

"So that's why I haven't seen him at your apartment recently," I said. "I thought you two had gotten into a fight about something."

Sasha shook his head and kicked a clump of dirt with a solitary weed growing out of it. "Want to buy his half?" Sasha asked me.

I was tempted. The lure of land ownership was strong, and the price was right. I could have a house and almost an acre of fertile soil for less than ten thousand dollars.

"You could move in with that new girlfriend of yours," he suggested. "That one-room apartment is way too small for two people to live comfortably. Right?"

36

Siburbia

I felt a nauseating sense of déjà vu after we moved into the new office. My frozen utopia had transformed into Siburbia. Instead of moving our homes far away from our workplace, we had moved our workplace away from our homes. The dislocation was just as sickening to me as was American sprawl, maybe even more so.

The way to work was no longer a pleasant stroll along serene paths in an idyllic village, but rather a gloomy trudge on dusty roads crowded with heavy machinery that billowed out noxious clouds of gray exhaust. So we drove. If the point was to elevate Siberians to an American lifestyle, I was succeeding. Everybody in our office now commuted to work in cars, just like Americans. Actually it was less like the way American workers commute and more like the way American kids get to school.

Our drivers would drive around for an hour gathering small groups of our employees at street corners. Everybody was at work by nine A.M. My brisk morning walk—full of sights, sounds, and smells that used to wake me up as I went along—was replaced with the stale smell of a climate-controlled car. When we arrived at work, the car's heater had lulled everybody back to sleep. Rather than feeling invigorated, we started the workday in a drowsy state that only coffee seemed able to hold at bay. By the time lunch rolled around, my stomach ached and gurgled from all the liquid caffeine.

Our standard of living kept rising along with the success of our company, but the quality of life was in free fall.

I would no longer be able to run home for nourishing sex during lunch. We were stranded in our comfortable office in the middle of nowhere. We were so far away from everything that there weren't even restaurants nearby.

Our employees complained about the situation.

Rather than bring our workers to the food, we brought the food to our workers. We converted one of the office rooms into a kitchen, and the adjacent room into a dining area. When it was complete, we hired a company cook, Elvira (pronounced "El-veera"). She was a Tatar woman who made heaping portions of fatty foods. Soon, everybody was gaining weight. The men in the office loved Elvira like a grandma. The women in the office hated her like a mother-in-law. The women sopped up every greasy morsel Elvira put on their plates but then cursed the evil cook immediately after lunch. The food was part of the problem; but more than that, it was the sudden reduction in daily exercise that caused clothes to tighten around growing bellies and sagging butts. Twice a day, these women were commuting in a car instead of walking. And since we were now located on the first floor, not the fifth, they now missed the equivalent of several Stairmaster workouts every day. For women who invested so much into their physical beauty, this was more than just disappointing. This was devastating.

Some of the women couldn't stand to let their bodies grow soft and pudgy; they ate food less often, but talked about it more often. Suddenly, a new industry popped up to meet this new demand. Aerobics classes were suddenly all the rage. Going to an aerobics class in Siberia seemed about as absurd as going to a tanning booth in Phoenix. Now, after a long day of work, Siberian women could scurry home, cook a meal for their husbands and kids, take a bus to a sports hall to jump up and down for an hour, then get back on the bus to return home completely exhausted. Sure, they were more worn down than ever, but they were slender, damn it!

Sasha and I also engaged in the battle of the bulge. Sasha wanted a shower installed at the office so that we could cross-country ski to work in the winter and jog in the summer. Instead, we bought memberships at a new sport club. We drove there on our lunch breaks and hurried through the weight room, frantically pumping iron on equipment imported from Germany. We didn't take the time to stretch properly. Then we slurped down some soup as we rubbed our sore muscles and stiff necks. There just wasn't enough time to drive to a gym, work out, eat a decent lunch, and then drive back to the office. Sasha suggested that we buy a few exercise machines for the office. Like so many exercise machines in America, our machines got used for about a week, then became furniture.

And it wasn't just our bodies that suffered. Using a lot of money and very little creativity, we fought the mental and emotional emptiness of our self-imposed isolation. We tried to buy back the things we had left behind. It was hard to know where to begin. We were suddenly filled with wants that we never had before.

Everybody in the office suddenly had new *needs*. The accountants, who took their teatime snacks seriously, needed a refrigerator. The drivers, who used to be happy as clams telling jokes in their tiny, smoke-filled room at the end of the submarine, now needed a TV for their new, spacious digs. And everybody needed cars. Lots and lots of cars. The accountants needed their own car to shuttle them from the bank to the tax police. The sales department lobbied for its own vehicle to make collections from clients. The logistics department, responsible for clearing our incoming cargo through customs and seeing it safely to the warehouses, also needed a car.

We bought a couple of Russian Ladas and a Russian van. Managing so many vehicles became a problem. Sasha bought half a dozen CB radios, one for every car in our growing fleet.

As an economist, I recognized that moving our office out to Siburbia was a great way to boost the economy. By simply dislocating ourselves from our community, we had become the ideal consumers. We had become insatiable. We also needed to hire more people to run, tend, and protect all our newly acquired stuff: drivers, janitors, and security guards. We also needed to hire people to manage the growing numbers of employees. Perpetual economic growth seemed assured. Happiness seemed ever more unlikely.

We hired Victor Petrovich, a retired submarine officer, to coordinate our growing fleet of cars. Victor Petrovich was a tiny man, but his silver hair and military posture made him seem larger than he was. He was the only one in the office, besides the chief accountant, who everybody spoke to using the formal *vui*, instead of the familiar *tui*. On holidays, Victor Petrovich put on his jet-black navy uniform with colorful medals adorning the chest. He demanded obedience from those who worked under him, and he gave it to those above him.

Even though much of the staff was racing around town in our growing fleet of vehicles, the office was remarkably crowded. People waited outside Sasha's door from morning until evening. Whenever he went to the bathroom, half of the waiting people followed him, firing questions like frenzied reporters chasing a politician plagued by scandal. By looking at the motley folks waiting to see Sasha, I could see the changing face of Siberian business. The power-hungry bureaucrats were gone, replaced with the profit-hungry wholesalers. Slippery loan sharks had transformed into equally slippery bankers. There were Indians from the subcontinent offering trainloads of tea; Chinese from just south of the border offering trainloads of peanuts; and Russians from all over offering to buy anything and everything. But, like Popeye's buddy Wimpy, they couldn't pay us now; they'd be glad to pay us next Tuesday for product today. Some things never changed.

At the end of one of the seemingly endless procession of long days, Sasha walked into my office while I was talking on the phone with Monika, our supplier of latex products—her workday was just getting started. Sasha leaned against the wall and waited.

"Okay, then," I said, wrapping up the conversation, "I'll see you in August."

Click. The phone went back into its cradle.

"Sanya," Sasha said in a tired, but urgent voice, "we need to take a vacation. If we don't, we'll miss summer entirely. Let's go. I'll take Lyuda and Alina and you can take Natasha."

"Natasha is in Kamchatka," I said, "which is even more reason for me to get out of here. Where do you want to go?"

"Baikal."

37
Getting Away from It All

A week later, we flew to Irkutsk, where we met Sasha's college buddy Sergei. He was a large man with a full red beard. Sergei let out a robust laugh when he saw Sasha. "Still shaving your head in protest, Mukhmedich?"

"That's right, Red. Until they win the championship, I'm going to keep protesting."

They growled, hugged, and slapped each other's backs.

Whenever the Russian national soccer team was eliminated from the summer European tournament, Sasha shaved his head bald. They had lost in an early round this year, and now Sasha's skull was perfectly round, his ears protruding like fins on a blowfish.

"You look ridiculous, Abdulich," Sergei laughed as he rubbed his friend's smooth scalp.

"That's the point," Sasha declared. "I'm supposed to look so awful that the Russian team will be ashamed. To avoid the hideous sight of my shiny head, maybe next time they'll win."

Lyuda groaned.

Sergei turned to Lyuda and gave her a hug. She almost disappeared in the large man's embrace. Alina was scared of Sergei and hid behind her mother when he tried to talk to her.

As we walked to Sergei's car, I pulled Sasha aside and asked why his friend called him by so many different names.

"Oh, Red is just making fun of my Tatar blood. He's been calling me Arab-sounding names for as long as I've known him."

"That's right, Akhmadich," Sergei said with a chuckle. "Your ancestors invaded on horseback and ruled us Russians for four hundred years. I figure I better make fun of you now, while I still can. With a little help from your American friend here, it sounds like you're determined to reconquer Russia, this time with chocolate. A barbarian and a bourgeois—now there is a deadly combination."

On the drive to Sergei's apartment, he told us the bad news. His yacht had a broken rudder. There were no yacht-supply stores out here, so he would have to make one himself. That, however, would take several days. So, we abandoned our plans to go boating and decided just to go camping on one of the Baikal's islands.

Because there wasn't enough room in Sergei's four-wheel-drive NIVA, we had to split up. Lyuda, Alina, and I went on a hydrofoil that streaked across the great lake's clear water at sixty kilometers per hour. Sasha and Sergei filled the NIVA with supplies and drove on rugged back roads.

The boat was so crowded with Siberians eager to get away from it all that Lyuda and I had to stand in the galley. Alina had a sugar fit after devouring an entire Snickers bar. She squirmed out of Lyuda's hands and ran up and down the boat's cluttered aisle. She tripped over backpacks and tents. She cried for a few minutes, then, when the sugar buzz faded, she fell asleep.

"In America," Lyuda asked, "how does marriage work?"

Her question seemed innocent enough, but, to me, it sounded like a police officer reading me my rights. Everything I said would be held against me or, more likely, against Sasha, my friend and partner. Whatever her gripe with her husband, I didn't want to get caught in the crossfire.

"You're asking the wrong guy," I said with utmost sincerity. "I've never been married."

She laughed, but persisted. "Seriously, how does marriage work in America?"

"As often as not," I said, "it doesn't."

"But your parents are still together, right?"

"Yes," I said with a bizarre sense of guilt. "My parents have been lucky, I guess."

That obviously didn't satisfy her. She was determined to learn the secret to marital happiness, or the source of her unhappiness. For the rest of the three-hour boat ride, she relentlessly interrogated me about the way marriage is supposed to work, as if my American passport was actually a marriage counselor's license. I was sympathetic to her situation, the lonely wife of a successful Siberian businessman. But I was also the partner of that businessman. It was an uncomfortable situation, to say the least.

I was glad to get out of the boat when it finally made a brief stop halfway up the deepest freshwater lake in the world. We stood on the bone-dry shore. There were no buildings, no signs of civilization except a dusty road and a man walking a hang glider up the steep slope of the lake's shore. Sergei and Sasha rolled over the hill in the little white car about twenty minutes later. The man flew his hang glider back and forth in a futile attempt to catch an updraft. The air was perfectly still. He just slalomed his way downward, landing several feet away from Sergei's car. Sergei yelled at the pilot for nearly hitting his car. The pilot yelled at Sergei for parking on his landing strip. Only after exchanging insults did they realize that they knew each other. They both laughed as they shook hands. Sergei complimented the man's hang glider and the man complimented Sergei's car.

Thirty minutes later, a ferry took us across the strait to Olkhon, the lake's largest island. We all crammed into the car like circus clowns and drove thirty kilometers north to an isolated cove where a large group of Sergei's friends had already set up camp. We spent five days on the shores of Lake Baikal. We played soccer, went for hikes, and even built our own ad hoc banya out of campfire-heated rocks and a giant canvas tarp. Sergei built a makeshift fish smoker out of an old gas canister and smoldering pinecones. We tossed freshly caught fish into the smoker, and within an hour, we savored the delicacy of smoked fish.

One afternoon, a Buryat man drove up in a UAZ. He was barefoot and had no shirt. He face was puffy from years of drinking. A raw side of bloody beef sat in the back of the UAZ.

"Buryat pizza delivery," Sasha said as he nudged me in the side. Sasha handed over a wad of rubles and the Buryat hacked off a slab of meat with a hatchet. We ate shashlik and smoked fish, all washed down with vodka.

Sergei told us about the local legend of Baikal's magic water. "If you stick your finger in the lake, you'll prolong your life by a year. If you go into the water up to your waist, you'll prolong your life by five years. If you go up to your neck, you'll live an extra ten years."

"How about if you go all the way?" Sasha asked. "What if I jump in over my head?"

"You'll cut your life short by thirty years," Sergei laughed. "You'll drown, Iatohlavich."

After a shot of vodka for courage and/or stupidity, we all jumped into the icy water and thrashed about for ten seconds. Our hearts accelerated as our breathing seized, our chest muscles too tense to expand. Our breathing quickly recovered, and then the adrenaline began to flow. For the next thirty minutes, I felt more alive, more vigorous than I could ever remember feeling. Maybe the waters of Baikal really were magic.

By placing a rotten log atop the embers of our campfire, Sergei made a self-sustaining fire chimney. We removed the log and placed it on top of four rocks. The log burned from the inside out, the flames greedily sucking in air from below and spitting dancing red sparks skyward. The red sparks flittered and faded away against the backdrop of flickering stars. Hundreds of miles from any city lights, the night sky teemed with the streaks and swirls of the Milky Way. I took my sleeping bag and slept atop a hill; the tip of my nose dipped into the stars overhead. I felt as powerful as a god and as insignificant as a flea all at once.

These kinds of moments were why I had moved to Siberia in the first place.

38
The Best of Times

Monika got her wish to see Siberia that summer. There was a medical trade show in Novosibirsk. The trade show was held in a former hockey stadium, now a year-round convention center. Monika got off the plane along with three middle-aged, barrel-shaped German men who represented various companies selling an odd variety of medical paraphernalia from catheters to herbal medicines. These four had apparently become good friends while on the Eastern European tradeshow circuit. These fun-loving Germans changed my impression of Germany as a stale land of precision and exactness. But they did it in an odd way: they agreed with my stereotype of Germany.

"Germany is such a boring place," Dieter, the curly-haired catheter salesman, said with a laugh. "That's why we all got jobs that take us to places like this."

"*Ja*," Mathius, the herbal medicine salesman, said with a nod. "God, you are zo lucky to live out here." He waved both his hands at the forest like a conductor, as if the trees made up his orchestra.

After the tradeshow was over and Monika declared it a success, we took her and her German colleagues on a cruise on the company boat. We colonized *Khrenovoye* (Horseradish), the smaller of the two main islands at this end of the Ob Sea.

The "cutter," as Ivan Ivanovich called it, could safely accommodate up to twenty people at a time, and thirty not quite so safely. Below deck were several rooms with beds for overnight expeditions. In front of the captain's bridge, the long, flat deck served as a dance floor. Ivan Ivanovich had rigged up several speakers that blasted out music, transforming the boat into a floating disco club. A spotlight panned over scantily clad, gyrating bodies.

Built behind the bridge was the pride of the ship: the onboard banya.

One of our young accountants, Alya, revealed on the cruise that she was a truly talented banya maid.

She was like a dancer, her motions graceful and purposeful. First, she ladled water onto the rocks that were inside a square cavity in the stove's wall. The steam came shooting out sideways. To protect her prone subject—in this case, me—she held the birch branches in front of the scalding geyser, dispersing the steam and simultaneously heating up the leaves. Once the room was sultry, she said, "A little more," and tossed more water on the rocks.

She turned to me like a surgeon turns to a patient lying on the operating table. She had two separate bundles of leafy branches. She laid one on my feet while she waved the other like a flame-throwing oriental fan over my entire body. I groaned. She switched bundles, grabbing the first bundle from my feet and quickly covering my feet again with the second bundle. She moved up my legs slowly, vigorously snapping the branches as if she were shaking water off a wooden spoon. She worked over my whole body, not slapping, but just touching the wet leaves to my wet skin.

She switched bundles again, and with a loud slap, the birch branches came down onto my back. Before I could cry out in pain, Alya put a comforting hand on my leg, and continued to slap vigorously with the other hand. Like the locomotive of a steam-driven train, the leaves came down rhythmically—*tsheuuuw, tsheuuuw, tsheuuuw.*

She put one finger over my nose and told me to breathe through one nostril. "It's good for you," she said. In awe of her expertise, I did what she said. I would have swallowed one of the bundles of birch branches if she told me to.

In the office, her voice was usually soft, cracking with meekness. In the banya, she bellowed out commands that were impossible to misunderstand or disobey. She didn't ask, "Could you please turn over?" She barked, "On your back! Cover your crotch with both hands!" I did, quickly. She then covered my face with one of the aromatic bundles of leaves, and used the other to work over my front side with care that was at once violent and tender. Alya switched bundles like a symphony percussionist going rapidly from xylophone sticks to timpani mallets without missing a beat. She ordered me to raise a leg, which she immediately seized tightly in her grip and pummeled with the branches as if she were angrily washing a flagpole with a wet mop.

When she finished, she said, "That's all. You're done." I was a pork roast and she had just stuck a fork in me. Without a word, I lifted my listless body, pocked with wet leaves, and stumbled to my feet. I staggered out the door and fell overboard into the cool water of the Ob Sea. I flailed about as a torrent of screams and whoops spewed involuntarily from my mouth.

"Next," Alya yelled from inside the banya. Sasha put his bottle of beer down and ran back for his pleasant pummeling.

The Germans lounged about on the sandy beach, drank beer, and soaked up the intense Siberian sun. In fact, from the moment they got off the plane until the minute they left, these Germans laughed, drank, and had a good time. They were visibly sad when they had to leave and go back to Germany.

The school year started in one week. Natasha's plane arrived in four days.

I wanted to surprise her pleasantly when she got back. I decided to buy some nice furniture for the apartment. Lyuda offered to go furniture shopping with me. She clearly reveled vicariously in my desire to please Natasha. We found a green couch with two matching soft chairs and a coffee table. I forked over the bundles of rubles and the salesperson promised that the furniture would be delivered the next day, the same day that Natasha was supposed to fly back.

The hours rolled by, but the furniture didn't come. An hour before I had to go to the airport, I called Sarah. I asked if she could hang out at my place in case the furniture came. She came over with her new boyfriend. Ivan was a tall, blond university student who was giddy most of the time. Just as they were walking up the steps to my apartment, the furniture arrived on the back of a flatbed truck. Ivan and I frantically hauled it into the apartment. But the couch wouldn't fit through the door. In my haste, I kicked it through the doorway, breaking it. Ivan promised to hammer it back together and Sarah promised to arrange things so that the place looked nice when I got back with Natasha. I thanked them both and scurried off to the airport.

I got there with five minutes to spare before the plane from Kamchatka landed. As the people filed off the plane, my heart beat with anticipation. But Natasha wasn't among the passengers. I waited for an hour, holding out hope that she'd walk through the rickety metal gate. Maybe she missed the plane, I thought. On the hour-long ride back from the airport I went over and over in my mind, trying to remember if I knew how to get in touch with her. I didn't know her phone number in Kamchatka. I didn't even know if she had a phone out there. I decided that I'd find her tall girlfriend to ask if she knew anything about Natasha's whereabouts. But it was already past midnight, so I'd have to wait until tomorrow. When I turned the corner into my courtyard, I saw that the lights were on in my apartment.

Having already experienced wrenching disappointment at the airport, I fought back the urge to run, to get my hopes up again. Sarah and Ivan had probably left the lights on. When I got close, I could see that the kitchen window was fogged over. I still didn't run. Maybe the village's hot water had been restored and I had left the faucet open. When I inserted the key and turned it I heard Natasha let out a cheer. My heart leapt. If her absence made my heart grow fonder, her reappearance made it nearly burst with joy.

Only after we had hugged, kissed, and halfway undressed each other, did I ask her when and how she got here. Why hadn't I seen her at the airport? She said in between planting kisses on my neck that she had managed to get on an earlier flight. There was no way to let me know. Sorry.

"I'm just glad that you're back," I said.

She kissed me on the nose. "I'm really glad to be back home, too."

I raised an eyebrow. "Home?"

"When I was in Kamchatka I realized that, even though my mom, dad, and brother still live there, it was no longer my home. My home is wherever you are."

"Did you tell your mother that you're living with a foreigner, an American?"

"Not at first," she said with a mischievous smile. "We were in the banya and she was giving me her usual lecture about how I was too headstrong, that no Russian man would ever marry a woman like me. 'You're not so young, anymore,' she said. I told her that she was right, that no Russian man would want to marry me. But I told her that I'd solved the problem. I said I was dating an American."

"What do you mean dating?"

"That's exactly what she asked. She clearly wanted to know whether I'd slept with you, if I'd given you my flower."

"And?"

"I said that I had; that we had."

"And?"

"She was shocked. I thought she was going to faint. Then she pulled my head to her breast and told me that I was still just a baby—that I was too young to be dating."

We both laughed.

"Your mom sounds like an intense woman."

"Like mother, like daughter," Natasha said. "You'll find out just how intense soon enough. She's flying out here next month to kill you for deflowering her daughter."

39
Unconditional Love

With each passing day, the sun came up a couple minutes later and went down a couple minutes earlier. The outside temperature dipped down a few degrees more than the previous night. The birch leaves flashed yellow then fell to the forest floor in a few short weeks. For a few days hoarfrost twinkled on the ground in the mornings. Then, after a night of flurries, the village was quiet and clean again, covered by a coating of creamy snow.

The flight with Natasha's mother arrived at three A.M. It was right on time. I was more surprised by the plane arriving on time than by the fact that somebody, somewhere figured that it was optimal to have a plane arrive at such an ungodly hour. I had been living in Russia for too long.

Natasha and I stood in the darkness with snowflakes tickling our faces as we watched the furry human forms pass through the gate and through the taxi-driver gauntlet. They all looked the same to me, but then Natasha waved her gloved hand and shouted, "*Mamulya.*"

A square-shaped woman walked up to Natasha. "*Dochechka,*" she said in the same baby voice Natasha used with me during intimate moments.

A chill went up my spine.

The woman engulfed her daughter in an embrace, clutching Natasha's head to her breast. After a few seconds, Natasha pried herself from her mother's embrace and turned to me.

"Mamulya, this is Shm..." she paused. Natasha didn't call me Sasha; there were so many Sashas in this part of the world, and she said that I was unique. So she called me by names that she thought up. And she thought up a new nickname for me almost on a weekly basis. This week it was "Shmarling," derived from "Darling." She laughed, then collected herself. "Mamulya, this is my man."

"Lyubov Vasilievna," I said with a polite nod. I knew better than to offer to shake a Russian woman's hand. It was an offense to her femininity.

She nodded formally, stoically, and said, "*Zdrasvuitye.*"

"Allow me to carry your suitcase," I said, reaching for her bag. She handed it over with a raised eyebrow. I couldn't tell if it was a suspicious or surprised look. Probably both.

Back at the apartment, the interrogation began in earnest.

"What are you doing in Siberia?"

"I import cocoa beans for the local chocolate factories," I answered, making an extra effort to look her straight in the eyes.

"Mom," Natasha jumped in, "you know what he does. I told you this summer."

Mother looked at daughter. "I'm just trying to determine what kind of man it is that thinks he can take advantage of my daughter."

"Mom," Natasha complained.

"It's okay," I said, putting my hand on Natasha's back and rubbing it to calm her down.

Her mother looked at my hand on her daughter. She lectured her daughter about the dangers of trusting people, especially men. And now that she had slept with me, she had no leverage.

"I don't need leverage," Natasha argued.

"*Dochka*, how could you have been so naïve. You were seduced."

"He didn't seduce me," Natasha asserted, then blushed. "I was the one who initiated sex. It was time. It felt right. He was tender with me."

Her mother let out an indignant laugh. "A man has to be strong. He has to be the solid wall you can stand behind."

"Look, Mom," Natasha said as she walked behind me. She put her hands on my shoulders. "Look at this wall. He's huge. You can't even see me behind him, can you? This is my wall. This is my man."

Her mother glared at me. "It's clear that my daughter loves you. Do you love my daughter?"

"Yes. More than anything."

After a long pause, her stern face broke into a smile. "Well, okay then. That's all I needed to hear." Then she leaned in toward me and asked, "How can you stand her? She's such a shark."

"Mom!" Natasha said, clearly both amused and offended.

"Well, it's true," her mother said, chuckling.

By the end of her weeklong stay, Natasha's mother was pestering her daughter to hurry up and get married. "It isn't serious unless you've got a ring on your finger. Unless you're married, a man can up and leave at any time."

"If he doesn't love you, a man can up and leave even after he's married," Natasha argued.

Her mother shook her head in resignation. "I give up. You seem to know what's best for you. That's all I want, you know? What's best for you."

"I know, Mamulya."

Lyubov kissed her daughter on the cheek and walked off toward the plane that would take her back to Kamchatka.

Natasha and I suddenly had no challenges ahead of us except the usual grind of work, school, and a long winter. Before the snow got too deep, we rented a pair of horses from a cash-starved collective farm nearby and galloped across the rolling fields near a frozen tributary of the Ob. Their hooves sent up splashes of snow that sparkled from the low-angled rays of the winter sun. They were farm horses, so they weren't all that fast. But with the temperature hovering around minus eighteen Celsius, going fast meant a bitter, biting wind. We pulled on the reins more than we nudged the beasts with our heels.

While she rode in front of me I suddenly felt a sense of déjà vu. I'd seen this woman before. I realized that it was Natasha who I'd seen on the horse in front of the university on April First (Math Day) over a year ago. I had seen her for the first time exactly one year before we met.

275

Soon after riding the horses, another beast entered our lives. While we were at one of Sarah's parties, a hungry, stray kitten appeared on her doorstep. Since Sarah was going back to the U.S. in a few days to apply for some grants so that she could expand her work fostering a generation of Siberian democrats, Natasha and I agreed to take the howling little bundle of black fur. Sarah named the cat Scout, but Natasha and I, after only a few days of having it in our apartment, changed its name to Pooper. In addition to trouble figuring out how to use the toilet I had built for him, Pooper wasn't weaned yet. He would stick his face into Natasha's long hair and start kneading her scalp with his claws and nuzzling his snout in search of milk. At first it was endearing, if a bit painful for Natasha. But when he did it seven times a night, Natasha had to wear a bandanna if she wanted to get any sleep at all.

It quickly became clear that this wasn't a feline prodigy. It fell off our fourth-story balcony, fortunately without suffering anything more than a broken claw. Natasha came home one day to find the cat with its head stuck in an empty, fogged-up mayonnaise jar. Slapping with its paws at the bubbles in Natasha's bubble bath, Pooper lost his grip on the slippery edge of the tub and vanished through the foam, sending up a spout of water. Since it became clear that leaving this cat at home alone was dangerous, I devised a harness that I wore underneath my down parka. Natasha and I would go walking around the village with Pooper's head protruding out like a baby kangaroo from between two of my parka's buttons. When he got too cold, the cat just pulled his head back inside. I suggested that we rename him Joey, the Australian name for baby kangaroos.

Once we ran into one of Natasha's classmates walking with George, his massive Rottweiler. The dog sniffed the bulge in my parka just as Pooper stuck his face out into the wet nose of the huge hound. Both dog and cat were frozen for a second of utter confusion. Pooper, once he figured out what he was looking at, snapped his head back inside like a turtle. The dog looked at its owner then back at my belly and gave a loud bark. A second later, I felt a warm sensation as Pooper urinated on me.

"Maybe we should change his name," Natasha said with a laugh.

We loved him despite his faults.

We celebrated New Year's Eve at Sasha's brick house in the 'burbs. Natasha's abstinence from meat became an issue. Not eating meat in Russia is hard enough, but not eating meat in a Tatar home during a holiday is a real problem. Baba Masha hassled Natasha to eat some of the meat dumplings that she had been making over the past few days. Natasha, just to get the old lady to quiet down, put one on her plate, but she didn't eat it. Seeing that Natasha wasn't eating meat, Alina decided that she, too, wasn't going to eat meat. This caused the mighty matriarch to get out of her chair and put two more dumplings on Alina's plate.

"You're going to eat until your plate is clean," Baba Masha declared.

Alina started to cry.

"Don't make her eat all that," Lyuda said. "That's too much."

"She's lucky to have meat at all. We didn't have meat for years when I was a kid. That's why I'm so small. No," Baba Masha said with gusto, "my granddaughter is going to eat meat."

Natasha and I were both glad to leave that big house and get back to our little apartment the next morning.

By midwinter, my parents wanted to meet Natasha. Rather than flying to the other side of the world, we decided to meet halfway, in Italy. Our company travel agent found a Moscow-based travel agency owned and operated by a thirty-year-old, self-proclaimed retired KGB spy. Through him, I bought a two-week customized tour for two. For a total of $1,100, we got train tickets from Rome to Florence to Venice to Milan, hotels and historic guided walking tours in every city, and plane tickets from Moscow to Rome and from Milan back to Moscow. The former spy also managed to get Natasha an Italian visa. All we had to do was get from Novosibirsk to Moscow, which cost forty dollars for each of us with our student IDs.

We left in the middle of March when the Siberian sun was getting high in the sky, but the needle on the thermometer was still well below zero. Twenty-four hours later we were strolling around the Colosseum in just our sweaters. The only problem was that our clothes started to smell like cat urine. Apparently, before we dropped him off at Aunt Sarah's, Pooper had sprayed our backpack. As it thawed out in the Italian spring weather, the smell became overwhelming.

The garish wealth of the Vatican made Natasha literally light-headed. After we left the Sistine Chapel, her feet started to drag and her shoulders began to sag as our guide gave a canned speech about the Vatican's decision to add fig leaves on the nude marble statues. Everywhere Natasha looked, there was incalculable wealth. Mosaics on the floors, frescoes along the walls, and murals across entire ceilings. She had to sit down on a bench while the rest of the tour group walked on ahead.

"This is a church, right?" she asked me as I rubbed her neck.

"This is *the* church," I said.

She just shook her head and groaned. We skipped the rest of the tour and went to a Chinese restaurant, which raised her spirits considerably. She was pleasantly surprised to find half of the menu filled with vegetarian and seafood dishes. She laughed at herself and her clumsiness with chopsticks, but eventually got the hang of it. As we left the restaurant, she declared that Chinese food was now her favorite food. We walked aimlessly through the streets of Rome. For dinner we stepped into a deli and bought fresh mozzarella cheese, fresh bread, pesto, and a few tomatoes. When we'd finished eating that, she declared that Italian food was now her favorite cuisine. When she had her first cappuccino, she declared emphatically, "This is my favorite drink."

After three days in Rome, we boarded a train and went to Florence. My parents had already been there for a few days. They met us at the train station. Natasha got a beautiful bouquet of flowers and a hug from my mom and dad. I just got hugs. They escorted us to our hotel through the narrow streets of Florence as if it was their hometown. My dad and I walked in front, while Natasha and my mom walked behind, chatting. I smiled as I eavesdropped on their conversation.

Natasha had studied English for years in her Kamchatkan high school and at the University of Novosibirsk, and she had always been an *otlichnitsa* (an A student). But when she heard me speaking English with Sarah for the first time, she dropped her jaw. She didn't understand a thing. It was as if she hadn't taken a single English class in her life. This had made her understandably apprehensive about meeting my parents, who didn't speak a word of Russian. So, in addition to her usual course load of exotic math subjects, she took it upon herself to bone up on English, especially the pronunciation of American English. We watched American movies on a VCR. She made me stop the movie every several minutes so that I could pronounce similar sounding words like "dock" and "duck." As I said them, she would stick her face inches from mine in order to scrutinize the way my mouth moved.

When Natasha noticed that I was listening in on her conversation with my mother, she gave me a friendly poke in the back. "Don't listen," she said, but she said it in English.

While emerging from an arched tunnel that led into a cobblestone square, I spotted Paula, a prematurely gray-haired but perpetually youthful family friend from Minneapolis. She lived a few months every year with her husband in Florence. She was buying flowers from a street vender. I tapped her on the shoulder. She turned and gave me a bright smile. There were hugs all around. Natasha got a hug from Paula before they were officially introduced. Turns out my parents had already told Paula about Natasha. Maybe it was the warm greeting of my parents; maybe it was all the walking; maybe it was running into familiar faces on the streets; but Natasha and I felt at home right away in this old Italian town.

My mom, who had raised two boys, was quickly enamored of Natasha and kidnapped her at every chance she could get. They would go for long walks about town. Dad and I would usually grab a couple of cappuccinos, find a bench in a crowded square, and talk about my bizarre business experiences in Siberia. My dad, an international entrepreneur himself, enjoyed my stories with belly laughs and shakes of his head. "Sounds like a lot of fun." Then he asked,

"Why does the factory buy cocoa beans from you guys? Couldn't they bypass you and buy from the source?" I didn't have a good answer for him, other than that we took the Director on trips to America every once in a while.

Paula took us on a trip to Greve, an ancient hill town outside Florence. We walked up a windy road through vineyards. As we walked back down, Natasha and Paula locked arms and skipped down the winding road singing "A Spoon Full of Sugar." We had watched *Mary Poppins* the week before we left for Italy.

After three days, Natasha and I had to catch our train to Venice. My mom didn't want to part with us, mostly with Natasha, so she and dad got on the train with us. They found a hotel a few canals over from ours and we spent two more idyllic days together. When they had to leave, we escorted my parents to the train station. My mom cried, which made Natasha cry.

On the way back to our hotel, we jumped into a gondola. While passing underneath the Rialto Bridge spanning the Grand Canal, I got an urge to propose to Natasha. My parents clearly approved of her, and I had her mother's approval. In fact, I was likely to earn her mother's disapproval if I didn't ask her daughter to marry me soon. I couldn't tell whether proposing in a gondola in Venice was incredibly romantic or incredibly tacky. It was April First. We had known each other for exactly one year, but like dog years, a year in Siberia is worth more than regular years.

I turned and looked Natasha straight into her green eyes. "Natasha, will you marry me?"

A smile stretched across her blushing face. She opened her mouth and three words came out. "*Da. Si.* Yes."

40
Bean Counters

Natasha and I arrived in Siberia just as spring did. The temperature surged above freezing, turning the streets of our village into muddy canals. Natasha joked that it looked like Venice. We both went back to our routines. She went back to her studies and seminars. I went back to faxes and phone calls. But something felt different for me. The thrill of doing business in Siberia had faded. My fervor for bringing the market to this part of the world was all but gone. The market was here, but it didn't feel like an accomplishment.

After the voucher fiasco, I realized that the poor in Russia would probably remain poor for a long time. The rich would be getting a lot richer before anything trickled down, if ever. That was a bitter pill for an idealistic economist to swallow, but even more disheartening was watching what the rich did with their *earnings*.

All I had to do was look at the things for sale to realize to what depths of hedonism the Siberian dream had sunk. The back pages of Novosibirsk newspapers were covered with advertisements for "full service" visits from Tanya, Katya, Natasha, and Lena. Most of the telephone numbers were Novosibirsk numbers, but a significant proportion of them were local to our village. Prostitutes were for sale in our little academic village. Prostitution was a cottage industry in Siberia, but it was an integral part of Moscow's service sector.

Sasha and I flew to Moscow to meet our suppliers and freight forwarders at least every other month. With each visit, the city looked more and more like a crass imitation of Las Vegas, if that's possible. On one particular trip, I went without Sasha because he had to deal with a tax audit. When I tried to check into the hotel, the hefty woman in the lobby said that she had no reservation in my name. I asked her to check again. The woman with dyed blue hair simply pretended not to notice me. I realized the problem: I had spoken to her politely and in Russian. I pulled out my U.S. passport and said in perfect English, "I want a room."

She looked up with wide eyes and a red face. She frantically started fingering through her little metal recipe box. "Why didn't you say you were an *inostranets* (foreigner)?" She pulled from the box a little card with my reservation written on it. "You shouldn't confuse a poor old woman like me."

I was disgusted by such blatant discrimination, even if I was the beneficiary of it.

Except for the dozen scantily clad women just hanging around smoking cigarettes in the lobby, the hotel hadn't changed much since the Soviet days. The warped floor squeaked as I walked down the hallway, a skeleton key unlocked my room's thin door, and inside there was a carpet on the wall, but the cold floor was bare. I took a shower to get Moscow's grime off of me and slipped in between the chilly sheets. Minutes after I turned out the lights, the phone rang.

"Would you like a girl?" a woman's voice asked me.

"No," I said.

Five minutes later the phone rang again.

"Want a girl? Not expensive," said the same voice.

"No," I said with a little laugh. Selling sex was bad enough, but haggling was pathetic.

Five minutes later the phone rang again. I picked it up and said in English, "I don't want a girl. Thank you," and hung up. For good measure I took the phone off the hook and tossed the receiver under the other bed's pillow to prevent the dial tone from keeping me up.

Five minutes later, there was a knock on my door.

"Come on," the woman's voice said. "Try a girl. Four hours for forty dollars. It's a good deal."

I thought prostitutes got paid by the job, not the hour. Ten dollars an hour *was* a good deal.

"No!" I yelled. "I don't want any girls. I just want to sleep. Let me sleep."

"Okay, okay," she said. "But you have to put your phone back on the hook. It's hotel policy."

It was then when I realized who this woman was. She wasn't a madam. She was the *dezhurnaya* (from the French *du jour*), the little old lady who sat at the desk by the elevators for a twenty-four-hour work shift. There was one dezhurnaya on each floor. Back in Soviet days, the dezhurnaya guarded the floor from raucous behavior; she was a babysitter for hotel guests. Today, however, the dezhurnaya did telemarketing, pestering the guests into having sex with young girls for dollars. The old lady probably got a commission from every transaction.

"I'll put the phone back on the hook if you promise to stop calling me and offering girls."

"Okay," she agreed.

Five minutes later, she called and asked, "Do you like boys?"

"No," I laughed. "Good night, babulya."

She laughed. "Sweet dreams, sonny."

When I flew back to Novosibirsk, I found the Saab in the airport parking lot. Sergei was smoking a cigarette and leaning up against the side of the car. He didn't wait inside the car for fear of falling asleep. One of our other Sergeis had made that mistake a year ago with the minivan. While he slept, somebody stole the Chrysler hood ornament off the front of the vehicle.

Sergei greeted me with a nod, shook my hand, then popped open the trunk. I tossed in my bag and briefcase. Sasha was asleep in the Saab. He wasn't here to meet me. He was escorting a group of chocolate executives to London for yet another "business trip." Even though I would have liked to visit London, I didn't have the stomach to chaperone another group of Siberian shoppers abroad.

When I opened the Saab's door, the cold air woke him. He smiled and stuck out his hand. I shook it. He rubbed his eyes, then let out a yawn, then a yawp.

"Base, this is car one," Sergei said into the CB radio's microphone. "I've got Richardovich. Still waiting for Kamilovich's plane."

"Understood," Victor Petrovich's voice came from the radio's speaker. "Base out."

"How'd the audit go?" I asked.

"Aaggh," Sasha grunted. "No big deal. They knew that we had paid our taxes, that we hadn't broken any laws. But they couldn't leave without finding anything. It would look bad for the tax inspectors. Those two inspectors actually pulled me aside and begged me to help them. We agreed that they could slap us with a symbolic fine and they agreed not to audit us for at least two more years."

"Nice work," I said.

"How'd your trip go?"

"Fine. The next shipment of beans is on its way."

Sasha's eyes brightened as he suddenly remembered something. He reached into the inside pocket of his coat and pulled out a cell phone. He handed it to me.

"What's this?"

"It's a cellular phone," he reported proudly.

I gave him a smile. "I know it's a cell phone."

"Sorry." Sasha laughed. "Sometimes I forget that you're an American."

"Does this thing work here?" I asked as I pressed the ON button. The keys lit up.

"No," Sasha said. "They haven't put up the antennae yet. That's why I got it so cheap. I'm going to see if it works in Moscow. By the time I get back from England, there should be a few antennae in Novosibirsk. They promised coverage in the village within six months. The guy who sold it to me said that I should be able to get reception within a month if I stand on the roof of my apartment."

"Convenient," I said.

As I handed the phone back to Sasha, I saw through the window behind him an old man snapping the reins of a shaggy horse. The horse was pulling a cart with the old man. Next to him on a bale of hay sat a large woman, made even larger by the thick coat she wore.

Like a steam engine, the horse sent out white puffs from its nostrils into the chilly morning air.

Sasha slapped me on the shoulder and said, "Oh, I almost forgot. The factory is claiming that there were less than fifty tons of beans in the last shipment. They say that we are trying to cheat them."

"The Director accused us of shortchanging him?"

"No," Sasha shook his head. "Of course not. He's on our side. It's one of the technicians raising such a fuss. The Director can't ignore these complaints from his employees. He has to appear to be looking out for the best interest of the factory."

"Even when he's not," I said.

"Right," Sasha said. "Anyway, I think it would be a good idea for you to go to the factory and inspect the shipment. I'm sure it's just a few kilograms short, but we need to let those peons at the factory think that we respect them. I think that you, as an American, would impress them more than I could. Just let them think that we care."

"Which we don't."

"No, not really," Sasha said. "We're trying to make money, not friends."

I laughed. "Let me get this straight. You want me to go to the factory and pretend to count beans?"

"You don't really have to measure all fifty tons. Just let them yell at you and accuse you of being a cheat, then say that you will look into it and make sure it never happens again."

After five minutes of silence I turned to Sasha, who was fiddling with his new phone.

"What the hell are we doing?" I asked.

He looked up, confused. "We're waiting for my plane."

"I mean our business. What are we doing?"

Now, even more confused, he just looked at me and said nothing.

"We're bean counters," I said.

He laughed. "Yes, but we're going to be rich bean counters."

"Maybe so." I sighed. "I almost hope that we don't get rich."

Sasha gave me a concerned look. "Sanya, there is a Russian expression: 'It's better to be rich and healthy than poor and sick.' Don't forget it."

"I don't want to be sick and poor. I'm just concerned about how we are making our money. Why doesn't the factory buy its own beans and cut us out of the deal?"

"They don't have the money," Sasha said.

"Neither do we," I said. "All of our money is borrowed."

"True," Sasha admitted. "But you're forgetting about the business trips to New York and London."

The economist in me groaned. "We're not adding anything to the equation. If anything, we are in the way of a more efficient means of getting things done."

Sasha, in a slightly defensive tone, said, "Sanya, we've kept the factories supplied with raw materials when they didn't have any. I don't see anything wrong with that. And we provide these trips to the factory directors because they are reasonably cautious about how they spend their money. Lots of people were killed in this country for being rich. The factory directors haven't forgotten that. They are rich, but they don't want anybody to know it. That's where we come in. We take them on trips to places where they can spend their money without having to worry about envious eyes. It's a service, just like any other. If they are willing to pay for it, why shouldn't we be willing to provide that service? Why shouldn't we be willing to profit from it?"

"I don't know," I admitted. "All I know is that it isn't supposed to work this way."

Sasha's plane eventually took off. On the ride back from the airport, we passed the horse-drawn cart after only a few minutes on the road. I was disappointed and disgusted to see the once expansive fields divided by a procession of billboards advertising little luxuries, brand name luxuries: Marlboro, Absolut, Snickers, Levi's. The colors on the billboards were bold, flashy, and, at this time of the morning, just plain obnoxious.

Sergei passed every car on the road as if they were standing still. He tried to pass a military truck but a snake of cars coming in the opposite direction made him use his breaks for the first time since we left the airport. Inside the army truck sat several dozen soldiers with rifles between their legs. They were obviously cold with only the canvas tarp over their heads to protect them. The soldier sitting closest to the tailgate looked at me. I wore a tie and a white shirt; I had taken off my parka and sport coat because it was so warm in the Swedish car. The soldier just stared at me with a bitter look. His eyes were accusing. Why was I sitting comfortably in a foreign car while he was freezing his ass off, sucking in diesel fumes in the back of an open truck? The soldier grabbed the rifle from between his legs and aimed it at me. After jerking the rifle back as if from the gun's recoil, the soldier slapped his buddy next to him and pointed at me. They both laughed at my pale face.

It isn't supposed to be like this, I thought to myself.

41
The Worst of Times

Overcoming the initial shock of post-communist life, some of the factories upstream sputtered back to life, resuming production. Soon thereafter, toxic waste flowed into the Ob Sea. There were no warning signs posted. But when Natasha and I found a rare opportunity to go for swim, my eyes swelled seconds after I jumped in the water. The whites of my eyes turned pink, then red. The skin around my eyes also changed color, first red, then purple. I looked like a zombie. The chemicals affected my vision, too. They stripped away the romantic blur. Now when I looked at Siberia, I wasn't seeing an idealized vision of what it could be; I saw a sober picture of what it actually was, and an even grimmer image of what it was becoming.

Our tenuous hold on the Siberian chocolate market required fastidious maintenance. Our profit margins grew and shrank periodically, but our free time only shrank. To improve our earnings, Sasha had begun negotiating with a Moscow chocolate concern that was interested in buying the Novosibirsk chocolate factory. Sasha wanted to become friends with these bigwigs. He figured that if he could help them buy the chocolate factory, he might be rewarded with a few hundred shares of the factory. So we spent much of our time in banyas with brokers with nervous tics, bankers with pot bellies, and other venal men.

The heat of the banya couldn't keep me from getting chills at the cold-blooded way these men talked about business. It wasn't about adding value, it was about capturing it, by any means necessary.

Natasha graduated, but I couldn't celebrate with her because I was on a business trip with Sasha in Moscow, more meetings to make shady agreements with disagreeable men. A few days after I got back, she flew to Kamchatka for a month. I promised that we'd go camping when she got back. When she did come back, we didn't go camping. I was too busy. A neighbor in our stairwell offered her a job at the Institute of Genetics. Even though the monthly salary wasn't enough to buy a decent meal at the local restaurant, Natasha took it in order to fight boredom. With me at work for twelve hours a day, six days a week, she had too much free time on her hands. She stepped up her exercise regimen, running for several hours a day. I was usually too hungover in the mornings from the previous night's business meetings to run with her. As her body grew more taut, my belly started to soften.

Natasha's feelings of neglect manifested themselves in passive-aggressive behavior. When I tried to take a nap on a rare business-free Sunday, she turned the television up to full volume.

"Your mother was right," I snapped at her, "you are a shark."

If Natasha was only in the first stages of neglect, Lyuda was in the advanced stages. She would go into tantrums when Sasha went to play soccer with his friends on weekends. She had years of loneliness and frustration under her belt. Lyuda wasn't sure what she wanted, but she knew she wanted something. There was something missing in her life and she was determined to find it. She decided that remodeling the apartment was what she needed. If they moved the kitchen to where Alina's bedroom was now, and knocked out a wall here and there, then she would probably feel better, more complete.

Sasha didn't like the idea. But Lyuda accused him of spending all of their money on the brick house in Siburbia, the one that Baba Masha had, in effect, claimed as her territory. Lyuda said that Sasha didn't deserve a son because he wasn't a good enough father to his daughter. How could he be a good father if he was always at work? And when he wasn't at work, he was either drinking or napping. Sasha relented to his wife's demands. She would get her new kitchen. Maybe then he'd get a son.

Baba Masha had her demands, too. She wanted the big brick house to be filled, not just with furniture, but with grandchildren, especially grandsons. Sasha obviously couldn't please both women in his life. However, that didn't stop him from trying.

Lyuda and Baba Masha played a vicious game of chess against each other. In this game there were two queens and everybody else was a pawn. The two properties showed dramatic material improvements, but the two women showed dramatic psychological wounds. Soon, Alina was brought into the fray. Lyuda and Baba Masha began to differ about how to raise Alina. Whereas Baba Masha was strict with Alina, Lyuda was permissive. Grandma's rules were non-negotiable. Mother's rules were nonexistent. The result was a confused little girl who acted like a stern woman one minute, then a spoiled toddler the next.

Sasha, working so hard to buy the things these women demanded, was chronically fatigued. He might as well have had narcolepsy. On weekdays, he'd nod off in the car no matter how short the trip between meetings. On weekends, he'd doze off at the table after eating one of his mother's large meals. Baba Masha just shook her head in disgust. He'd fall asleep while his wife nagged about how the workmen were messing up the remodeling job. Sasha told me that he often woke up from a catnap to the sight of Lyuda crying.

"I don't know what I'm supposed to do," he complained. "If I tell her that the kitchen is too expensive, she cries. So I go to work on weekends to earn the money for her damn kitchen, and she cries because I'm never home."

One morning, just as her husband was about to go to work, Lyuda swallowed an entire bottle of sleeping pills. Sasha forced his wife to vomit out the pills by thrusting his finger down her throat.

Baba Masha, not to be outdone by her daughter-in-law, tried to throw herself underneath a speeding truck just as Sasha was getting ready to leave the cottage one Sunday evening. He pulled his slow-moving mother out of the road after a couple of trucks swerved around the little old kamikaze.

"I should have gone down to the train tracks," his mother said as he walked her back to the house. "Trains can't turn."

The two women came much closer to driving Sasha to an early grave than they had at doing themselves in. Sasha aged a decade in one month.

Back at the office, the fax and copy machine operator, Ramzia, was pregnant. The man who left his sperm in her soon thereafter left Russia. He had found a computer-programming job in America. Ramzia had to move back to her parents' village in Tatarstan. To replace her, we hired Pasha, one of the kids Sasha used to tutor in physics. Pasha didn't want the job, but his dad insisted: "You can't just wander around with your friends doing nothing."

Back at home, Pooper had run away. He had hit puberty and had squirmed out the door one evening when Natasha and I came back with our arms full of groceries. He slipped down the stairs and out the front door. He had done this several times before and always come back the next morning. But this time, he didn't come back.

Angry arguments had replaced appetizing aromas as the most noticeable thing coming from behind the doors in our stairwell. Several times a week Natasha and I would wake up in the middle of the night to the sound of fierce fights raging in neighboring apartments.

Sashka, the enterprising little boy who lived on the first floor of our stairwell, stopped picking up our empty bottles on Thursdays. When I finally ran into him early one morning, he looked five years older, but not an inch taller.

"Where's Phil?" I asked. I hadn't seen his dog in a while.

"Dead," he reported in a matter-of-fact voice. Then he walked away without another word.

The babushka who sat on the bench in front of the apartment for several hours each day (all year round) knew what had happened. She knew everything that went on in this courtyard.

"That little boy's dad is an alcoholic," she said in a loud voice. As she spoke she looked at the apartment window on the first floor. She wasn't just talking to me. "He doesn't have enough money to feed his habit and his family. So the family goes hungry. Phil went crazy with hunger. He killed a cat the other day and ate it."

My stomach turned.

The old lady continued her rant, "The poor, hungry dog attacked Nina Markovna. She lives on the third floor. When Sashka's father found out, he lost his mind. He killed Phil with a hatchet." The old woman's condemning eyes remained fixed on the window of the apartment.

It wasn't just hungry dogs that faced the threat of murder.

Every day the news reported professional-style murders of bankers and factory directors. The dogs that fight for scraps around the dumpster fight the fiercest. With Russia's economy teetering on chaos and its politics bordering on anarchy, about the only thing organized in Russia was crime. Soon enough, however, crime in Siberia became more egalitarian, more democratic. Random violence quickly became a problem, then it became an epidemic. Our little Siberian village had taken another step toward being like America. The streets weren't safe at night, which meant they weren't safe all winter long.

The woods, everybody's playground and sanctuary, were now the stalking grounds of a pack of teenage predators. This gang of pubescent hooligans ambushed solitary pedestrians. With pipes and tree branches, they savagely beat people, putting a dozen complete strangers in the hospital. Pervasive fear emptied the woods, exacerbating the danger for the stubborn few, like Natasha, who refused to surrender the woods to a bunch of teenagers. One day Natasha found herself alone in the woods with this pack of hoodlums. They were blocking her path. She stopped in her tracks. They started to run at her. She ran away, her athletic legs too strong and too fast for the young punks. She venomously conceded the woods to them. She ranted about how they had no right to steal her woods away.

A few of the teenage hoodlums got cocky and tried to assault somebody near the edge of the woods. Some other pedestrians saw what was happening and ran in to help. They caught a couple of the punks; the others ran off. One of them turned out to be Pasha, our fax boy.

Sasha, with all the responsibilities of running the company, furnishing his mother's house in Siburbia, and remodeling his wife's kitchen, simply didn't have the time to tutor his neighbor's children anymore. Obviously, nobody else had time for these kids either.

Once the seal had been broken, a genuine crime wave washed over our bucolic village. A stocky young man wearing brass knuckles punched Natasha's former roommate, Marina, in the face. The mugger took her fur hat and left a ghastly scar across her face. She joined the other victims in the quickly filling-up hospital ward. Except for muscle-bound ruffians and their trashy girlfriends, the streets of our village emptied at sundown. Friends stopped visiting each other, preferring the safety of their apartments with only the violent American action movies and sappy Mexican soap operas to keep them company.

Walking by day also took on added risks because the village was fast becoming overrun with cars. It was no longer possible to stroll with impunity down the center of the wide streets. Cars buzzed and whirred up and down the streets, filling the air with blue exhaust. Accustomed to sleeping on the sun-warmed streets in summer, dozens of cats perished. I actually witnessed a cat crossing the street get run over by the back wheel of a Russian car full of young men and their trophy dates. The girls screamed as the back of the car bounced over the feline speed bump. The car sped off. I walked up to the cat that was, to my surprise, still alive. The cat's claws were imbedded in the asphalt. I pried its claws from the road and carried it to the side of the road. It looked side to side stiffly, then it gingerly walked off into the woods. To die, I assumed.

Cats weren't the only ones at risk. Because some of the drivers were inevitably drunk, there was a spike in car accidents. In Siberia, drivers don't exchange insurance numbers after an accident and go their merry way. I once saw two drivers, already bloodied from crashing into each other, get into a fistfight to determine who was at fault. I saw a motorcycle sidecar (with a person inside) slide like a bobsled down the street after a car blindsided the bike. I saw a little red car swerve to avoid a huge pothole only to careen off the road and into a birch tree. The driver was thrown into the passenger seat where I found him. I asked if he was okay. He was so drunk that he wasn't even aware he had been in an accident. He just looked with confusion at the dashboard in front of him.

After a few moments, he turned to me and asked, "Where did my steering wheel go?"

Another problem with the infusion of cars was that there were not enough places to park them. Fortunately, an enterprising person cut a swath into a large portion of the woods in order to create a parking lot where about fifty cars could park, for a fee. It made me furious. Even worse for this economist, it was the result of the market doing what it does best, meeting high demand with increased supply.

For years I had been promoting the market as Siberia's salvation, and now the market had become a monster. So this is what Dr. Frankenstein felt like.

Faith in Siberia

Television commercials, even more than the shows they interrupt, are real-time windows into the soul of a society. People's hopes, fears, and ambitions are all exploited by television commercials. As Russian television commercials became more sophisticated, Russian capitalism became more savage.

One of the first bank commercials I saw in Russia was a cartoon. A little round man, looking like a combination between Tevye from *Fiddler on the Roof* and Mario from "Donkey Kong," stood on one side of a river. He had just harvested honey from a beehive. He had more honey than he needed. On the other side of the river stood another man, this one looked like Santa Claus in a baker's uniform. He held two armloads of bread. The two men spotted each other from opposite sides of the river. The look in their eyes conveyed that they both had the same idea; each could trade a little of his surplus for some of the other's surplus. But there was a problem. The river was too deep and the current too strong. Then, as if by magic, a glittering bridge appeared. The men met each other on the bridge, conducted their trade and lived happily ever after with a balanced diet of bread and honey. The advertisement faded to black. The words MOST BANK appeared.

In Russian, *most* means "bridge."

This was the kind of market fairy tale that could bring a tear to the eyes of a free-trade economist like me. Every transaction requires that both parties are made better off, or, one is made better off and the other is left the same, but never worse off. Free trade increases value, by definition. Or did it?

As time went by, the Russian commercials became more and more like beer ads in America. They were flashy, entertaining, and expensive, but not particularly informative. One bank put out a series of advertisements that were caricatures of great historical figures, from Caesar to Napoleon. These sixty-second commercials were short movies. One showed Alexander the Great crying after conquering the known world. Then, with a glimmer in his eyes, he ordered his soldiers to pile all of the loot to be burned. As Alexander inspected his troops, the shimmer of a ring caught his eye. The soldier with the ring was embarrassed and began to remove the ring, but it wouldn't come off. He began to bite and tug, but it still wouldn't come. By then, his fellow soldiers were laughing at him. Alexander gave a knowing smile to the camera. The camera zoomed in on the large knife at Alexander's side. The next scene showed a pile of burning treasure. The ring, covered in blood, rested atop the burning pile. The commercial faded to black. The words BANK IMPERIAL appeared.

In Russian, *imperial* means "imperial."

I came to Russia with the hope of speeding up the process of converting the economy from communist to capitalist. But capitalism didn't need any help. It washed over Russia like a tsunami. There were no levees, dikes, or dams to slow down the mighty wave of market forces. I now realized that, while communism's greatest liability was its impotence, capitalism's greatest liability was its potency.

When our glove sales began to wane, rather than lower our prices or increase advertising, Sasha suggested that we *persuade* (i.e., bribe) the mayor of Novosibirsk to mandate the use of rubber gloves in all commercial food preparation.

"Food gets safer. We sell more gloves. Everybody wins," Sasha declared proudly.

As far as I was concerned, the free market was a means for competition among sellers to create more freedom for buyers. As far as Sasha was concerned, the free market was about the freedom to become a monopolist. Compared to most Russian businessmen,

Sasha was a moderate. Most of them had a Malcolm X attitude about business—destroy your competition by any means necessary. Fighting competition, rather than fighting to compete, was the Siberian businessman's chief objective. My economist soul was in conflict with my businessman exterior. It was becoming clear to me that I couldn't be a faithful free market economist *and* a successful Siberian businessman.

My frustration at work spilled over into my personal life.

Five months after coming back from Italy, things were so bad between Natasha and me that we had stopped talking about wedding plans. We lived together but we spent very little time together. It was as if the honeymoon was over and we hadn't even gotten married yet. Somehow my mother sensed the growing rift between Natasha and me. She called me to ask how we were. I told her that things had been better.

"You know," she said, "you can't expect to be loved if you aren't lovable."

"I know."

After a pause, she asserted herself. "I want you to know that your father and I already love Natasha. We don't want to lose her."

"I don't want to lose her either," I said.

"Why don't you two come here for Christmas?"

"I don't think she'll be able to get a U.S. visa. We're not married yet."

"Oh, come on. You've accomplished harder things. You can do this."

We flew to Moscow, spent an entire day in lines at the U.S. embassy, and managed to convince the INS officer behind the glass of our intentions to return. In fact, it was an invoice for condoms to be delivered the following January that convinced her. She gave Natasha a multi-entry visa. We spent Christmas in Minnesota. Without the pressure of being a Siberian businessman on my shoulders, I had time to spend with my fiancée. We took long walks around and sometimes across the city's frozen lakes. We rediscovered each other. We fell in love again.

"So," I said as we walked on the ice underneath a bridge between Lake Calhoun and Lake of the Isles, "what do you think of my country?"

"It's not as nice as Italy," Natasha said as she got down on her hands and knees to look at the channel's sandy bottom through the clear ice. "But I'll tell you what I do like. You don't hide your hand-icapped. Every day I've been here, I've seen either a blind person or somebody in a wheelchair. Riding the bus, shopping, doing normal stuff. You never see that in Russia. And it's not because we have less blind or handicapped people. We just hide them away in Russia."

"What don't you like about America?"

"People driving in their cars to get to sports clubs where they walk on treadmills. Fast food. Insincere smiles. Don't get me started," she said with a sigh. She rolled onto her back and put one of her new Christmas mittens over her red nose. "I love you and I love your family, so I'm no longer an objective judge; but I think that there are more good things in America than bad things."

I looked out at the cluster of ice fishermen dotting the lake's frozen surface. Maybe not all Americans were addicted to comfort after all.

"When we go back to Siberia," Natasha said as she held out her two hands to me so that I could pull her to her feet, "I want you to drink less, work less, get more exercise and, most importantly, make love to me more often."

"*Postarayus* (I'll try)," I said. As I heard my own voice echo in my ears, a shiver ran down my spine. My comment sounded eerily similar to Sasha promising Lyuda that he'd be a better husband, father, etc. "*Budu* (I will)," I corrected myself. "I'm not willing to lose you just to become a Siberian cocoa king. I'll quit that job and become a writer if I have to."

Back in Siberia, I did what I could to get home before seven. But with Sasha in no such hurry to get home to his perpetually bit-ter wife or unwaveringly critical mother, the business meetings often transitioned into dinners, which inevitably led to vodka. I was lucky if I got home before ten. A couple of times a week I would excuse myself from these meetings of business and booze and hitch a ride with the rest of the employees in the company van.

At least once a week, Natasha and I visited Sarah's apartment. Sarah, now forty years old and engaged to her twenty-two-year-old Ivan, had slowly transformed her apartment from a bohemian pub into something more like a communal library. Books crowded nearly every horizontal surface. Her rules were simple: you could borrow any book as long as you returned it within a reasonable amount of time, and every time you went abroad you had to bring back books to add to the collection. It was a rule I obeyed dutifully. I didn't want to risk losing my library privileges. While I perused the shelves for the next book to read, Natasha practiced speaking English with Sarah.

On one visit, we found her spitting mad.

"Alex, you're not going to believe what the missionaries are saying now. I heard that one of the instructors in those Bible studies is a real piece of work." Changing her voice into a high-pitched shrill with a southern drawl, Sarah said, "'Y'all cahn't be shoo-ah that condoms work. Theh got teeny tiny howls in 'em.'" Sarah laughed an incredulous laugh. "They're telling the kids here that condoms don't work. Can you believe it? I feel like I spend half of my time trying to clear up the confusion those missionaries cause. I'm tempted to go to one of those Bible studies, just to see what they are preaching behind closed doors."

"You won't go," I said.

But a few days later, she did. I was surprised that she actually had the guts to go into the heart of the beast. Even more surprising, she managed to persuade me to go with her.

There were Russian-language Bibles available for everyone. A young couple, a newly ordained minister and his wife, led the meeting. They were from Wisconsin.

"*Zdrazvuite*," he said clumsily but confidently. "Welcome. My name is Derek."

"*Zdrazvuite*," his wife said with a shy smile and a slight blush. "I'm Carol. We feel blessed to be here, and we're glad you could join us."

As the translator conveyed Carol's words, I found myself thinking about how Carol and Derek looked like a dozen of my friends from back home in Minnesota. It was disorienting. I'd been in Siberia for a long time. I was now old enough to have pastors as peers? On the way to the meeting, I was coiled up like a spring, ready to pounce on anything offensive that the missionaries said. But I sat silent throughout the meeting. They never gave me a reason to speak up. No demands that everybody give up their savage ways. No promises of eternal damnation for transgressions like masturbation. Not so much as a single mention of teeny, tiny, little holes.

We cracked the new Bibles and poked around a bit, but the majority of the questions the Russians asked were simply about religion in general. How often do most people go to church? How many years did Derek study to become a minister? Derek and Carol listened respectfully to the questions. They shared what they knew and admitted what they didn't.

When it was over, the visitors got to keep the Bibles. These two were providing information, not suppressing it. Even if I didn't agree with the information they had to share, I couldn't see anything wrong with them having the right to share it. Neither could Sarah. After preparing to face off with an enemy, we ended the day with two new friends; and in Siberia, friends are dear indeed.

On the walk back to the American Ghetto, I turned to Sarah and said, "I think I've been in Siberia for too long. When the missionaries seem like reasonable, decent folk, you know it's time to get out of town."

She laughed for a few paces, then stopped and turned. "You're not serious?"

I nodded.

"Things not going so well in business?"

"They're going fine. Sasha will always find a way to clear a profit. I just don't feel like my efforts are improving life here in Siberia."

"You've lost faith in capitalism?"

"Maybe a little," I confessed. "When two kids are fighting over a candy bar, a wise mother will step in and tell one to cut the candy bar and the other to choose which half he wants. She knows that it's the surest way to guarantee that the candy bar is cut right down the middle. That's how I think of market economics. Self-interest harnessed for the common good. Maybe I just can't see the big picture anymore, but I don't see much common good in bribing chocolate factory directors."

She nodded sympathetically.

"Besides, I don't think my marriage or my liver can survive much longer in this environment."

"Do you want to move back to America?" she asked with a look of disbelief. "Back to sprawl and malls? Does Natasha?"

"I don't know. Maybe we'll move to Italy."

Leaving Siberia scared me. I had found my utopia in Siberia and then lost it. But life in Siberia had become so familiar to me that I couldn't imagine any other place to live. There were days when staying in Siberia seemed like the easiest choice, the comfortable choice. And that, perhaps more than anything, convinced me that it was time to leave.

On Russian Orthodox Easter, Sasha insisted that the Christians (Lyuda, Natasha, and I) show him how we celebrate Easter. Lyuda made the traditional Russian custard in a special mold. Natasha and I went out to buy some eggs to decorate. It took us well over an hour to find what we were looking for. The days of shortages and long lines were gone. There were plenty of eggs for sale. The only problem was that they were all brown eggs, not very good for decorating. We finally found a little babushka sitting on an upside-down crate. In front of her was a plastic bag full of twenty white eggs. After a little polite haggling, we bought them and went home.

We didn't have any egg dye or food coloring, so we had to improvise. We boiled some beets for an hour, then boiled the eggs for a few minutes in the purple liquid. To our great astonishment and disappointment, the white shells came out exactly the same brown color as all the other eggs being sold in the streets. How could a purple liquid turn a white surface brown? It was like a magic trick gone terribly wrong, we'd tried to pull a white rabbit out of a hat, but instead pulled out a pair of dirty underwear.

Natasha grabbed a candle and started drawing invisible wax designs on the ten remaining white eggs. Again using the purple beet water, we managed to produce brown eggs covered in white spirals, stars, and crosses. Natasha nearly peed in her pants with laughter when she pulled out the egg that I had decorated. I'd drawn a sickle and hammer on one hemisphere and the classic Soviet slogan *Slava Trudu* (Glory to Labor) on the other.

We went over to Sasha and Lyuda's the next morning.

Lyuda was supposed to have gone to the church to have her custard blessed, but she had slept in.

"Don't worry," I said, "we were supposed to hide these eggs."

"Well, then," Sasha said, "why don't the ladies go to the church while Sanya hides the eggs."

Lyuda said that getting the blessing wasn't that important. Sasha, her Muslim husband, insisted that she be resolute in her Christian faith. While Lyuda, Alina, and Natasha were at the church, Sasha and I hid the eggs around the apartment.

Sasha was very impressed with the decorated eggs. "This is incredible. How did you get these white lines onto brown eggs?"

Figuring that this was as good a time as any, I said, "Sash, I think it's time I leave."

"What for?"

"For good."

43
Success and Happiness

We had until June, when my return ticket would expire, to get ourselves ready to leave.

Natasha flew out to Kamchatka to say good-bye to her folks. Before she left, she purchased a little Pekingese puppy for her mom, as a kind of consolation prize—you're losing your daughter, but here is a cute dog. The dog was tiny and had a fierce temper. She named the dog Bonaparte, Boney for short. When Natasha got back to Novosibirsk, she spent a month saying good-bye to friends. In the meantime, I tidied up all the loose ends at work. I told our suppliers that I was leaving and that they now had to deal with Sasha directly.

We gave Sasha and Lyuda our furniture. The couch, of course, didn't fit through the doorway, so we broke it and hammered it back together again. Lyuda said it looked perfect in her new kitchen/dining room/den. Sasha was just glad he didn't have to buy new furniture on top of all the other expenses. Natasha and I cleaned our apartment all night the day before our flight. By four in the morning, the place was bare except for a box of ragged, worn-out clothing. I put the box next to a nearby store's dumpster, and when I returned fifteen minutes later to dump a final plastic bag of trash and floor sweepings, the box was gone. The store's trash was still there. Somebody had obviously spotted something of value in the box and picked it up. Russian recycling.

Sasha and Lyuda invited us over for a farewell breakfast. Lyuda wanted to christen the newly remodeled kitchen. After six months of arguments, destruction, construction, and reconstruction, Lyuda still seemed unsure if she liked the final result. She was still unsatisfied.

Something was still missing. Sasha liked it. In fact, he loved it, if for only one reason — it was done. Wearing a thick wool sweater knit by Baba Masha's wrinkled hands, Alina watched television with a vacant stare on her face. Her little hands repeatedly, mechanically, dressed and undressed her Barbie doll.

Of course, there was vodka. Lyuda protested that vodka for breakfast was disgusting. Sasha insisted that it wasn't really breakfast; it was a late supper. That made it okay. At least, it did for him.

In the four years that I had lived in Siberia, I had developed a frightening tolerance for alcohol. I could now drink as much as Sasha. The acquired ability didn't give me much reason to feel proud. It's not exactly the kind of thing you put on your résumé under the heading "Other Skills and Abilities."

Lyuda made tea for herself and Natasha. She no longer made tea in the ritualistic Russian way. She now bought Western tea bags. "Don't you just love these?" she asked Natasha. "They're so convenient."

Natasha just nodded politely.

"*Za druszhbu* (to friendship)," Sasha toasted. He said the word that had always been sacred to him as if it were now foreign.

I had spent the past four years persuading Sasha to separate friendship from business. Now he was director of a successful company. He was also very much alone. One by one, almost all of his friends were gone. Now it was my turn to leave. Over the past four years, Sasha had taught me to put friendship before business. It seemed that he had learned my lesson better, but I learned the better lesson.

"*Za druszhbu*," I said, blushing with shame.

Swallow, sniff, sigh.

Lyuda groaned in disgust. Alina imitated her mother with a little groan and a roll of her eyes, but her eyes quickly returned to the television set.

"Listen, Sasha," I said, "if it wasn't for your friendship, I would have left a long time ago."

"When that stupid soldier pointed his gun at you?" Sasha asked.

"You know, he probably didn't have any bullets in the gun. Besides, there are idiots everywhere, even in America."

"Especially in America," I said. "We're not leaving because that punk pointed a gun at me. America is the last place for refuge from nuts with guns. We're leaving because there is nothing left for us to do here. Natasha is done with school and I'm done being a Siberian entrepreneur."

Sasha gave me a confused look. "What are you talking about? We still haven't made our millions. We're not rich yet."

I reached under the table and grabbed Natasha's hand. I felt plenty rich.

"And now that we are buying stock in the factory," Sasha continued, "it's only a matter of time before we're rich enough to sit back and let interest accrue on our fortunes. We still have to enjoy the money we make. What's the point of earning money if you don't get a chance to spend it?"

"I didn't come here for the money," I said.

Sasha raised a skeptical eyebrow.

"I'm still a fireman at heart," I said, referring to the two years of volunteer firefighting I had done in college. "Putting out fires is the most exciting part of the fireman's job, but if that's all he did, he wouldn't be a complete fireman. If a fireman is really serious about fighting fires, he works to prevent them from starting in the first place. A good firefighter works to put himself out of a job. And I've done that. You don't need me anymore to run the company. You can handle all the foreign suppliers yourself. I've taught you everything I know about market economics."

"Yeah, and I've probably taught you more than you ever wanted to know about Russian economics."

"True," I acknowledged. "Strange as it may seem, Sash, this is success."

Sasha was silent. He poured another round of vodka and raised his glass.

"*Za uspekh.*" He made the word sound like a curse.

"To success," I repeated.

Swallow, sniff, sigh.

More shaking of heads from the peanut gallery.

"Actually, I think we've been a little too successful," I said. "You've already achieved the American Dream, the capitalist utopia. You've got a house in the country, you drive around in a Saab, and this..." I waved my hand at their newly remodeled kitchen.

"So this is utopia?" He wore a disappointed expression. He poured another round of vodka, then raised his glass.

I raised mine.

"To happiness," he said as if he were toasting a long-lost girl-friend on her wedding day. She was marrying somebody else.

"To happiness." I looked at Natasha as I said it. She winked at me.

As our glasses hit the table, Sasha said, "One more joke before you go?"

"All right."

"An American, a Frenchman, and a Russian are stranded on an island. A few years go by. They grow long beards. Their clothes become frayed rags. While sitting around the campfire one day, they notice something floating in the water. It turns out to be a lamp with a genie in it. The genie says he will grant three wishes, one wish for each of them. The American wishes to be a Hollywood movie star swarmed by big-breasted women. The genie snaps his fingers and poof—the American disappears. The Frenchman wishes to become a wealthy owner of a château surrounded by vine-yards. Again, the genie snaps his fingers and poof—the Frenchman vanishes. 'Ah, what great friends I had,' the Russian says with a sigh. Then, he suddenly smiles as he turns to the genie, 'I wish for a crate of vodka and my two friends back.'"

Sasha looked at me and snapped his fingers. "Poof."

Epilogue

"You go to heaven for the climate,
but you go to hell for the company."
—*Mark Twain*

I stumbled upon profound happiness in Siberia, an infamous land of suffering. But if happiness were the only thing to happen while I was there, I never would have bothered to write down a single word.

While I came to enjoy daily life in my little Siberian town, Russia endured three simultaneous but distinct revolutions—one economic, one political, and one cultural. The magnitude of this triple trauma is nearly impossible to appreciate, especially for us First Worlders. Imagine an economic depression as severe as America's Great Depression, a cultural upheaval as great as Japan's after Commodore Perry used mighty battleships to pry open the backward, isolated island, and a political implosion akin to Napoleonic France after Waterloo. All at once. All in the same country. Yes, Russia is a mess right now. Actually, calling it a mess is too kind. It is a catastrophe. But, by all accounts, it should be much, much worse. There is unfathomable hardship. But there is also defiant joy. This is particularly true in the worst part of Russia: Siberia.

Over the years, many Siberians enchanted me with their steady hope amid hopeless chaos. I knew that these were terrific times; I also knew that these were terrific people. It was a privilege to be among them. It was an honor to be accepted by them. I went to Siberia in search of a place severe enough to satisfy my lust for extremes. Siberia did not disappoint, but it did surprise. Siberia, it turned out, was also a wonderful place of sublime subtleties. It was a pleasant surprise.

There were, of course, plenty of unpleasant surprises. I was surprised by how quickly all the debasing aspects of democracy and capitalism took root while the ennobling aspects withered. I had falsely assumed that democracy and free markets were both inseparable from each other and indivisible in and of themselves. Democracy and the free market, the best institutions the West had to offer, stormed over the borders and ran deep into Russia. But, as with all foreign armies throughout history, they quickly were spread too thin and became diluted. Unfortunately, that left only the worst qualities: greed and indifference. It was too much to watch my dreams of a free, prosperous Siberia turn into a nightmare of a despondent, destitute Siberia. I needed to get away for a while.

Immediately after leaving Siberia, I was confronted with the torrent of bad news that is the bread and butter of Western media. Modern Russia, as abundant in bad news as it is in natural resources, is a dream come true for Western news media eager to mine only two types of stories: one based on pathos (*Russians are so poor...how poor are they?*), the other based on fear (*Russia's military is so fouled up that it actually poses a bigger threat to us now than did the Soviet Union's military*).

After a short while, I completely stopped watching the evening news, and soon thereafter gave up on reading newspaper articles as well. Not that the reports weren't true (Russia is poor and the military is in shambles); they just weren't the whole truth. The picture they painted of Russia (and of America) was both too apocalyptic and too naïve all at once. They gave extended coverage of the sensational calamities that made Americans shudder in horror, but these were the very things that seemed to roll off the backs of most Russians. All the while the news reports gave short shrift to the countless disappointments and setbacks that hobbled the hopes of even the most resilient Russians. Most annoying to me was how the news flatly ignored the few, the precious positive things that were happening in Russia. While they covered another businessman (a Western businessman this time!) murdered by the Russian mafia—as if there was just one Russian mafia—the news ignored the thousands of entrepreneurs (Russian entrepreneurs, no less!) that overcame long odds to make a profit.

Given the crooked playing field and that for seventy years it was a crime against society to earn a profit, it is downright miraculous that every Russian entrepreneur isn't a con artist or thief. But most Russian entrepreneurs today are at least as enterprising as the average American, no less honest, and motivated by what has jingoistically been credited as a uniquely American characteristic: the pursuit of happiness.

Sergei never gave up his dream to own a big rig. He made enough money driving the Kamaz to buy it back from the company. Soon after buying it, he sold it. With that money he bought a Maz, a slightly bigger truck made in Belarus. I gave my favorite Siberian trucker a real American air horn and a metal bulldog hood ornament. I'd purchased them at a Mack Truck dealership during one of my trips to America. Even though Renault, the French automaker that once manufactured the diminutive Le Car, had recently purchased Mack Trucks, Sergei still considered Mack the ultimate symbol of American long-haul greatness. He mounted the horn on top of his Maz. He had the loudest truck on the tundra. With a single tug on the cord above his head, Sergei could scare the fur coat off a woman crossing the street in front of his truck. He fixed the metal dog to the dashboard rather than to the hood, from where, he said, it would surely be stolen. The missing metal Chrysler star that used to be on the hood of the minivan we'd imported a few years back was testament to Sergei's wisdom. Besides, like the Kamaz, his new Maz didn't have a hood. It was a flat-faced truck, which made the bulldog emblem seem all the more appropriate.

Sergei made a couple of very profitable trips up north, hauling tons of television sets along ice roads atop frozen rivers to desolate outposts. He drove the Maz for slightly over a year. When he heard about a Mercedes truck dealership in Moscow, he sold his Maz (after removing the air horn and metal bulldog). The money he pocketed from that sale, plus the profits earned from hauling cargo, plus much of his life's savings, all fell short of the purchase price of the German vehicle. So he borrowed the rest.

He was the envy of his trucking buddies. He had what he had always wanted: a Western rig. He also had a Western-sized debt. But he had the means to pay it off. All he had to do was profitably drive his truck for a few years and he'd be back in black. And drive that truck is really all he wanted to do anyway. So, his debt wasn't really such a burden after all. Unfortunately, that soon changed. He had borrowed his money in deutsche marks. So, when then–Prime Minister Sergei Kirienko said that the Russian government would no longer artificially support the ruble, Russia's currency lost almost half its value. Sergei earned his profits in rubles, but had to pay his debt in marks. Suddenly, he would have to work twice as long in order to get out from under his debt. When I asked him whether he regretted buying the truck, he lit a cigarette and puffed out a Russian expression: "Those who want to drink champagne must take risks."

Another risk-taker was Lena, the woman who had been the company's in-house travel agent. Not content to arrange travel for chocolate executives, she expanded her activities and her client base. She was the one who organized the fateful trip I took with Natasha to Italy. Pretty soon the company could no longer contain her. Encouraged by her success, confident of her abilities, Lena started her own travel agency and opened offices in the very heart of the city, just a block away from Lenin Square. If you meet Siberian tourists drinking vodka and taking pictures of themselves in exotic places around the world from Milan to Miami, Bombay to Boston, Cairo to Canton, there is a chance that Lena had some-thing to do with it.

Shura, Sasha's entrepreneurial friend, after taking one too many risks, finally found a business that didn't require him to borrow money from loan sharks. He quietly moved back from Italy to

Russia, bought a computer, and discovered the Internet. In short order he was selling Soviet and Russian stamps on eBay to collectors as far away as Texas. He has no employees and virtually no overhead. The business is essentially self-financing. He hardly ever has to freeze up capital in inventory. Instead, he goes around town with a portable scanner, records a digital image of the stamps people are willing to sell, then posts the stamps on the Net. If (and only if) he sells them, he buys them from the original owner and puts them in the mail to the far reaches of the globe.

Shura can earn as much as $2,500 a month, or as little as three hundred. He's not going to be filthy rich anytime soon, but, when the average Russian wage is equivalent to between thirty and fifty dollars a month, he's doing relatively well—in any case, he's got enough to afford a little champagne now and then.

Sarah is still in Siberia, doing what she has always done: leading the horses to the waters of civil society. Her nonprofit has grown to the point where the all-Russian staff can handle almost everything. She really doesn't have to come in to the office every day, but she does. She continues to take the train on business trips to "neighboring" Siberian cities. She is simultaneously Siberia's staunchest supporter and most ardent critic. When she tells Siberians what to do, it is not as an outsider who thinks she knows best. She meddles because she is a concerned local. She cares so much about what happens there, not because it is her job, but because Siberia is her home.

Sarah recently married her boyfriend Ivan. Rather than take his Ph.D. in economics from Princeton to the IMF or World Bank to become a macroeconomic analyst, he decided to brave the wilds of his hometown and opened a high-end mattress manufacturing company in Novosibirsk. Even Siberians need to sleep.

Sasha, my friend and partner, well, his life since I left almost deserves another book. One of the reasons I threw my hands up in the air and left Siberia was that I was spending too much of my time in smoke-choked, vodka-soaked meetings with avaricious men. Sasha was one of those men. If a man I cared so much about could become one of *them*, so could I. I have vague memories of arguments over quantities of shares, prices of stocks, terms of promissory notes, and variables of interest rates. But one thing remains very vivid in my memory. During those meetings I knew that I'd rather have been with Natasha than with those men. I knew that the free market would eventually force these free-for-all capitalists to stop fighting over how to divide the pie amongst themselves and start figuring out how to make the pie bigger for everyone. If they didn't, they wouldn't survive long. In the short run, however, it wasn't their survival that was in jeopardy.

Less than a year after Natasha and I left Siberia, the Novosibirsk Chocolate Factory underwent a revolutionary change of leadership. A faction of long-time workers forcefully took over the factory and wouldn't allow the Director through the front gates. They said that their goal was to prevent him and his rich friends from selling the factory to a gigantic Moscow chocolate concern.

The workers who led the revolt selected someone from their own ranks, a middle-aged woman, to assume operational direction of the factory. Once at the helm, she immediately cut off all business contacts with Sasha and the company we had worked so hard to build into a viable enterprise with more than forty employees. I felt disappointed that all those years of work now appeared for naught. I felt even more depressed that all the employees who had hitched their fate to our company, worked so hard to make it successful, were now on the verge of unemployment. But this was Siberia, so just when things seemed their darkest, there was an eclipse and it got even darker.

Soon after the mini-coup at the factory, two bullets, one to the chest and one to the skull, brought an end to the rebellion. The provisional director died in the stairwell to her apartment, as did the rebellion. Order, or some sinister semblance of it, was restored.

There were many suspected of committing, or at least ordering, the murder: Sasha, the Director, the deputy director, some of the brokers and bankers, as well as many of the Moscow investors. All were interrogated extensively by the police. None were convicted.

The Moscow concern eventually acquired a majority share in the factory. It immediately appointed a new director. The former Director was forced into early retirement. The deputy directory also left the factory to work for a company that supplied the city with coal. A few weeks later, Sasha became the deputy director for the Novosibirsk Chocolate Factory. He now sits in the same room where he and I, just four years prior—from the other side of the desk—negotiated the first beans-for-chocolate barter.

I asked him if, hypothetically, two guys, one American and one Russian, walked into his office and offered him a beans-for-chocolate barter deal, would he agree to it? Sasha laughed and shook his head. "Those were different times, Sanya."

Sasha was recently offered a job as deputy director for, of all things, a *Khladocombinat*, or "cold factory." He bragged to me over the phone, "It's got the largest refrigerator east of the Urals."

"Sasha," I said, "everything east of the Urals *is* a refrigerator."

"True, but this operates year round, and what with global warming and all, we should get more business in the future." Sasha, the eternal optimist and relentless salesman. If anybody can sell ice to Eskimos, he can.

From America's vantage point, everything in Russia appears too chaotic to make heads or tails of, and Siberia is simply off the radar screen. But there is a growing sense of order. The anything-is-possible anarchy that was Siberia from 1992 to 1996 is now a matter of history. I'll let history judge what opportunities were lost and what ground was taken in the name of progress during that time. For me, those four years have left me with a lifetime of rabid ambivalence to chew on until I've got no teeth left.

Capitalism is no longer the universal cure-all that I once thought it was. In fact, I'm convinced that, like democracy, it is the worst way to organize society until you consider all the alternatives. I'm still just as determined to crusade for free markets, but my motivation has changed. I don't consider it a panacea. It is not a means by which to reach happiness. It is a means to escape misery. It is a salve, not a salvation. Sasha's life is a case in point.

Although his manic efforts at work had put him well ahead of the game—hell, being alive in Siberian business meant that you were ahead of the game—things at home were far from unambiguous for Sasha. His parents felt too isolated in the giant brick house in the suburbs. The rest of the family, despite Sasha's best intentions, wasn't moving out to the house. Lyuda had no intentions of moving in with her dominating if diminutive mother-in-law. Alina had school and friends back in Akademgorodok. Sasha's commute to work in the city was already too long; he simply couldn't move still farther away. So, if the family wasn't going to move out to Baba Masha and Kamil, then the grandparents demanded to be moved closer to the family.

Soon thereafter, Sasha sold the big house and moved his parents into a smaller house closer to the village. The younger generations still stayed in the apartment, but at least now they were closer, which meant more frequent visits. This worked for a while, but Lyuda soon wanted a home of her own. Sasha borrowed some more money and had Victor, the former wrestler, build him a new house to his wife's specifications. But before the house was finished, Lyuda received a grant to study for three months at a university somewhere in America. Los Angeles and New York were her top choices. She ended up at Kent State. And it was more than she had ever hoped. After seeing the bright lights of Cleveland, Lyuda realized that she would never be happy living in a house in Siberia. She told her husband that she wanted to move to America. He said that he liked it in Siberia and didn't want to move. They were at an impasse. They were both strong-willed and each stood their ground. At some point, they concluded that marriage wasn't supposed to be a battle of wills. They agreed to stop fighting each other. They agreed to separate from each other. Lyuda couldn't just pick up and move to America. But she didn't want to remain with a man who didn't share, or at least support, her dream. So one of them had to move out.

Sasha didn't want Alina to have to move from the apartment that had always been her home; her parents' separation would be traumatic enough. Realistically, Sasha knew that he wouldn't be able to spend much time with Alina; he was too busy earning money to cover all the accumulated debts of trying to support such a dispersed family. Lyuda would stay with Alina while Sasha moved out and got his own apartment, which meant that he had two apartments to pay for as well the two houses. Curiously, as Sasha's marriage fell apart, he moved into the same apartment building that I had lived in when my relationship with Katya fell apart.

While I was in that apartment, I had recovered from heartbreak and, after several painful (for everybody involved) missteps, I found Natasha. So, today I am hopeful that Sasha will find a lovely woman who finds him lovable. I'm hopeful that Sasha will find happiness. His rabid enthusiasm has been tempered by hard-earned wisdom. He realizes that he can't have everything that he wants, no matter how hard he tries, no matter how successful he becomes. Accepting limitations, ironically, may be the very thing that brings him happiness.

Happiness, it seems, grows thickest along the thin line separating the naïve optimism of America and the futile fatalism of Russia. For four years, I straddled this narrow line between bliss and despair. That I found it in sweet Siberia may have been an unlikely coincidence. Who knows? All I know is that I was most successful at walking that fine line when I was least aware of it.

But I'm not content to simply accept happiness as a fortunate accident. I must understand it. Not surprisingly, I have yet to feel the same sense of bliss that I felt in Siberia. My mind tries to tackle the matter in terms of economics.

The Soviet Union was criminally inefficient at producing wealth. Soviet production techniques required great expenditures of labor and repulsive expulsions of pollution in order to transform mountains of valuable raw materials into nearly worthless molehills of finished goods. Never have so many exploited so much to produce so little. The United States, on the other hand, is criminally inefficient at consuming wealth. Overwhelming abundance in America brings little more than temporary relief from our constantly increasing cravings. Never have so many consumed so much for so little happiness.

Part of the fun of living in Siberia was watching just how much happiness one box of chocolate could bring. Knowing that I was responsible, if only indirectly, for putting thousands of boxes of happiness on the tables of Siberians made me sleep like a baby and wake like a child, full of anticipation. It took so little stuff to bring so much happiness to Siberians. Better still, I was a part of disassembling the archaic Soviet production calamity, and building on top of those ruins a new, efficient foundation. In time, I knew, Siberia's economy would become much more productive. Was it so unreasonable to assume that happiness would increase likewise? Unfortunately, yes.

While Siberian productivity made marginal progress at best, Siberian consumption suffered a devastating collapse in efficiency. The stores filled up faster than Siberians wallets emptied out. Waves of imports flooded the once barren Siberian markets, but waves of hyperinflation wiped out the average Siberian's ability to buy those imports. Hope at finding something worth buying had been replaced with the despair of not having anything to buy it with. To me, even more significant than the average Siberian's ability to purchase the basics of modern life was his growing inability to appreciate it. Sasha had more than he ever could have hoped for: two homes, two apartments, two cars, two trips abroad a year, and yet, happiness was receding away from him faster than ever.

He has won all the battles, yet lost the war.

To me, America, the lone superpower left standing at the end of the Cold War, reeked of the same pyrrhic victory. We had won all the battles yet failed to convert it into something meaningful, something great.

I'm writing this on a commuter train in the heart of Silicon Valley, surely one of the most comfortable places in one of the most comfortable states in one of the most comfortable countries in the world. The train just passed a small house with a huge motor home parked in the driveway. The motor home has American flags all over it and one mural-sized word, KOMFORT, painted on the side. It seems that comfort, even if misspelled the way Russians would, is an integral part of the American way. Being comfortable is downright patriotic. For me, this feels like the poor spoils indeed.

Clearly, I'm still uncomfortable with comfort. Four years in Siberia only exacerbated these feelings. Comfort, more than ever, seems like a sacred verb, but an insidious noun. Food comforts the hungry. Warmth comforts the cold. Love comforts the lonely. But what comforts the well-fed, the well-clothed, the well-loved? Do these people even need to be comforted? *Can* they be comforted?

We instinctively pursue comfort with the assumption that it will bring us happiness, even though it will only bring us relief. Relief is all it has ever brought. Relief is all it ever can bring.

I would argue that most Siberians need more comfort, while most Americans need less. And for those who think there is no such thing as too much comfort, I will bang my hand on the table to remind them that there are costs to pay for our comforts, not just the price we pay to acquire those comforts, but the intrinsic costs of ownership.

There are many reasons why I wrote this book. It frustrated me that Americans were miserable despite opulence, while Siberians eked out surprising levels of bliss amid turmoil.

I'm still haunted by Siberia. She is like an ex-girlfriend. Almost daily, when certain old vehicles drive by, I'll catch a whiff of Siberia in the blue oil-and-gas exhaust. I know that too much will kill me, but I can't help but take a deep breath. The memories conjured up are just too sweet to resist. Try as I might to deny it, I'm still in love with Siberia.

Acknowledgments

If I had known beforehand how hard it was going to be to run a business in Siberia, I would have gone to Novosibirsk anyway. If I had known beforehand how hard it was going to be to write a book, I wouldn't have written a single paragraph. Between living in Siberia and writing a book about living in Siberia, writing the book was by far the more challenging endeavor. Fortunately, I had plenty of people to help me along the torturous path to publication.

Special thanks to Pam Schwandt, the first writing professional to see my manuscript, for using encouraging green ink, instead of an admonishing red ink, when editing my early manuscript. Considering the shear quantity of edits, she probably had to go through several green pens. I know that my self-esteem couldn't have withstood that much red ink.

Thanks to Ann Kindschi for reading my entire book out loud to me so that I could hear how my words actually sounded; and to Dan Kohn, the most optimistic cynic I know, for keeping me engaged in the world when my instincts urged me to withdraw.

Deepest thanks to Yuri Krugavoy, my loudest and most beloved professor, for introducing me to the dual passions of Russia and literature. Combining the two caused him to shout, stomp, and spit during his lectures. He, after reading a still crude version of the manuscript, forbade me from giving up until I had published my book. In fact, he wrote a check to be drawn against his retirement account to keep financial concerns from inducing me to give up my quest for publication. I never did cash the check, but I will always remain indebted to him.

To Joe Regal, my agent, thanks for reading my year-old manuscript and writing the foreboding, yet fortifying words: "Within your manuscript is the germ of a remarkable book. You'll basically have to rewrite the whole thing." On many occasions when I contemplated the very sane prospect of abandoning the book and getting my life back, these words kept me focused ruthlessly on improving the manuscript.

Thanks to Susan Hartman, director of Connect US–Russia, for opening the door to the wonders of Russia way back in 1988. What a Pandora's box it has turned out to be. I couldn't resist. Now it seems as if everything has spilled out except for hope.

To Sarah Lindemann, queen of the American ghetto, thanks for being so supportive of my entrepreneurial dreams while I was in Siberia and of my literary dreams after I left.

I owe my eternal gratitude to Natalya Blakely, my lovely wife and closest friend, for believing in me, no matter how many times I had to start from scratch. For tolerating me even when I was at my most intolerable. From the first time we met, you've always brought out the best in me. You still do.

Finally, thanks to Sasha, for not only taking me under his wing, but for flying with me. His wings weren't very protective, but they were plenty adventurous, which is just the way I wanted it. I wanted to fly recklessly and relentlessly, like Icarus. If I hadn't met Sasha, I would have left Siberia sooner than I did, and much poorer in every respect.

About the Author

Alexander Blakely grew up in Minnesota and graduated from Swarthmore College with a bachelor's degree in economic theory. He spent the next four years living in Novosibirsk, Siberia, cofounding and managing a successful business. Since returning to live in the U.S. in 1997, he has been a trade analyst for the Foundation for U.S./Russian Economic Cooperation, an editor for *Russian Far East Update*, and the first employee of KnowNow Inc., a technology firm developing next-generation Internet infrastructure in post-bubble Silicon Valley. He lives in San Francisco with his wife Natasha. This is his first book.